MEDIA CONVERGENCE

ISSUES in CULTURAL and MEDIA STUDIES

Series editor: Stuart Allan

Published titles

Violence and the Media
Cynthia Carter and C. Kay Weaver

Ethnic Minorities and the Media
Simon Cottle (ed.)

Global Crisis Reporting
Simon Cottle

Mediatized Conflict
Simon Cottle

Moral Panics and the Media
Chas Critcher

Critical Readings: Moral Panics and the Media
Chas Critcher (ed.)

Culture on Display
Bella Dicks

Game Cultures
Jon Dovey and Helen W. Kennedy

Media Convergence
Tim Dwyer

Perspectives on Global Cultures
Ramaswami Harindranath

Media, Politics and the Network Society
Robert Hassan

Museums, Media and Cultural Theory
Michelle Henning

Domestic Cultures
Joanne Hollows

Media Talk
Ian Hutchby

Citizens or Consumers
Justin Lewis, Sanna Inthorn and Karin Wahl-Jorgensen

Media Technology: Critical Perpectives
Joost van Loon

MEDIA CONVERGENCE

Tim Dwyer

Open University Press

Open University Press
McGraw-Hill Education
McGraw-Hill House
Shoppenhangers Road
Maidenhead
Berkshire
England
SL6 2QL

email: enquiries@openup.co.uk
world wide web: www.openup.co.uk

and Two Penn Plaza, New York, NY 10121–2289, USA

First Published 2010

A catalogue record of this book is available from the British Library

ISBN-13: 978-0-33-522873-7 (pb) 978-0-33-522872-0 (hb)
ISBN-10: 0335228739 (pb) 0335228720 (hb)

Library of Congress Cataloging-in-Publication Data
CIP data applied for

Typeset by RefineCatch Limited, Bungay, Suffolk
Printed in the UK by Bell and Bain Ltd, Glasgow

Mixed Sources
Product group from well-managed forests and other controlled sources
www.fsc.org Cert no. TT-COC-002769
© 1996 Forest Stewardship Council

FSC

The McGraw·Hill Companies

For my parents, Isabel and Wilfred

CONTENTS

SERIES EDITOR'S FOREWORD

The word 'convergence' is increasingly being used to describe the imperatives reshaping media industries around the globe. Typically signalled out for attention in this regard is the influence of digital technology, which is widely credited with or condemned for (depending upon one's point of view) dramatically transforming familiar assumptions – not least where business and regulatory models are concerned – about how media institutions operate. Excited claims made about technology-driven 'revolutions' risk obscuring what is really happening, however, especially where the impact of technological change is overstated as a sudden, prodigious departure from previous convention. The appeal of this illusion, where one startling breakthrough follows another in a logical, rational sequence unfolding under the rippling banner of progress, is difficult to resist. But resist it we must, I believe. The identification of technical innovations is crucial, yet equally noteworthy are the uneven ways in which these innovations are taken up, modified, and recrafted to render them fit for purpose. Such a focus on the situated materiality of technology pinpoints the ways in which media institutions are being recast by the lived negotiation of its affordances and possibilities, as well as by its pressures and constraints. Hence the importance, I would suggest, of seeking to complicate some of the more technology-determined accounts of media convergence so as to discern the basis for a more nuanced treatment of these issues.

It is precisely this challenge which informs Tim Dwyer's book *Media Convergence*, which endeavours to situate our everyday engagements with diverse media forms and practices in relation to the forces that are restructuring the media industries with such astonishing swiftness. The ways in which people are using media, he contends, is directly linked to complex, multi-layered interactions between 'traditional' (or 'old') communication cultures and emerging ('new') online, mobile media. In documenting the nature of these interactions, he proceeds to explain why it would be naïve to simply accept claims made about technological change at face value. He suggests, in contrast, that the perceived influence of various rhetorics of convergence (ranging from upbeat utopian to grim dystopian scenarios) needs to be critically assessed against the backdrop of actual developments underway in media industries in different national contexts. Dwyer argues that convergence is a new media ideology, one that facilitates a neoliberal re-organization of global markets – a process with serious consequences for the future of democracy. Accordingly, he shows us why efforts to rethink policy frameworks for media and communications infrastructures will require an integrated approach, if they are to achieve their aim of ensuring a sufficient degree of diversity in content, platforms and ownership to fulfil the aspirations of citizen-led initiatives to enrich and expand democratic participation in public life.

The *Issues in Cultural and Media Studies* series aims to facilitate a diverse range of critical investigations into pressing questions considered to be central to current thinking and research. In light of the remarkable speed at which the conceptual agendas of cultural and media studies are changing, the series is committed to contributing to what is an ongoing process of re-evaluation and critique. Each of the books is intended to provide a lively, innovative and comprehensive introduction to a specific topical issue from a fresh perspective. The reader is offered a thorough grounding in the most salient debates indicative of the book's subject, as well as important insights into how new modes of enquiry may be established for future explorations. Taken as a whole, then, the series is designed to cover the core components of cultural and media studies courses in an imaginatively distinctive and engaging manner.

Stuart Allan

ACKNOWLEDGEMENTS

My principal thanks go to the Series Editor Stuart Allan who has been untiringly supportive, and always willing to draw on his extensive experience and knowledge. I also want to thank the editorial team, and in particular, Melanie Havelock, Stephanie Frosch and Claire Munce.

Numerous colleagues and friends have made the book possible. My departmental colleagues in Media and Communications at the University of Sydney have all contributed in various collegial ways. Thanks to Marc Brennan, Antonio Castillo, Sean Chaidaroon, Stephanie Donald, Fiona Giles, Alana Mann, Steven Maras, Megan Le Masurier, Penny O'Donnell, and Richard Stanton. I am grateful to research colleagues Fiona Martin, Anne Dunn, Andrew Kenyon (at Melbourne University) for their collaboration in the preparation of an ARC Linkage Project application during the hectic period I was writing the book. Virginia Nightingale was her usual generous and supportive self, making insightful suggestions on earlier draft chapters. Graham Murdock has been a source of inspiration over several decades, and also very generous with sage advice. Terry Flew has been a long-term interlocutor whose similar research interests have influenced me over the years. Thanks to Adam Lucas and Bill Pritchard for their friendship and advice in relation to a broad range of issues.

Steve Keen very kindly agreed to read and make comments on the private equity arguments in Chapter 3. Many thanks to Bill Rosenberg at the Campaign Against Foreign Control of Aotearoa in New Zealand, and various international colleagues including Kari Karpinnen in Finland and Phil Napoli in the USA who were happy to provide copies of their conference papers or assisted by responding to my questions.

Ofcom and the OECD kindly gave permission to use data from their

Communications Market/International Communications Market Reports, and international broadband usage data series, respectively.

My thanks are due to the original publishers for the several arguments aired elsewhere. They first appeared in 'Traditional Media Buys Online: Not All Good News for Audiences,' in Andrew Kenyon's *TV Futures: Digital Television Policy in Australia*, Melbourne University Press, and in my previous book with Virginia Nightingale, *New Media Worlds: Challenges for Convergence*, Oxford University Press. I owe a debt to colleagues and co-authors, Derek Wilding, Helen Wilson and Simon Curtis, then at the Communications Law Centre, for research data first published by the Communications Law Centre, at UNSW/ Victoria Universities in *Content, Consolidation and Clout: How will Regional Australia be Affected by Media Ownership Changes?*

I am grateful to the organizers of the International Association of Media and Communications Researchers Conference (IAMCR) conference on 20–25 July 2008, at Stockholm University, Stockholm, Sweden, where I gave a paper entitled *First Impacts: Dismantling Frameworks for Cross-owned Media in Australia*, and which was subsequently published in the UK in *Communications Law* by Tottel Publishing. In this regard, my thanks go to Wolfgang Kleinwachter, then co-chair of the IAMCR's law section.

Thanks to Annette, Rod, Lilly and Nina for providing the country ambience and hospitality, which facilitated writing during the summer break. Finally, I should acknowledge that Susan and Declan helped in countless ways; and they showed incredible tolerance for not reminding me too often that I should be doing more family-focused, and less computer-oriented activities.

Note on the text

In the text, bold indicates that the term is defined in the Glossary of Key Terms at the end of the book.

INTRODUCTION

How will people access media content in the future? What combination of TV, computer or mobile device, and which kinds of content will become common? Although issues of bandwidth, speed, networks and business models dominate industry, policy and academic debates, the important issue from an audience perspective is which screen devices will be used to view specific shows, genres and websites. And how much news, sport, music videos, games, drama, documentary, reality or social networking will there be? Will we be watching the same content on large home screens that we will while we are on the move? Or will using different types of content depend on where we are situated, and what we are doing at that time? There is emerging evidence to suggest that a ubiquitous, higher bandwidth Internet will see people accessing their favourite TV shows or Internet sites no matter whether they are at home, work, chilling out in a café, or somewhere out and about on the move.

This book is concerned to analyse the political, economic, cultural, social, and technological factors that are shaping these changing media practices. More critically, we will explore how powerful industrial and governmental actors interact to determine the way networks control the distribution of resources for consumers and citizens. My argument is that the principal consequence arising from such changes in our media industries are nothing less than the role media perform in a democracy.

The implications for the education of future media content makers are stark too. This point was succinctly made in *The Baltimore Sun* in the USA, noting that 'readers and advertisers are migrating online, where competition for eyeballs and ad dollars is fierce. Almost 16,000 jobs were lost at U.S. newspapers last year' (Kiehl 2009). The author observes that although the traditional career path for young journalists, starting out by working at a small paper or TV station and then working your way up is disappearing, this will be replaced by new pathways for those graduates with the right mix of skills. It is suggested that this will be a multimedia expertise involving 'digital storytelling', research and communication skills, and the ability to work with audio, video, graphics and Web design as the core job requirements. These are also 'cross-media' skills, in that they allow content to be made for distribution over several 'platforms': for television, radio, newspaper and online and mobile media.

Throughout this book my understanding of *media convergence* is the process whereby new technologies are accommodated by existing media and communication industries and cultures. The fact that the term is used to describe this adaptation, merging together and transitioning process, is an indication that the ongoing confrontation of old and new technologies is complex and multi-layered. When the process is mentioned, invariably it is referencing the intersection of distinct media and information technology systems that have previously been thought of as separate and self-contained. Innovative media production or consumption is often an important component. For example, **Internet Protocol TV (IPTV)** blurs 'Internet' and 'television' media, recombines them in a new distribution mode over various platforms and access devices, but then also creatively innovates existing 'television' cultural forms.

In this book as well as evaluating the practical operation of 'convergence' in terms of the structural and cultural transformations within media industries, we will also be considering convergence as a rhetorical construct by particular agents. The assumption is made that the term often obscures important shifts in work practices, editorial processes and publishing strategies. For instance, Erdal has argued: 'One of the main synergetic strategies for cross-media work is to get more news published on more media platforms, with the same, or fewer resources' (2007: 78). Such a mode of production is sometimes referred to as 'convergent or convergence journalism' (Erdal 2007; Quinn 2004, 2006), where production strategies are implemented 'not only between media organisations with the same owners, but also within the same organisation' (Erdal 2007: 78). And yet it is these very processes that may have important implications and which affect, for example, the construction of news diversity or policies concerned with fostering local content production.

Democracies are sustained by and through the ability of well-funded and resourced media organizations to analyse, and hold important institutions, such as our parliaments, courts, government agencies and their officials, and politicians at all levels to account. My argument at its core is about how the influence of the rhetorics of convergence needs to be critically assessed against the actual developments in media industries, audience, and in policy and regulatory contexts. Convergence is a new media ideology too: that is, a way of thinking that facilitates the operation of neoliberal global markets. Media owners in the twenty-first century strive to continuously expand their output across media platforms. In this sense, the economic and ideological dimensions of media convergence work together in the interests of a further consolidated ownership base.

As a dominant ideology, 'media convergence' has its practical ideological effects on the way people think about the unfolding media and communications industries. The ideological representations of convergence that circulate in the media, often inflecting ideas about the inevitability of industry conglomeration and concentration, can work to prefigure people's expectations and understanding. This is the business of news reports of mergers and acquisitions that occur on a daily basis. To take one example, before it eventually came to pass, there had been a long-running news story about how Microsoft would 'team up' with Yahoo! following the earlier failure of the software giant's $US44 billion takeover attempt of the number two search engine corporation (Johnson 2009). Typically there are several interconnected claims assumed in media convergence media reports. First, there is the claim about the unquestionable benefits that sheer scale brings. It asserts that in order to survive in a global economy where a handful of corporations control the production and distribution of media content, there is a need to constantly acquire, co-opt, and merge, whether on a 'friendly' or 'hostile' basis. Second, there is a claim about the synergistic benefits that will inevitably arise from new and improved ways of doing business. Third, these ideological claims of the benefits of expansion and business rationalization are enacted within broader discursive frameworks of neoliberalism and technological determinism. These frameworks provide ready-made explanations (as ideologies or assumed meanings) in relation to what exists, what is possible and what is necessary. Now whether these claims are always true in part or in full is not the key point. Rather, the issue is whether such claims have causal or practical effects among policy-makers, industry actors and wider publics. If people believe such claims to be an inevitable feature of the media, then we can reasonably argue that ideologies of media convergence are implicated in the power relations of the unfolding media industries.

But the ideologies of convergence have their specific practical affects too: the ways that people are using media *are* fragmenting. At the end of the first decade of the third millennium, the available evidence suggests that across western democracies newspaper circulation, TV audiences, and advertising revenues are all in a slow decline (House of Lords 2008a), and this partially explains why traditional media have been so keen to expand into online and mobile media. This transforming usage is an important element for consideration at a time when governments search for appropriate broadband policies that will improve business and public access to 'internetworked' media and communications platforms.

There are various definitions of 'convergence' available, and I will discuss these again shortly (and elsewhere in the book). But to begin, here is a fairly standard technically-oriented definition used by the UK's 'convergent' media regulator: 'The ability of consumers to obtain multiple services on a single platform or device or obtain any given service on multiple platforms or devices' (Ofcom 2008a: 1). This, they explain, is in a context where 'Convergence is all around us – mobile phones with video, radio and the Internet, radio over TV platforms and the Internet and TV over mobile platforms including digital radio, and the Internet – all facilitated by the move to digital technologies.'

To foreground the 'consumer' in policies is of course an important role for a regulatory agency whose mandate it is to act on behalf of various media populations, including its broader public interest constituencies. Yet unfortunately it tends not to be accompanied by any discussion or show of intent in relation to the equally important remit to advance the citizens rights of audiences. Indeed, there's a kind of privileging of media convergence *consumer* experiences: mobile phones that take pictures, video and play digital music files, and handheld broadband Internet access devices 'acting as the gateway to a multiplicity of services', for example, to receive free-to-air or on-demand television or radio.

To these we need to add other equally widespread everyday activities like reading newspapers or listening to radio online, or watching audiovisual material that originated on television or was first released at the cinema over various small screen devices. Importantly for the discussion that follows in subsequent chapters, the talk is often now about how convergence means media companies no longer occupy their own historical turf: in the UK, a satellite broadcaster like BSkyB provides broadband and a telecommunications company like BT provides digital television on demand ('BT Vision'). Another consequence of convergence for consumers is the way services are now offered to them as 'bundled' packages. A 'triple play' offering is broadband Internet, television and fixed line phone services from the same provider. A 'quad play' combines these with a mobile phone service.

When we come to look at policies for controlling concentration of ownership in later chapters, it will be apparent that this issue is particularly important, especially through a cross-medial lens. The global–local axis is part of this equation too. Global media corporations can develop both horizontal (across similar products and services) and vertical ownership strategies (across platforms or **value chain** segments), and audiences will be accessing the full spectrum of content genres, no matter where the provider is located. Geography is even less limiting when the software has a **peer-to-peer** (**P2P**) **architecture**. At the same time, media convergence can explain why Internet giants Google and Yahoo! are increasingly involved in traditional media markets right along the value chain from content creation, through to packaging and distribution.

Studying media convergence

Media convergence can be studied at a number of distinct levels including cultural, industrial, technological, or regulatory levels – and these will often be present in different combinations. For example, one infrastructure service that has arisen exponentially is **Voice over Internet Protocol (or VoIP)**. VoIP has elements with implications at all these levels in what, at first encounter, appears to be just a fairly geeky technology. It is a 'catch-all term that covers a range of services, including computer-to-computer communications and VoIP services that act as an effective substitute to standard PSTN (or Public Switched Telephone Network) landline services' (ACMA 2008). The way it works is by converting your voice into a digital signal (using **Internet Protocol** or **IP** packets) that travels over the Internet via a broadband connection. Using specific software, VoIP converts the voice signal from the caller's telephone into a digital signal, then converts it back at the other end to enable voice communication with anyone with a phone number. However, to limit an appraisal to simply this technical assessment would be to severely curtail its wider cultural, industrial and regulatory significance (VoIP is discussed further in Chapter 5).

Another increasingly important example of media convergence can be seen in Internet Protocol TV (IPTV): it combines new methods of TV programme distribution over IP platforms and access devices, but it's also innovating existing 'television' forms. IPTV, quite literally, combines a managed Internet broadband network with elements of traditional TV, in terms of content, scheduling and generally its overall packaging for audiences to view. At the time of writing, France was the clear leader in IPTV, both in terms of number of subscribers (3 million) and as a share of all digital TV subscribers (approximately 20 per cent) (Ofcom 2008a: 112). Yet, as Henton and Tadayoni point out, while IPTV and IP-VoD (Internet Protocol-Video-on-Demand) began offering services using streaming TV over the Internet:

> In the last five to six years, we have witnessed the emergence of a huge amount of 'on demand' video services on the Internet, specific 'Internet TV' Channels, and 'time-shifted' versions of parts of programming from traditional broadcasters. Furthermore, broadband operators deliver IPTV services in their managed IP networks.
>
> (2008: 57)

Such IP developments are becoming a competing delivery infrastructure, affecting the provision of television, including HDTV, terrestrial, satellite and cable systems and content providers themselves who are all responding with 'on-demand' approaches. These authors anticipate that while the current IP-VoD is mainly based on client server architectures, in the future they will be characterized by more efficient P2P architectures. However, and perhaps of greater significance, they argue that the underlying protocols of the Internet 'will increasingly function as a common technology platform for convergence developments among the different media branches' (2008: 63).

Mediatizing convergence and cultural change

The introduction and rapid diffusion of digital media have brought about profound changes in the nature and organization of contemporary mediated communication. Access to new media, and especially to mobile and online media, means that people are able to organize their everyday contacts and their personal, leisure and work activities while on the move. New media increase the versatility of human action. In other words, much of this change is experiential: media audiences are *experiencing* media convergence in the situations they find themselves in while connecting to network infrastructures. Joining wireless networks in the activities of our everyday lives *is* a new and different way of accessing content. But these experiences are diffuse, and as Mackenzie highlights:

> There is no pure experience of wirelessness. Feelings of wirelessness are 'verbalised' in a mass of images, projects, products, enterprises, plans and politics concerning networks and communications infrastructures. Wireless networks such as Wi-Fi are quite heavily mediatized as convergent.
>
> (Mackenzie 2008)

There are numerous popular Internet video distribution (IP VoD) and Internet Protocol television (IPTV) providers (Figure I.1 shows a selection: YouTube, Apple TV, BT Vision, Current TV, Joost, Miro and Now TV).

Mediatization, then, is itself an important component of media convergence. We can understand the term as referencing experiences of how the media are implicated in the production and transmission of messages about convergence and changing media industries (Thompson 1995; De Zengotita 2005; Fortunati 2005). Circuits of mediated meaning are thus embedded in discourses of media convergence. This kind of self-referentiality between disparate contexts is a consequence of living in a mediated world. Certainly, it would be a mistake to view convergence process as a linear, homogenous, neat unfolding of media and communications products and services. There are numerous critical commentaries that point to industry *divergences* and contradiction, especially when studied at comparative transnational or regional levels (see Ludes 2008; Storsul and Stuedahl 2007). Taking a wider societal and media change perspective and

Figure I.1 Selection of IP VoD and IPTV providers: YouTube, Apple TV, BT Vision, Current TV, Joost, Miro and Now TV

eschewing any convenient unifying of experiences that the 'convergence' label tends to imply, Ludes notes,

> The emergence of a so-called European Information and Knowledge Society is a multidimensional, non-linear, long-term process of shifting balances of disinformation and information, ignorance and knowledge as well as media and culture specific frameworks of evaluation and

interpretation. The concepts of 'convergence and fragmentation' appear too static for an adequate understanding of this process . . . they should be replaced by converging and diverging trends, implying media and social changes and allowing for 'unity in diversity'.

(Ludes 2008)

In tracking media and social change we can make the observation that the application of digital technologies in personal communication devices, such as mobile cellular phones, MP3/MP4 players and PDAs/smartphones, has provided the impetus for change in the traditional media industries and revitalized the confidence of Internet industries damaged by the **Nasdaq tech crash** in 2000. This date is sometimes also used to delineate the end of the 'first Internet era' (Kung et al. 2008: 126).

One aspect of the shifting balance of power between 'old' and 'new' media before the tech crash was the collision of content and communications and the policy issues this brought to the fore. Arguably the first phase of convergence occurred around a decade before the tech crash with the introduction of the Mosaic WWW browser (see Figure I.2 on p. 13), when it seemed to many that digital media would totally eclipse traditional media, and that the media convergence world would be dominated by one medium – the übercomputing device. Today, however, this mono-medium scenario has been replaced by a new ideal. In this scenario, individuals are equipped with multiple media devices, all of which talk to each other wirelessly. Ubiquitous computing and intelligent user-friendly interfaces are the new black. Coordination of our personal devices has become a measure of the alacrity of the way an individual customizes their devices. It is important, however, that we place discourses about events like the dotcom bubble in a wider historical context, as part of a narrative about communication technology going back to the telegraph (Carey 1989; Mosco 2004).

Convergence is never just a technological process but is implicated in, and expressed as, profound and ongoing social, cultural and economic change. That said, the pervasive pleasures of new media devices, and their popularity within everyday popular cultures, tend to self-evidently promote technological determinism as a potent way of explaining their role in society. Device mania is an important component of mainstream teen culture: what's the latest 'must have' cool phone, media player or gaming device? But this needs to be placed in a context of the broader debates of inclusion/exclusion, the digital divide and ICTs, education and learning in information/knowledge societies and who profits from particular developments in media and communications industries.

Industrial convergence

As always with new media technologies, their introduction is shaped by competing interests, with governments being involved to varying extents, and they are always underwritten by prevailing ideologies, or ways of imagining their utility (Carey 1989; Winston 1998; Hesmondhalgh 2007). Some commentators suggest the ideological framing in the development of media in this early period of the twenty-first century can be summed up in the word 'marketization'. Murdock has criticized the process the term describes, noting that it involves the steady erosion of public interest values. Indeed, the rhetoric of marketization promises an opening up of markets, ensuring free and fair competition and promoting the interests of consumers. However, as Murdock notes, in this formulation the actual requirements of full citizenship, though at times ritually evoked, trail some way behind (Murdock 2005). For him, full citizenship in democracies with pluralist mediaspheres entails access to a range of ICT resources to allow audiences to exercise their social, cultural, economic and political rights.

Hesmondhalgh, in his analysis of convergence in the cultural industries, emphasizes the historical and ideological dimensions of media convergence. He writes:

> Information and entertainment would, it was envisaged, increasingly be consumed via some kind of hybrid of the computer and the television set and transmitted via cable, satellite and telephone lines as well as, or instead of, via the airwaves. Such convergence is still a long way from happening, even in the most prosperous countries, but the idea of convergence fuelled many of the more recent changes in the cultural industries . . . It is now sufficiently advanced that extremely important mergers and alliances have been formed across the different sectors, including most notably AT&T's purchase of TCI (1999) and the merger between AOL and Time-Warner (2000–2001). Many new technologies have been introduced because companies perceive that profits will be made out of such convergence. The most important of these are the various forms of digitalization and the provision of broadband channels . . . *Because powerful companies that provide jobs and prestige envisage such profits, national policymakers have introduced policies clearing the way for further rounds of convergence-led activity.*
>
> (Hesmondhalgh 2007: 131–2; emphasis added)

Hesmondhalgh describes four waves or identifiable periods of marketization (2007: 114–35).

1. The first occurred in the 1980s and 1990s with the deregulation and privatization of telecommunications markets in USA. The breaking up of 'Ma Bell' (AT&T) into seven 'Baby Bell' local phone companies was the most significant element of these processes, and the quid pro quo for AT&T agreeing to this was the US government allowing it into previously forbidden cross-industry sectors in IT (computer) markets.

2. The second wave of marketization concerned how Public Service Broadcasters (PSBs) were restructured through a range of market-oriented measures, usually financial, but also in terms of a more adversarial relationship to their national governments. The general intent of these measures was to position PSBs more competitively against commercial broadcasters, and to wind back their public service ethos.

3. The third wave of marketization has been about the 'transitional societies' of India, Russia, Eastern Europe and Latin America entering into major transformations from 1989 onwards, which allowed them to engage with major international corporations involved in cultural production. He writes: 'It is fair to say that, as the end of the Cold War coincided with the rise of neo-liberalism, a great number of the world's economies were brought under the aegis of marketisation, including their cultural sectors' (2007: 128).

4. The final wave he calls 'towards convergence and internationalization', and he sees this wave developing from 1992 onwards. The prospective convergence of the cultural industries with telecommunications and IT (including broadcasting, computing and IT), indeed, its figuring as 'inevitable' in policy discourses, marks the arrival of this final phase or wave of marketization. 'Convergence' became an autonomous and legitimating discourse to be deployed by corporations and governments alike. Hesmondhalgh explains how the US Government introduced the 1996 Telecommunications Act on the back of this discourse. In a similar way, the EU's Green Paper on Convergence in 1997 was 'heavily pro-marketisation', argues Hesmondhalgh. 'Convergence functions as a self-fulfilling prophecy: policy change is both brought about by perceived convergence and, at the same time, is likely to accelerate it' (2007: 135).

We will consider specific strategic 'convergence' mergers and alliances throughout the book, but another key argument is that the process of media convergence is inevitably tied to relentless industry consolidation and sectoral cross-ownership, and to the prevailing ideological and policy framings that underwrite it. There is abundant evidence that *convergence discourses* are continuing to play a strongly legitimating role in relation to media industry consolidation as much at the level of common-sense ideologies as in policy-making contexts.

In liberal democratic nation-states the terms plurality and diversity have been used to account for the architecture of service provision and the range of available formats and content genres. Indeed, the idea of sustainable media diversity in distributive platforms, as well as in relation to content itself, is emerging as a contested site for media policy in the twenty-first century. Policy goals for diversity and pluralism in broadband Internet, and access policies for higher bandwidth cellular mobile and digital television platforms are becoming increasingly important as traditional media move online, and more content is accessed through these channels.

My interest in the book also lies with the implications of media convergence and for audience usage of media. Nightingale identifies three challenges confronting the media convergence process that have significant consequences for audiences (Nightingale and Dwyer 2007):

- The first challenge arises from the fact that old media and cultural industries were unprepared for, and often resistant to, the impact digital media have on their core business activities. Online activity means people are no longer dependent on the media releasing information when it suits them – people now routinely create, borrow, share and even steal content that has been created by others.

- These activities have brought the second challenge into focus – the problem of how content might be 'protected', copyrights enforced and how the established media industries might access some of the income they believe they have lost through illegal file sharing. The content problem is central to the understanding of media convergence. It is both about protecting copyrighted content and simultaneously concerned with the problem of how to develop enough new content for the digital environment. Fortunately for the industry, in regard to the creation of new content, users came to the rescue by demonstrating that economic value can be extracted from the content users create for their own enjoyment. User Generated Content (UGC) is both a solution and an additional challenge for the media convergence process. UGC requires a quite specific environment in which to grow – that environment is usually described by the terms 'social networking' or 'social software'.

- The third challenge for media convergence arises because social networking is based on 'sharing' while media industries repurpose shared content for commercial transactions. The disjunctions between social networks, new audience formations of the World Wide Web, and consumer markets therefore arguably represents the most challenging issue facing governments and their regulatory agencies worldwide.

Technological convergence

One major difference between media industries today, and their predecessors is the proliferation of delivery modes and media platforms. There are many implications and challenges for media policy formation implicit in these changes. Where once it was imagined that convergence meant that all media would be delivered via the personal computer, it is now recognized that the new media reality is a multimedia one. Stories, news, commentary and gossip are packaged for delivery via media as different as domestic television sets, laptop computers and the personal mobile phone screen. This is seen in the newsrooms for major metropolitian newspapers where multi-skilled journalists are filing copy first for the online site to be followed by a video report and then a more in-depth article for the traditional newspaper product. And similar trends have been underway for several years now in the newsrooms of major broadcast organizations (Patterson and Domingo 2008). News from a consumption perspective, as Allan argues, citing comments made by Peter Chernin, the former president and chief operating officer of News Corporation,

> is a form of content that needs to be 'repurposed' so as to comply with the demands of the 'time-shifting' consumer, who interacts and engages with the possibilities created by an explosion of choices otherwise constrained by the 'old analog world'.
>
> (Allan 2006: 170)

While communications media are constantly undergoing significant transformations, in an era of deregulation (and frequently, re-regulation) and the Internet, it is important to recognize that the fundamental debates involving communication and society both change and stay the same. This underscores what Finnemann refers to as the 'co-evolution' of old and new media (Finnemann 2006). This analysis is not inconsistent with the flexible position advocated by the UK's communications regulator Ofcom, that 'The rapid evolution of convergence means that it may be better not to attempt to define the term, but rather to describe its impact, both in different parts of the value chain, and in different regions of the world' (Ofcom 2007b: 90).

Figure I.2 shows how from a UK perspective, communications markets have been converging for several decades, but that the pace has accelerated since 2005. Broadly similar evolutions with their own specific alliances and local inflections have developed elsewhere in the EU, in Australia, the USA, Canada and New Zealand. These developments mean that consumers are now faced with a set of communications services not just profoundly different from those in the 1970s, but even from those in the mid-1990s.

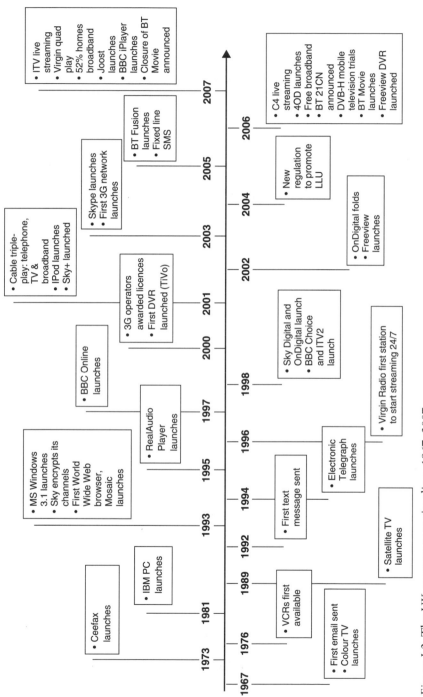

Figure I.2 The UK convergence timeline, 1967–2007

Regulatory convergence

These industry changes have necessitated changes in the policies developed for media regulation. While in the past it was adequate to treat the regulation of each medium separately (for example, to treat television as a different media industry from radio or the press), the current situation demands that the old media 'silos' be opened.

In other words, an important implication of these trends is that the traditional media of television, radio and the press are all evolving along with the rising popularity of new media forms. Accordingly, many laws, policy and regulation that have been developed in the context of existing media may often also be relevant to new IP media. These enduring concerns will include the wider set of law, policy and regulation which grapples with issues such as the media and democracy; media concentration and ownership; public service media and market liberalism, universal service and net neutrality; the representation of race, ethnicity and other diversities; news and the coverage of elections; the availability of a full range of programming genres; protection of the child audience; and the provision of services for less able audiences. Clearly traditional concerns do not just disappear because of new media delivery modes. We can safely predict that new modes will change social and cultural uses as a result of innovation in provision, for example, developments in the way people are using media while in transit based on their specific locations, accessing content that originates almost anywhere in the world, the ease of falsifying identity, or the altering content itself, through software which enables such modification, and other forms of as yet unseen creative media use.

Transformations in communications media industries are requiring governments and their regulatory agencies to respond to these changing mediascapes on behalf of market and audience constituencies. Several countries have dedicated, purpose-built 'convergent' regulatory agencies to oversee Broadcasting, Telecommunications (including the Internet) and Radio Communications industry sectors: Australia and the UK fit into this category with the Australian Communications and Media Authority (ACMA) and the Office of Communications (Ofcom), respectively. Italy has its Communications Authority, the Autorità per le Garanzie nelle Comunicazioni (or AGCOM). Other regulatory agencies were in some respects already convergent, at least to the extent that their sectoral regulation (for telecommunications, radiocommunications and broadcasting) were nominally housed within the same agency. Japan has a combined broadcasting and telecoms regulator: the Ministry of Internal Affairs and Communications (MIC). The Canadian Radio-Television Communications Commission (CRTC) and the US Federal Communications Commission (FCC) agencies fall into this latter category. Others are partially convergent, such as the Singaporean Government's Media Development Agency (MDA) that has a content regulation remit arising from the combining of broadcasting and film regulatory functions in 2003.

In these new networked mediaspheres, existing laws, policies and regulation for content, ownership and control will need to be supplemented with a broader set of access rules focusing on network delivery speed (for both downloads and uploads), mobility, privacy, network interconnection, and diversity in genre and origin of content (Nightingale and Dwyer 2007, see Table I.1). Moreover, the shift from a predominantly wireline telecommunications network environment to a competitive telecommunications data market and Next Generation Networks (NGNs), requires fundamental rethinking about coverage, funding and other arrangements concerning universal service. In this process, a core issue now on the agenda is whether broadband ought to be part of universal service requirements, and this is an issue we will discuss further in Chapter 5.

Table I.1 models the evolving concerns of media policy-makers in the transition from analogue (or legacy) systems to digital Internet Protocol-based new media worlds. The model assumes that the issues applying in column 1 may also apply in column 2.

In the likely event that governments use broadband to deliver certain education, health and other public services more widely, it can be seen that these might become as essential for households as emergency services over a telephone are today (OECD 2006).

Table I.1 Media policy evolution and ICT connectivities

Delivery infrastructures	1 Analogue/legacy	2 Digital IP
Wired (copper, HFC, optical)	Content • cultural maintenance/ localism • accuracy and fairness • classification Ownership and control	Access • speed/mobility/privacy • network interconnection • consumer price Diversity and genre choice
Spectrum/Wireless (broadcast, cellular, WiFi, WiMAX)	Licensing	Origination
	Codes of practice USOs	Authentication Intellectual property rights
Satellite (GPS)	Price controls	Network architecture

Industry consolidation, media convergence, democracy

A clear implication of such continuous industry change is that powerful corporations will always lobby and apply pressure to liberalize public interest protections to suit their own particular interests. Famously, Bagdikian (2004) has argued that only five corporations, 'The Big Five', absorb the lion's share of the 37,000 different media outlets (daily newspapers, magazines, radio and television stations, book publishers and movie companies) in the United States. These corporations are Time-Warner (AOL), Disney, Viacom, Vivendi-Universal and the Bertelsmann group. Bagdikian's core argument is that concentrated ownership of the media means that the public is only exposed to the viewpoints and opinions of five corporations whose interests are actually quite similar. Messages that do not fit within the prevailing attitudes, values or revenue goals of these corporations get little, if any, exposure. Democracy is the poorer for this reduced diversity in available media messages.

In his analysis of concentrated media ownership, US legal academic C. Edwin Baker (2007) identifies a number of adverse effects on democracy arising from a concentrated structure of media ownership. He marshals a series of interconnected reasons to explain why ownership matters. First, he argues that the goal of a more democratic distribution of 'communicative power' as source diversity will be more likely to be achieved under dispersed ownership of media. In this context he draws an important distinction between source diversity as a *commodity* value and as a *process* value, where the latter matters more for maintaining democracy. Second, Baker argues that the 'widest practical dispersal of media ownership' provides safeguards of 'inestimable value'. And, third, ownership based more on quality and less on the bottom line should be the measure for policy-makers (2007: 6–37).

It is interesting to note Baker's take on the 'convergence of media forms' and the argument that the Internet reduces media concentration. He argues that, at best, the question becomes to what extent the Internet 'reduces a comparatively few companies' share of the audiences in relevant contexts, and 'increases the number of independent, significant media outlets effectively accessed by diverse groups'. His conclusion is that the evidence on this count is mixed, and typically discussions involve 'sloppy thinking' which fails to consider the specific nature of problems with the 'old order and precisely what solution the Internet, whatever else it does, offers to *these* problems' (2007: 123).

Industry sectoral convergence can be interpreted as a multidimensional process involving various combinations of the earlier silo structures. One of the most fundamental has been the coming together of the Internet and telecommunications industries: this is also seen to be essential to the 'shift from voice to data' infrastructure, as we've already discussed in relation to VoIP (see Chapter 5).

Telecommunications corporations have been re-engineered as Internet Protocol (IP) businesses where voice is now just one category in an array of data services. The complexity of these transformations is underpinned by the fact that different content services (voice, video, music, radio) are capable of being delivered by a diversity of suppliers or 'platforms' (including telecommunications, digital terrestrial broadcast, cable and Internet corporations). Moreover, all content, sometimes made originally for a particular platform (e.g. television or 3G mobile telephony) is increasingly repurposed for delivery over the Internet.

Web 2.0 and network convergence

The rising popularity of social networking sites and social networking software, allowing multitasking of interaction, is now a favoured destination of choice for audiences, especially in younger age cohorts. It is standard practice for these groups to do any number of combination of activities such as instant messaging, audiovisual 'conferencing', play games, watching virally distributed videos, download music or television programmes simultaneously. In a comparable way, the mobile phone has also become a hub for many functions that were previously only provided by stand-alone devices. However, not all mobile applications have met with immediate success – handsets which can switch between fixed and mobile networks not only face the challenge of reconciling personal and household use, but also compete with other functionality and tariffs which offer the customer a similar proposition.

The spread of these access technologies is, however, very uneven throughout the developed world (let alone the developing world), and depends on cultural practices as much as the actual availability of specific technical infrastructures. In Australia, Asia and the EU in particular, growing numbers of people are now accessing the Internet on mobile networks. In Japan, where the total population is around 127 million, they easily lead the charge: the mobile (or 'Keitai') Internet is more popular than the fixed internet with over 100 million subscribers in 2007. In terms of the applications used on the Keitai, email is very popular with a recent survey indicating that 80 per cent use it, and the same proportion say they have downloaded music. TV for mobile is regularly used by over half of its subscribers. Some 75 per cent of users say they enjoy online clothes shopping with their mobile at least once a month, making Japan a model for m-commerce. Surprisingly perhaps, video calling, as in the UK, is used by less that 10 per cent of Keitai net users (Fitzpatrick 2007).

For media regulators, many of these usage trends are pointing to the need for policy development to be based on (delivery) platforms rather than particular media 'silos'. In the past, the link between the service (such as broadcasting or voice telephony) and the platform over which it was delivered was clear. Now proliferating wireline and wireless network infrastructures (DSL, satellite, cable, 3G mobile, WiFi and WiMAX) are blurring the distinction between the service and the platform. In these circumstances, the flow of formats across different platforms, often repurposed, and different ways of accessing content become the focus of our interest.

The Internet, advertising and search businesses

Industry transformations are closely implicated in the reconfiguring of traditional businesses. As digital distribution platforms have converged, the traditional packaging strategy for audiovisual content – the advertiser-funded television channel – has come under increasing pressure from the growing popularity of online advertising. For example, IT search businesses have streamlined traditional media advertising. Google has become the powerhouse in advertising largely by selling short text advertising on highly targeted topics people are searching for, or reading about, on the Internet (Vise 2005: 3). And it now competes with television advertising by placing short video ads on many of the websites where it sells advertising. Google and other businesses dependent on alliances with search engine-driven advertising businesses are investing heavily in the research and development of so-called 'search engine optimization' algorithms. Competitive advantage in the way searched material is ranked has become a key element in e-commerce, including businesses such as news organizations that have traditionally not been motivated in the first instance by advertising or mass marketing imperatives.

It can be seen that in this period of neoliberalism media corporations have developed new ways of amassing audiences for the purposes of building and maintaining profitable consumer media cultures. Traditional media corporations have rapidly re-engineered their businesses as multi-platform ones with integrated online outlets, for the milieu of digital capitalism. Intensifying Internet protocol networks and e-commerce underpin the rise of online platforms. These platforms have either been built from the ground up, or are acquired and then adapted to suit the requirements of the particular media corporation. As we discuss further in Chapter 1, the resulting adaptations by media corporations are called upon by the hegemonic demands of the neoliberalization project in a global marketplace. Neoliberalism requires the technologies of information, including the massive interactive databases of social networking websites, to 'compress the rising density of market transactions in both time and space' (Harvey 2005).

And bringing audiovisual material and targeted advertising together with social networking is an area that has been rapidly developed by Google and other corporations. Further evidence of this trend can be seen in the announcement of the billion dollar alliance between News Corporation and Google in 2006. The deal was an agreement making Google the exclusive provider of search and keyword targeted advertising for New's Fox Interactive Media Group, the entity responsible for managing News Corporation's growing stable of online sites (Shultz 2006).

Similarly, an alliance announced in 2007 between Google and DoubleClick to cooperate in the provision of Internet advertising has extended Google's existing dominance in online search and text advertising to image and video ads (Rampell and Ahrens 2007). The suggestion of regulators and fear of privacy advocates is that the marriage of Google database and DoubleClick advertising technologies will bring targeted display, and video advertising, straight to the consumers who are most likely to be interested in particular goods and services. With deep pockets and billions to spend on acquiring wireless spectrum, Google sees the future of the wireless industry is in advertising on small, mobile, handheld screens. The challenge for Google will be in working successfully with powerful carriers such as AT&T, Verison Wireless and Sprint-Nextel and handset manufacturers, to install their own operating software (Hart and Goldfarb 2007).

As a consequence of the rise of search businesses such as Google, eBay, MSN, Yahoo! and Amazon, the advertising industry has been forced to respond to these altered practices by more strategically matching fragmenting audience consumers to goods and services through specific media providers. For Christina Spurgeon, these developments are part of a 'shift from mass media to the new media of mass conversation' and that 'new media based on ICTs, such as the internet and cell phones, invite us to think in exciting ways about advertising, as an industry and marketing communication process, as well as a crucially important influence in consumer and public culture'. She writes:

> Conversational media are the communication services of the global network economy and information society. They overlay rather than supersede mass and niche media, and, as the older media forms are digitized, conversational media also augment and converge with mass media to produce new, niche and one-to-one media forms.
>
> (2008: 2)

Castells has referred to them as 'mass self communication' (Castells 2007). The advertising industries are closely implicated in processes of industry transformation that now exhibits a distinctively bifurcated structure: 'a small number of larger firms with an international orientation . . . have expanded horizontally into other marketing communication specializations, and large numbers of small firms with a primarily local (national) orientation' (Daniels 1997: 109, cited in Spurgeon 2008: 18).

Computer giants such as Microsoft, Intel, IBM, Cisco and Apple are a fundamental component of this mosaic of change too. Their vast investment strategies have an impact on the direction and shape of new media developments as social shaping of technology theorists have argued (Winston 1998; Sørensen and Williams 2002). Market-leading corporations structure arrangements that allow their business interests to be advanced. Often there is more benefit to one party than the other, although occasionally there may be a mutual benefit. For example, when Microsoft formed a strategic alliance with Viacom in 2007, the agreement was to cooperate in advertising, content distribution, event promotions and games on Viacom broadcast and online networks for a five-year period. It is reported that the deal facilitates Microsoft's access rights to Viacom TV and film content for use on Microsoft properties such as MSN and Xbox 360. In return, Viacom's 300-plus websites will use Microsoft's Atlas division as their ad server (abandoning their existing DoubleClick arrangement). Apparently this deal allows Microsoft to have the exclusive right to sell 'leftover' display ad inventory on Viacom's US sites (Hayes 2007).

The US internet advertising market was reported to be worth between $US20–40 billion in 2007, and some commentators expect it to grow to $US80 billion by 2010 (Schneider and Whoriskey 2008). Clearly, there is much at stake in these new Internet advertising markets, and they significantly contribute to the shape of the media and communications markets that audiences access.

Conclusion

In this chapter I have argued that unprecedented structural transformations are occurring throughout the media and communications industries, suggesting that they are no longer dominated by the traditional broadcasting or publishing industries. Media convergence is a process embedded within the networked informational economy, and is therefore a part of a much broader set of societal discourses that we discuss in the next chapter.

This book is concerned to focus on the impact of 'convergence' on traditional media, and this includes how new convergent media, such as the Internet, are affecting traditional media. But my argument is also at its core tracking how the rhetorics of convergence need to be critically assessed against fragmented, historically contingent developments in media and communications industries, audience, policy and regulation.

In this context, commercial Internet businesses and broadband infrastructures are shaping the direction of change and relations with audiences. The consequences of these transformations resonate through our everyday lives: socially, culturally, politically, economically, and technologically. Yet, paradoxically, in many ways, we can also observe that the development of commercial Internet cultures echoes the narrative histories of the telegraph, radio or broadcast television: stories about the accelerating consolidation of information-based entertainment and e-commerce markets (Williams 2001).

Media convergence is a multilayered object of study that warrants interdisciplinary analysis. A brief overview of the chapters to follow will provide a sense of how they will be approached in the book:

*   In Chapter 1, we begin by taking stock of the numerous instances of media convergence in our everyday lives. Models of interpreting media convergence are evaluated in the context of neoliberalism as a key framing ideology. We also consider a range of theoretical concepts and perspectives together with case studies of changing industry practices.
*   Chapter 2 provides an account of how major traditional (or 'legacy') media players are moving into the online space. Online platforms are either being built from the ground up, or are being acquired or co-opted, and then adapted to suit the requirements of particular media corporations. The acquisition of the social networking site MySpace by News Corporation is assessed as a case study which illustrates this trend. The global financial crisis highlights a need to more closely scrutinize the way media corporations are financed and operated.
*   In Chapter 3, the focus turns to national regulatory regimes for media ownership. The chapter begins by examining the underlying concepts behind these cultural and economic policy mechanisms in Australia, Canada, New Zealand, the United Kingdom, and the United States, before considering the extent to which their unique cultural expressions of media ownership regulation may inform generalizations for future policy development.
*   Chapter 4 considers how commercial media businesses are closely implicated in the performance of neoliberal ideologies, and argues that new audience engagement strategies can be seen as imagined responses to the 'segmenting tendency' in media industries. They also signal a shift away from the 'society-making' of traditional mass media forms to social

networking in new digital media usage. However, the argument is made that it remains to be seen whether people find this restructuring emancipatory, or ultimately merely a new variation of the underlying power relations in democratic media systems.

- Chapter 5 argues that policies for broadband by national governments have assumed centre stage, and are increasingly important elements in twenty-first-century infrastructure projects. The chapter considers how universal service provision must be rethought in twenty-first-century economies where broadband plays a vital economic, social and cultural role. If the Internet is the archetypical example of media convergence, then broadband infrastructures and applications are its preeminent forms. In this context we examine the restructuring of traditional telecommunications by VoIP and the rise to prominence of 'net neutrality' debates.

- Chapter 6 concludes that changing industry and audience practices, including the increasing uptake of online and mobile media, and the continuing liberalization of media ownership rules are closely interconnected. The chapter canvasses the argument that regulation of traditional media's ownership and market structure is no longer necessary because the Internet provides a robust and viable alternative, suggesting that such arguments are essentially moot, as the Web becomes more like traditional media. In these circumstances, there is renewed merit, and substantive appeal, in revisiting 'welfarist' media communications policy models: recent events in global financial markets make this return more salient than ever. The book concludes with the argument that welfarist theories of governance provide positive frameworks for citizen-centred media and communications infrastructures, advocating that these will need to be based on media systems with an integrated approach to diversity of content, platforms and ownership.

Further reading

Baker, C. E. (2007) *Media Concentration and Democracy: Why Ownership Matters.* New York: Cambridge University Press.

De Zengotita, T. (2005) *Mediated: How the Media Shape Your World.* Bloomsbury: London.

Hesmondhalgh, D. (2007) *The Cultural Industries* (2nd edn). London: Sage.

Kung, L., Picard, R. and Towse, R. (eds) (2008) *The Internet and the Mass Media.* London: Sage.

Nightingale, V. and Dwyer, T. (eds) (2007) *New Media Worlds: Challenges for Convergence*. Melbourne: Oxford University Press.

Spurgeon, C. (2008) *Advertising and New Media*. New York: Palgrave-Macmillan.

Storsul, T. and Stuedahl, D. (eds) (2007) *Ambivalence Towards Convergence: Digitalization and Media Change*, Göteborg University: Nordicom.

INTERPRETING MEDIA CONVERGENCE

Convergence

A word that describes technological, industrial, cultural and social changes in the ways media circulates within our culture. Some common ideas referenced by the term include the flow of content across multiple media platforms, the cooperation between multiple media industries, the search for new structures of media financing that fall at the interstices between old and new media, and the migratory behavior of media audiences who would go almost anywhere in search of the kind of entertainment experiences they want. Perhaps most broadly, media convergence refers to a situation in which multiple media systems coexist and where media content flows fluidly across them. Convergence is understood here as an ongoing process or series of intersections between different media systems and not a fixed relationship.

(Henry Jenkins 2006)

Introduction

In this chapter, my aim is to make connections between new media practices in our everyday lives and broader ideological framings, which can help us to contextualize these developments. For instance, we know that YouTube is a massively popular video-sharing website, but can its success be mainly attributable to media convergence? An article in *The Guardian* recently teased out some of these ideas. It asked, 'Does YouTube make any money'? Probably not was the quick answer. But it conceded that there was some mystery in Google's sibling's *modus operandi* despite it being a publicly traded entity, for which it paid $US1.65 billion in 2006. The author notes that the main problem with the site is that it will lose $US470 million in 2009, and this stems from an inability to sell ads on 97 per cent of pages of mainly user-generated content.

Arguably, the 'business model' will need to come up with other alternatives, such as 'broad sponsorships, sweetheart deals and product placement' (Johnson 2009b).

But let's assume that the popularity of the 'second most used search engine' and video-sharing site is in some way connected with media convergence: what else, besides its vague business model, makes it so appealing? It's probably worth delving into some history to reflect on this question. Convergence, as Jenkins notes, was used as early as 1983 by Ithiel de Sola Pool (in *Technologies of Freedom*) to describe a force of change in media industries:

> A process called the 'convergence of modes' is blurring the lines between media, even between point-to-point communications, such as the post, telephone and telegraph, and mass communications, such as the press, radio, and television. A single physical means – be it wires, cables or airwaves – may carry services that in the past were provided in separate ways. Conversely, a service that in the past was provided by any one medium – be it broadcasting, the press, or telephony – can now be provided in several different physical ways. So the one-to-one relationship that used to exist between a medium and its use is eroding.
>
> (Pool 1983: 23 cited in Jenkins 2006: 10)

While this physical infrastructure focus is important, by 2001, Jenkins had himself identified convergence as a multidimensional process with technological, economic, social (or organic), cultural and global forms that was not dissimilar to the transition and transformations of the Renaissance period (Jenkins 2001). While the **Gutenburg Galaxy** had been the driver of change for the older monastic order,

> Media convergence is sparking a range of social, political, economic and legal disputes because of the conflicting goals of consumers, producers and gatekeepers . . . the digital renaissance will be the best of times and the worst of times, but a new cultural order will emerge from it.
>
> (Jenkins 2001: 93)

Jenkins highlights the importance of the 'cultural logic of media convergence', involving matters beyond simply merging technologies and 'commercially produced materials and services traveling along well-regulated and predictable circuits'. Rather, convergence means 'entertainment content isn't the only thing that flows across multiple platforms'. For him, 'our lives, relationships, memories, fantasies, desires also flow across media channels' (2006: 17). In other words, his definition of media convergence is a deeper cultural one, covering a great deal more than just 'content' flowing through various utility 'infrastructures' like water, gas or electricity. Judging from the popularity of

YouTube, I think we can agree with this more complexly nuanced argument deriving from cultural logics.

Production, distribution, consumption

At the level of everyday media production, distribution and consumption, significant global industry trends indicate profound shifts in the way audiences increasingly receive their daily media (Croteau and Hoynes 2006). In particular, changing patterns of distribution are underpinned by the complex processes we refer to in convenient shorthand as convergence, to account for the evolution of communications media in society. Since the 1990s, the term 'convergence' has been applied most commonly to account for the development of digital technology, the integration of text, numbers, images and sound (Briggs and Bourke 2002: 267). But the technical conversion process we refer to as 'digitalization' is only one element of multidirectional industry change, albeit a fundamental one, and indeed, in some cases continuities are the key feature.

The Internet offers the prototypical example of the changing way media are made, distributed and consumed. However, we need to bear in mind that unlike traditional broadcast media, the Internet is *both* a point-to-point and point-to-multipoint (or mass) medium: it connects individuals but it also speaks to and interacts with vast numbers of people simultaneously. It's worth recounting some of the new media practices referred to in the Introduction that have emerged within the past decade:

- music and videos being downloadable from the Internet to portable players;
- mobile phones with music, video, a built-in camera and Internet access;
- games consoles which are also CD and DVD players with Internet; connectivity and a hard drive capable of storing music and video;
- proliferation of blogs and uploading of videos to sites such as YouTube and Current TV;
- massive growth of social networking sites such as Facebook, MySpace, Bebo, and interaction in online worlds like Second Life, Habbo Hotel or World of Warcraft;
- ubiquity of search engines, and dominance of Google as an Internet access point;
- digital media replacing and supplementing analogue products and services with interactive and multi-platform convergent ones;
- broadcast TV and other news and entertainment content distributed over broadband telecommunication (including mobile) networks;
- audio and audiovisual telephony over the Internet ('VoIP');

- Internet access, including email, and audiovisual packet communication by mobile telephony, and other handheld devices;
- proliferation of 'intelligent' wireless networks, which allow products and services such as location-based devices.

It can be seen that in this process of change the earlier **silo structures** of broadcasting, telecommunications, publishing, and information technology industries in the twentieth century have been shaken by more flexible industrial dynamics and technological changes in advanced capitalist societies (Harvey 1990, 2001).

Flew (adapting Barr 2000) uses three overlapping circles to diagrammatically represent 'the three C's of convergent media' to explain a model of convergence and new media: convergent media involves 'the combination of the three Cs – computing and information technology (IT), communications networks, and digitized content' (Flew 2008: 2). In Flew's view, we should not underestimate the magnitude of convergent media, since all aspects of our lives, including art, business, government, journalism and education, health and so on are touched by interactive digital media environment and 'a plethora of ICT devices' (Flew 2008: 22).

The implications of these developments require significant rethinking by governments, policy-makers and industry regulators. And as the lines blur between industry sectors, there is a gradual convergence of the functions of governance bodies and responsibilities: it no longer makes sense to have totally separate governance systems for telecommunications, the Internet and broadcasting, as discussed in the Introduction.

Hesmondhalgh's understanding of the convergence process emphasizes the key drivers of change in the cultural industries, but he also argues that policy-makers 'worked hard to enable it for fear that, otherwise, corporations in their domain would lose out in the global competition for profits' (Hesmondhalgh 2007: 261). He refers to Murdock's (2000) useful categorization of the three principal clusters of convergence meanings: *convergence of cultural forms*, including the idea of a 'grand fusion' of multimedia; *convergence of corporate ownership*, as an economic and organizational phenomenon recognizable at the level of corporate strategy and structure; and *convergence of communication systems*, describing the manipulable and recombinant nature of digitized media technologies (Hesmondhalgh 2007: 262).

Convergence and market freedom

As I argued in the Introduction, 'convergence' is often used in discourses attempting to explain burgeoning developments in media and communications markets. We need to evaluate media convergence in terms of both ideological and production processes under neoliberalism more generally. In fact, it's critical that we begin to consider this relationship and its significance, and how we might conceptualize it, in the context of wider trends within capitalism and globalization.

In *A Brief History of Neoliberalism*, David Harvey defines neoliberalism as based on an idea that 'the social good will be maximized' by 'bring[ing] all human action into the domain of the market' (2005: 3). Harvey argues that neoliberalism 'requires technologies of information creation and capacities to accumulate, store, transfer, analyse, and use massive databases to guide decisions in the global marketplace'. 'Hence', he continues, 'neoliberalism's intense interest in and pursuit of information technologies (leading some to proclaim the emergence of a new kind of "information society")'. Furthermore, 'these technologies have compressed the rising density of market transactions in both time and space'. As a result, he suggests, they have produced a particularly intensive burst of what he referred to in his earlier book *The Condition of Postmodernity*, as 'time–space compression'. But in terms of its explanatory power for processes of media convergence, neoliberalism must underpin our understanding. Its shibboleths for the unfettered operation of free markets are ineluctably tied to new ICT and new cultural industries practices (2005: 4). Proponents of unbridled market transactions and consolidation in media and communications draw on these ideological legitimations, as they do for merger and acquisition activity in other industry sectors. Most importantly, few would deny that as leading-edge 'new economy' activities, there is a close affinity between these burgeoning media and communications alliances and the political-economic rhetoric that paves their way.

Harvey's account of the neoliberalization project forms the broader context of media and communications industry change. His narrative of its rise through complex constructions of consent, which varied quite markedly between the UK and the USA, its tensions, contradictions and uneven geographical spread throughout the globe, and its conditions that have generated alternative political movements is one that needs to be at the centre of our analyses. Certainly the neoliberalization turn from the 1970s, with deregulation of legal and regulatory frameworks, and privatization of former state-owned and state-controlled assets, created the conditions that allowed new ICT alliances to prosper.

Neoliberal theories, and in particular those advocated by the UK (Thatcher) and US (Reagan) Governments in the 1980s, but implemented throughout the globe from China to South Africa, from Japan and other Asian 'tiger' economies, to Sweden and West Germany, all had their distinctive modes of implementation. Harvey describes four processes that were critical to these transformations beginning in the 1970s, put in place during the 1980s and consolidated in the 1990s (Harvey 2005: 90–3):

1. A process of 'open financialization' created business environments conducive to foreign direct investment and portfolio investments (or 'vulture capital'). In this process, markets internationally experienced 'a wave of innovation and deregulation'.

2. There was an expansion in the 'geographical mobility of capital' arising from the removal of barriers to its free flow and the widespread adoption of free trade agreements under the auspices of the World Trade Organization.

3. The 'Wall Street–IMF–Treasury complex' was hegemonic in economic policy thinking, and this was used to persuade developing countries that the neoliberalization path was the best to follow. This often involved 'preferential access to its huge consumer market ... the US, riding a wave of technological innovation that underpinned the rise of the so-called "new economy", looked as if it had the answer, and that its policies were worthy of emulation'.

4. Harvey argues, the replacement of the residual Keynesian policies with monetarist ones in research institutes and universities was determinative, emphasizing the control of inflation and constraints over public finances, ahead of full employment and a social safety net. The sum of these technical and ideological conditions constituted the 'Washington Consensus' from the mid-1990s, paradigmatically represented in US and UK neoliberalization models (Held 2004).

Whether the excesses of market freedom and its debasement into absolute 'free enterprise' play out in more extreme forms of hegemony in the media industries, as seen in the oil industries and the intervention by the USA in the Middle East, remains to be seen. For McChesney (1999), it has already reached such a level. However, what is clear, is that neoliberalism constitutes, in Bourdieu and Wacquant's terminology, a 'new planetary vulgate' that pervades international economic policy (2001). A whole schema of ideological oppositions underpins the new common sense, where fundamentally 'the state' is positioned in opposition to 'the market'. They argue:

> The new planetary vulgate rests on a series of oppositions and equivalences which support and reinforce one another to depict the contemporary transformations advanced societies are undergoing – economic disinvestment by the state and reinforcement of its police and penal components, deregulation of financial flows and relaxation of administrative controls on the

employment market, reduction of social protection and moralizing celebration of 'individual responsibility'.

(2001: 4)

Their argument is also one that describes processes of neoliberal globalization
and the role of the state: in turns, withdrawing from marketplace interventions,
or with equal necessity, developing and implementing the policies and regulations, which facilitate investment capital.

Against this background of the broader societal and economic conditions,
we need to also focus on ways of thinking about how the media industries
themselves are transforming. It is to these theorizations that we now turn.

Co-evolution of old and new media

The ways in which we conceive the relations between existing and new media
are pivotal to debates surrounding media convergence. Niels Finnemann identifies a number of theories on this relationship, arguing that a *co-evolutionary*
framework is more suitable than those of general replacement or convergence.
His argument concerns how the Internet contributes to a change in the overall
media system through the 'coexistence' of paid and unpaid news and other
content; 'individualization and globalized reach'; and public spaces fragmented
according to specialized, professionalized and individualized needs and interests
(Finnemann 2006).

Case study
Finnemann's review of theories of relations between old and new media

Reviewing a number of theories dealing with the relations between old
and new media, which assumes a wider diversity than the term *convergence*
often implies, Niels Finnemann has usefully distinguished a series of
theories in four principal clusters:

1. *Theories of cyberspace* suggesting the emergence of a new separate
   universe beyond real life, a parallel virtual community (Rheingold
   1993), a City of Bits or E-topia (Mitchell 1996, 1999), or just *Being
   Digital* (Negroponte 1995). In the 1990s, the idea of cyberspace as
   a new, separate, autonomous and virtual space of its own was prominent. The main problem with this way of conceptualizing media
   change was that it inadequately explained how the Internet is actually integrated with everyday living. Indeed, Flew has argued that the
   research of Miller and Slater in their *The Internet: An Ethnographic*

Approach was valuable precisely because it engaged with how media usage was empirically embedded in everyday Trinidadian life and cultural practices (Flew 2008: 69).

2. *Theories of complete replacement* (McLuhan 1964; Boltz 1993; Negroponte 1995; Poster 1995; Deibert 1997; Nielsen 1998; Moravec 1998, 2000). Finnemann notes that replacement theories exist in varying degrees of radicalism, ranging from those such as Moravec (1998 and 2000) who argues from an evolutionary position that computers (or artificial intelligence) will outperform the human mind (and bring the history of man as dominating creature in nature to an end), to theories based on McLuhan's idea that electronic media bring with them the end of the Gutenberg Galaxy because of their combined auditory and visual capacities. Similarly, Deibert (1997) juxtaposes print culture to digital culture, while Poster (1995) distinguishes between (analogue) electronic culture and digital culture.

3. *Theories of a new hegemonic superstructure* identified by Finnemann are those that consider the Internet/digital media to be hegemonic media. Figuring pre-eminently in this connection is Castells' (1996–1998) 'new social morphology' in the form of 'an internet-supported space of flows on top of all societies'. Finnemann notes that

    > Even if it might turn out not to be completely false, it underestimates the role and function of old media – which in turn are also digitized. Since the new millennium there are many indications that old media have become dominant actors in the development of the Internet.
    >
    > (See Chapter 2)

4. *Theories of actual convergence*, as we've discussed earlier, such theories popularly conceived in the notion of 'convergent media' are well established, and probably the most popular conception of the relation between old and new media. But as Finnemann points out, 'Unfortunately, it is very unclear. Some of the former theories (foremost complete replacement theory) can be considered as variants of convergence theory' (see also Barr 2000; Flew 2008). There are several key foci of convergence theories (see the discussion at pp. 9–15), which may be summarized as follows:
    - converging networks;
    - institutional and organizational mergers of the ICT, telecoms and media corporations;
    - content convergence.

For Finnemann, any one of these clusters of theoretical approaches by itself would not be capable of identifying various relevant issues. He suggests that instead, these diverse arguments 'point to a need for a theory of co-evolution of old and new media within a new more complex set of media'. Drawing on Hallin and Mancini's *Comparing Media Systems* (2004), he sees specific forms of interactions between old and new media as a matter of history, geopolitics and culture. Intensified interaction between print media, electronic media and digital media, and cross-medial relations are all critical factors, and

> The filling out of this new media matrix depends on the different social and cultural drivers, whether commercial or noncommercial – not least civil society and public service broadcast institutions. Their drive may lead to different developments on a variety of parameters for possible cultural variation, such as in the spread of and forms of hypertext, multimedia and interactive communication as well as utilizations of a) private–public communication, b) local, national and transnational use and c) differentiations according to personal and professional interest.

In summary, he advocates a complex view of the co-evolution of old and new media:

1. The Internet and digital media provide new features and facilities and digital media contribute to a general change in the overall media matrix.
2. They do so, though, not by replacing old media. Rather, what we have is a process of co-evolution, including the development of a variety of new inter-relationships.
3. While old media are refunctionalized/repurposed, they are also influential actors in the development of Internet forms.
4. An implication is that existing cultural and social processes – not least those inherited in existing media systems – may lead to the development of varied forms for the integration and utilization of the Internet in different cultures (Finnemann 2006).

Internetization and mediatization

Several commentators have provided accounts of the evolving relations between traditional and new media as resembling a pincer movement. For example,

Fortunati refers to convergence as a process of *internetization* and *mediatization*, where traditional media are internetizing, and the Internet is mediatizing itself. For Fortunati, convergence is a process that both unifies media (they all become digital in form) and yet at the same time promotes diversification. While the traditional media were initially slow in responding to the challenge of internetization, they have become more adept at developing strategies that link their offline activities to online 'enhancements' (Nightingale and Dwyer 2006: 25–42; 2007: 25). Arguing for a similarly more complex interpretation of convergence, Dallow (2007) notes a movement characterized by

> further penetration into these newly mediatized online spaces by the older media, of newspapers, television, movies, radio, as well as by marketing and advertising more laterally. These kinds of changes are not merely summative (convergent), but exponential (emergent).

The point of his observation is that we need to recognize that there is a complex evolutionary, adaptive and organic process at stake, not just a kind of media 'building-site'.

From different, but related perspectives, other media theorists have examined changing meanings of mediation in the interactions and 'embedded compromises' between old and new media (Bolter and Grusin 1999; Manovich 2001; Evans and Wurster 2000). Our capacity to conceptualize mediatization, then, is supported by the inclusion of a range of perspectives. If Jenkin's (2006) view of media convergence figures the flow of content across different platforms (in *transmedia story telling*) as well as through a cultural convergence in audience agency, then De Zengotita's view is that mediatization in a postmodern world is operating at the level of common sense and 'in that awareness, the ethos of mediation is established' (De Zengotita 2005).

In his far-reaching account of world systemic historical development, *Critique of Information*, Lash argues that 'informationization' has erased distance between media theory, society and culture. He writes: ' "Media theory" for its part emerges when the principle of information which is also that . . . of "media", becomes so predominant as to engulf the realm of theory too. As society becomes increasingly like information, theory becomes increasingly like media' (Lash 2002: 76). At the same time, his view of mediation itself is distinctive, and interconnected with his view of media as machines:

> Mediation becomes machinic in the media age. With the proliferation of digital media, the experiential density of mediatic objects becomes so significant that we can speak of a parallel space. With mass media, mediation took place through a parallel realm, but one comprised of signs that were still one-dimensional or linear narrative, or two-dimensional

(painted or photographic images). With digital media and the generalized brand environment, the signs become three-dimensional. They become tactile. They constitute and inhabit a space in which we orient ourselves. Representations-of-space for Lefebvre suffocated the life from spatial practice in homogenizing the grain of their particularity under the sign of an unhappy universal. But in the information age, as these representations transform into objects, they, themselves become spatial.

(2002: 125)

The implications of this spatialized understanding of mediation for culture and cultural studies are immense. In Lash's opinion, the subject matter for media and cultural studies is about *objects* not audiences, writers, texts, signs or narratives. Translated to an assessment of media convergence and its devices, we might speculate that the time/space significance of iPod usage is likely to be the point of analysis, not so much the meaning of a specific, personalized set of tunes. Arguably, the meaning of this shift in mediation overlaps with De Zengotita's ubiquitous, commonsensical understanding too. Distinctively though, for Lash, the valorization of capital is patterning this world of mediatized objects, in an intellectual property sense: 'And with the increase in images, of culture machines, of information, of icons of brands and the like, narratives now just become one of many types of cultural thing' (2002: 126). In the next section, I want to turn to some actual applications of ideas of mediation.

Video and the new 'distribute-it-yourself' ethos

New ways of distributing our narratives are now ubiquitous in our media-spheres. An industry change emerging from the early years of the twenty-first century that has been rapidly increasing in popularity is the practice of distributing 'viral' videos, through Internet peer-to-peer (P2P) software, video-sharing sites and plain old emailing. Industry data confirms the increasing popularity of viewing online video (ACMA 2008b; Hitwise 2007; Ofcom 2008a).

The author of 'Viral Video Hall of Fame' in *PC World* with the comical subtitle, 'From crooning politicians to a grocery store manager who can crush windpipes with his mind, these are the greatest hits of the YouTube Age' makes the claim that 'it's possible to list "25 Classics" since the advent of YouTube in 2005'. One implication of this telescoped new media history is that people can remember these virally circulating 'hits', even though they may not have appeared, at the time of first viewing to be all that significant. For example, the *Lonelygirl15* video blog is cited as one such recognizable moment in this short history. It's been suggested that part of the video's memorability arises from the fact that it was caught out as a fake, hatched by a Californian screenwriter Ramesh Flinders and filmmaker associate Miles Beckett. The star of *Lonely-girl15*, a fictional teenage girl named 'Bree' is played by a New Zealander, Jessica Rose. For a period of time, those who viewed the video were under the false impression that this series of bedroom reflections was an 'authentic' video blog until *Los Angeles Times* reporters finally outed the creators and their starlet in September 2006 (*PC World* 2007).

It was reported that on the basis of the success of *Lonelygirl15* the creators had constructed an alliance with social networking site Bebo to create a British spin-off story that will use brands to help define the characters (Holton and Cowan 2007). But this time the focus of attention is 'Kate Modern', who has a profile on Bebo that allows fans to interact with the character and her videos. The principals of the project freely admit that the idea is to provide a vehicle for advertisers to display branded products and services at a teen market that has now moved online (see Chapter 2).

In addition to being a new media form in its own right, *Lonelygirl15* was also symbolic of wider DIY trends too: to make your own content and to 'distribute-it-yourself', which became popular for various genres of movies and television programming using peer-to-peer (P2P) sharing software, and shorter clips or more professionally produced 'mobisodes' (Goggin 2007) using the Internet or mobile net. In downloading and viewing videos like this, people separated by geography, social and cultural differences are linked into a social network; thus a community of interest was created or augmented by the video itself. In this sense, such video distribution practices were a harbinger of the rich media possibilities of participatory '**Web 2.0**'; sites like Google's YouTube, Facebook, Bebo, MySpace, Wikipedia, and their ilk. To these highly popular sites can be added growing second-tier video sites such as Hula, a joint venture between News Corporation's Fox and General Electric's NBC Universal, Veoh, Joost and the Sony-owned 'Crackle'. Major branded portals including AOL, MSN and Yahoo! rely on audience strategies based on video aggregation, as do incumbent traditional media corporations (including newspaper outlets) who increasingly use video content to attract audiences who might otherwise use broadcast media.

Case study
Copyright Protection and Video Distribution

These developments in video-sharing have not been left uncontested by powerful owners of copyright interests. In 2007, the US television giant NBC Universal and Viacom joined forces in a suit filed in a US district court in California to pressure YouTube (and their owners, Google) to filter copyrighted material from its popular video-sharing website. In an earlier US$1 billion suit, Viacom had claimed it was able to identify 150,000 of its clips on the YouTube service and that these had been viewed 1.5 billion times with each characterized by Viacom as deliberate copyright infringement (Anderson 2007a). NBC and Viacom then together backed Los Angeles newsman Robert Tur, who sued YouTube for letting users post his very well-known video of trucker Reginald Denny being beaten by police during riots in Los Angeles in 1992 (Agence France Press 2007). In the case NBC and Viacom depicted themselves defending the rights of less powerful individuals against Internet giant Google's vast financial and legal resources.

Lawyers for Google argued that they 'meet and exceed our responsibilities under the Digital Millennium Copyright Act (DMCA), which balances an easy takedown process and provides complete safe harbor for hosts such as YouTube' (Agence France Press 2007).

It has been reported that YouTube has been sued by other organizations, including a class-action copyright violation suit filed by the UK's Premier League in New York State. The League's suit was filed on behalf of copyright owners 'whose works were reproduced, distributed, publicly displayed, performed or otherwise transmitted or disseminated on youtube.com without authorisation' (Agence France Press 2007).

Earlier in 2007, US media giant Viacom had already launched a billion dollar lawsuit against YouTube, accusing it of illegally showing clips from its television shows. The Tur case marked the first time NBC took copyright concerns about YouTube to court. It also indicated the complexity of interests in this emerging old/new media alliance. NBC and YouTube entered into a strategic partnership in 2006. Google and YouTube lawyers argued that the Tur case ought to be dismissed on the grounds the website is protected by the DMCA, which simply requires it to remove copyrighted material after the owners complain. Their defence team argued that 'To accept the plaintiffs' unreasonable interpretation of the law would be disastrous for our dynamic industry, the backbone of the information economy.' Viacom and NBC's view was that if YouTube can filter out other illegal materials such as pornographic materials, and certain copyrighted content, then it can do the same for those protected by copyright (Agence France Press 2007). As class actions against YouTube/ Google grew, a new system of copyright protection for video clips has been announced by YouTube. That new video filter system is being developed in response to pressure applied by several large traditional media companies (including Disney, News Corporation, NBC Universal, CBS, Viacom and Microsoft), to agree to a set of principles to govern the way that copyright law and anti-piracy measures should be applied to video and music on the Internet (Chaffin 2007). The new filter system is a proprietary solution to inhibit the posting of copyrighted files. Commentators suggested that Google was in a rush to introduce the new system because once an industry initiative was formed, Google would be forced to accept the common model (Anderson 2007b).

Clearly, we cannot underestimate what's at stake in how the Internet is governed (Lessig 2004; Goldsmith and Wu 2008; Zittrain 2008). In *The Times Online*, Graham Smith, a partner in a British IT and intellectual property law firm, wrote:

> Earlier this month, a national tabloid newspaper won an online industry award for best use of video. One can hardly imagine a better example of convergence: an ink and paper publisher now transformed, thanks to the internet and broadband, into a purveyor of moving images.
>
> (Smith 2007)

In making this point, Smith wanted to construct a broader deregulatory argument: he was suggesting that the Internet is not broadcast TV and therefore should not be regulated in a like manner. Although video distribution over new media platforms certainly raises unprecedented regulatory issues, there are many continuities with existing legal and regulatory frameworks. In the next section, the history of capitalism itself will help us to interpret our changing media industries.

After 'Web 2.0'

The story of Tulipmania that gripped the Dutch economy in the 1630s has been used for centuries as a cautionary tale of speculative folly; and, not surprisingly, it was often retold around the time of the Dotcom bubble crash at the turn of the millennium. Anne Goldgar, a specialist in modern European history, argues that the Dutch mania for tulips has been heavily mythologized by historians. Her take is that there is much more to the story than greed, market madness and gullibility of crowds; in fact, the tulip became such an object of intense desire for Dutch citizens in the seventeenth century (Goldgar 2007).

Several elements of the Tulipmania story resonate with contemporary change in new media industries – the sheer rate of take-up for one, and the previously unseen impacts of *intangible* value under market forces. Graham, in *Hypercapitalism*, uses a Marxian framework to analyse the social perceptions of value in language and new media products, often as 'fictitious commodities' within a global knowledge economy. He argues:

> [T]he problems of understanding a knowledge economy become analogous to the problems facing classical political economy in its day: namely to identify the historical differences in production, distribution, and consumption; circulation, exchange, and value, that characterize new forms of social relatedness peculiar to a global knowledge economy as historically unique. As a 'substance' knowledge is ultimately ineffable. As a process, it is incredibly complex. Nevertheless, any knowledge economy based on the logic of capitalist commodity production must involve specific forms of labor, the products of which can be owned separately from the people that produce them . . . New property laws and new technologies are presupposed in the full development of any knowledge economy – new laws to distinguish between the conscious activity of people and ownership in the products of that activity; new technologies for the production, distribution, circulation, and exchange of knowledge commodities.
>
> (Graham 2006: x)

Graham's arguments attest to the changing social relations of production in a Knowledge Economy. For him, 'hypercapitalism' contains a contradictory set of relationships embedded in the logic of capital,

> those between production, circulation speed (or the speed of mediation), wealth, legitimacy, power, language and value . . . the products of powerful and 'sacred' dialects are rendered digital and propagated globally as binary bits representing numerical measures of economic wealth, or money (itself a mode of meaning), increasing and decreasing in value with each revolution.
>
> (Graham 2006: 7)

His theorization of globalized production processes within the Knowledge Economy goes some way to explaining both the affordances and constraints of new media and how it interacts with industry change more broadly. He argues:

> In a system with such a singular and ephemeral focus, production, consumption and circulation converge to form a temporally inseparable moment, and 'value creation' becomes an immediate, continuous process that analytically collapses the formerly separable spheres of production, distribution, exchange and circulation. I argue that there can be no analytical usefulness in separating these spheres within hypercapitalist political economy because the boundaries – conceptual, practical and temporal – between them are dissolved by new media's ubiquity; by the work habits

engendered by new mediations; and by the mass, and more importantly, the speed of hypercapitalist exchanges as they expand to encompass a global totality.

(Graham 2006: 8)

Undoubtedly there's a high level of generality and abstraction required to make sense of these ideas connected with new media ownership and those with a stake in the 'thin air' business (Leadbeater 2000). Perhaps equally abstract, as Graham (2006) notes, is the fact that 'the genomes of entire nations have become corporately owned'. Nonetheless, these transformations in value creation mean there are also important implications of such shifts in the production, distribution and consumption of information, and therefore knowledge.

Intangibility in new media has various dimensions. For McGuigan, a discourse of 'coolness' is actually a dominant tone in capitalism today. Corporations have incorporated counter-cultural traditions and deployed signs of 'resistance' simply in order to market their wares (see Frank 1997; McGuigan 2006). He writes:

> This is the era of *cool capitalism*. The original 'spirit of capitalism', often associated with puritanical Protestantism, emphasized deferred gratification and hard work. The 'new spirit of capitalism' (Boltanski & Chiapello, 2006 [1999]) is much more hedonistic and, indeed, 'cool'. Immediate gratification is sought and sold in the sphere of consumption. Consumers are, in effect, seduced by the delights of high-tech and 'cool' commodities, promising to satisfy their every desire, especially if they are 'different' and vaguely rebellious in tone. Great stress is placed on individual autonomy and the more complex notion of 'individualisation' (Beck & Beck-Gernsheim, 2002 [2001]). The individual perpetually on the move, accompanied by a personal soundtrack and in constant touch, is the ideal figure of such a culture (Agar, 2003; Jones, 2005).

Proliferating access to and usage of new media devices suggest that these changes in the sphere of consumption need to be factored into our explanations of incessant corporate realignments in the media and communications industries. Above all, our assessments of media convergence need to be cognizant that there are very particular connections between the corporations that own the cultural industries, and the media products, services and experiences they structure for consumption. The role played by networking structures in the media industries also warrants further analysis.

The network society and network intensification/ extensification

Various commentators have analysed the intensified/extensified contribution of networks to production and the accumulation of wealth in the late twentieth and early twenty-first centuries. For example, Hassan's view is that 'the evolution of the network society is a world-historical development' (2004) and the far-reaching social, political, economic, cultural, legal and technological changes it ushers in have been examined in a great deal of detail by scholars such as Castells ([1996], 2000, 2001, 2007), Benkler (2006), Lash (2002) and Schiller (1999). Hassan's approach in reading these positions is to recast them by making 'explicit the elements of the power/ideology nexus that underscore perspectives on the network society' (Hassan 2004: 31). In making his critique, he identifies four 'principal dynamics' or 'scapes' (see Appadurai 1996) to assist in focusing on this power/ideology nexus: 'Digital Technology', 'Digital Capitalism', 'Digital Globalisation' and 'Digital Acceleration'. In my opinion, each of these categories assists our understanding of evolving mediascapes, and together they are shaping the network society/networked information economy structures.

In sifting through this material that is theorizing the network society, Hassan has made some important observations. Noting the dependency of digital globalization on the 'ICT revolution', he argues that together the two have 'mutually reinforced one another to evolve into a supercharged capitalism'. Furthermore, this marriage has resulted from a multilayered process of convergence that

[has] brought capitalism to a higher order of organization, complexity and flexibility . . . it is my contention that the convergence of neoliberalism and the ICT revolution has meant that the economic dimension is the one that carries most of the power and momentum. To a very substantial degree, it underpins and facilitates the 'globalization' of both the cultural and the political. This is not to argue that the economy is the sole driver of the cultural and the political, but simply that the levels of cultural and political globalization attained today would not have been possible without the convergence of ICTs and neoliberal capitalism.

(Hassan 2004: 23)

If we then ask, how are networked media different from traditional media, as Hassan does, and what do these changes mean for the spaces of difference 'that are vital for the production of cultural diversity', his reply is that the media and what they do (as part of the informatized sector), have become *intensified* and *extensified* through the convergence (of neoliberal globalization and ICTs)

(2004: 50). In a McLuhanesque echo, following Lash's argument in *Critique of Information*, in Hassan's view, this means that media *are* the network society. As mediatization embraces all areas of society, mediatized culture seeps 'into every nook and cranny of social and cultural life' (Hassan 2004: 50).

It is in this scenario spaces of difference where cultural diversity are produced are erased. In my view, this asserted lack of difference between media and society, and media and culture, requires treating with some caution, however. The role of corporations in respect of different cultural productions is not evenly distributed, and this has enormous consequences in terms of media concentration. In this connection, we need to distinguish between processes of informationization and commodification. In the end the outcomes of these processes may be similar, but the means are different (although still connected): the former refers to a flattening out of cultural diversities through digitization/mediatization, while the latter occurs under a logic of media convergence and industry consolidation.

Castells has updated his well-known thesis in the *Rise of the Network Society*: the idea that networks now play a fundamental role in the constitution of economic, social and cultural infrastructures. He now argues that the development of interactive, horizontal networks of communication has induced the rise of a new form of communication, so-called 'mass self-communication', over the Internet and wireless communication networks (Castells 2007: 238–66). The implications of these conditions are that insurgent politics and social movements are able to intervene more decisively in the new communication space. Not surprisingly, corporate media and mainstream politics have also invested heavily in this new communication space where mass (traditional) media and horizontal communication networks are converging. In his revised formulation, the public sphere has been transformed by new configurations of power relations.

At a more fundamental level, some network society theorists are researching the specific impacts that the sum of individual activity can make to the information economy, rather than society or polity. Benkler (2006), in his influential book *The Wealth of Networks*, is concerned to provide an account of the new economy as a *networked information economy*. Like Castells, Benkler interprets the role of the Internet and networked ICTs in general as making an enormous contribution to this economy. His thesis is one that explores a fundamental shift in the economy and the relations of production. For Benkler, *social production* in the networked information economy underpins and is driving a new material capacity. Consumers have become more active and creatively interventionist in producing goods and services, through individuals mobilizing expanded knowledge by using networked computers. Social networking sites such as YouTube, Facebook, Bebo and other 'Web 2.0' sites like

Wikipedia are cumulatively generating vast amounts of information and knowledge. Through their coordinated networking efforts, individuals are reconfiguring productive capacities in both commodified and non-commodified ways.

While Lévy (1997) saw 'collective intelligence' operating at the level of knowledge, Benkler argues that as well as knowledge, transformations are occurring culturally, socially and most significantly, economically. In particular, his argument privileges the 'increased capabilities of individuals as the core driving social force behind the networked information economy' (Benkler 2006: 15).

Mobilities

As a conceptual field within new media studies, mobility has emerged as central to explanatory frameworks of the network society, including in relation to the usage of convergent media devices. Co-existing with the expanded knowledge base of social networks, commentators have begun the empirical and theoretical exploration of the interdependencies of *mobile network societies* (Larsen et al. 2006: 20). For example, Larsen et al. argue that social networks underpin modern living on an unprecedented scale of significance in local and global workplaces and families, indicating:

> Most people's biographies and mobilities are relational, connected and embedded rather than individualized. They are, though, individualized in the sense that each person's networks and relations are specific to the individual . . . People are enmeshed in social dramas that have social and emotional consequences.

Networks both enable and constrain possible 'individual' actions (Larsen et al. 2006: 26).

Obviously the consequences and meaning of different mobile wireless experiences for individuals are fundamental for industry stakeholders and the introduction of innovative products and services: devices, user-friendly interfaces and network platforms are all dynamically linked with how consumers actually make use of these communications in their daily lives.

Larsen et al. (2006) describe five 'interdependent mobilities' that arise in the relations between communications systems and physical travel 'within the specific context of mobile workers, teleworkers and the coordination of everyday mobility':

1. *Physical travel* of people for work, leisure, family life, pleasure, migration and escape.
2. *Physical movement* of objects to producers, consumers and retailers.

3. *Imaginative travel* elsewhere through memories, texts, images, TV and films.
4. *Virtual travel* often in real time on the Internet, transcending geographical and social distance.
5. *Communicative travel* through person-to-person messages via letters, post-cards, birthday and Christmas cards, telegrams, telephones, faxes, emails, instant messaging, videoconference including Skype-like software (see Chapter 5).

For Larsen et al., the case of the mobile cellular phone shows how all these mobilities intersect. People travel with their mobiles and organize their lives for business and pleasure, and as well use it for imaginative (diversionary) and virtual (Internet) activities (2006: 47). Yet these authors caution that mobilities and *network capital* go hand-in-hand to structure how people communicate and travel. Indeed, their overriding position is that 'transport and communications are complexly folded into each other'. They conclude that travel, communications and social networking work together:

> These sets of processes reinforce and extend each other in ways that are highly difficult to reverse. This also means that crucial to the character of modern societies is network capital, comprising, most importantly, access to communication technologies, affordable and well-connected transport and safe meeting-places. Without sufficient network capital people will be socially excluded as social networks have become more dispersed.
>
> (2006: 125)

'Mobile media cultures', then, have become richly layered experience contexts of everyday media usage. Goggin's (2006) assessment sees the full range of these industrial and commercial realities where

> Equipment manufacturers, cultural and content producers, and user groups and creative communities are now focusing on the possibilities of mobile media – with mobiles and wireless technologies, platforms, services, applications and cultural forms being designed, manufactured and reconfigured as convergent media.

In tracking the rise of this usage, there has been a shift in the role of users relative to that of producers. The significance of these developments is that 'mobile media are being heralded as a new site for consumption, democratic expression, individualism, citizenship and creativity' (Goggin, 2007).

But, as Bull (2008) argues, using mobile media can be a privatizing experience opposed to ideas of cosmopolitan citizenship. In his view, users of a device like the iPod are immersed in an 'individualizing of cultural experience' at the expense of sharing space with others.

In his analysis of 'mobile privatisation', McGuigan demonstrates how the pursuit of communicational mobility and privatized living and organization of life have driven the development of 'cool capitalism'. His analysis contextualizes the study of digital media within a long-standing sociological tradition of investigations about society and technology.

In broad terms, McGuigan is arguing that in considering the sociality of newer information and communication technologies, the concept of mobile privatization suggests that, while communicational mobility is enhanced, privatized living and organization of life are also accentuated. McGuigan shows how Williams' original formulation of mobile privatization was to make sense of the sociality of television. For Williams, the use of television was evidence of a new patterning of everyday life associated with urban-industrial society in general as much as with the specific use of communication technologies. McGuigan notes that when returning to the concept of mobile privatization several years after formulating it, Williams (1985: 188) remarked, 'It is an ugly phrase for an unprecedented condition.' It was not just that people in urban-industrial societies were living in small family units (the nuclear family replacing the extended family) but that many were comparatively isolated and private individuals while 'at the same time there is a quite unprecedented mobility of such restricted privacies' (cited in McGuigan 2007: 11).

He suggests that for Williams, these privatized phenomena are synecdoche for a larger whole, 'a now dominant level of social relations' observing how Williams links them to a larger whole of the market system: 'The international market in every kind of commodity receives its deep assent from this system of mobile-privatised social relations' (McGuigan 2007: 12).

And, as McGuigan notes, these arguments can be applied to contemporary sites of private consumption and mobility: desk-top computing online and portable telephonic and music-playing devices. 'An additional point to make, of course, is to do with screening, certainly in the convergence of computing and television, whereby everything is seen, literally, through a screen, mediated and packaged for consumption, sometimes quite active consumption' (McGuigan 2007: 12). In the context of the sociality of newer information and communication technologies, the concept of mobile privatization assists us in explaining the characteristics of new forms of privatized living and ways of living.

Reflecting on the implications of these transformations in social communication modes, including the use of mobile-screened devices in the network society, Allan (2007) observes that 'there appears to be a growing awareness that what counts as journalism is being decisively reconfigured across an emergent communication field supported by digital platforms'. In taking Castells' intervention as its conceptual point of departure, Allan has offered an analysis of one instance of 'mass self-communication' which has since proven to have engendered a formative influence on journalism in the network society (see also Allan and Matheson 2004; Allan 2006). Allan examines the spontaneous actions of ordinary people who were compelled to adopt the role of a journalist in order to bear witness to what was happening during the London bombings of July 2005. He construes the social phenomenon of citizen journalism as a form of Castells' 'mass self-communication', and yet he also critiques the ways and meanings in which its public significance is registered. On the potential of citizen journalism 'to bear witness', he notes: 'Its intrinsic value was underscored by Mark Cardwell, AP's director of online newspapers, who stated "The more access we have to that type of material, the better we can tell stories and convey what has happened." ' On the other hand, 'Others emphasized the importance of exercising caution, believing that its advantages should not obscure the ways in which the role of the journalist can be distinguished from individuals performing acts of journalism.' Allan quotes Roy Greenslade in the *Guardian* newspaper, who said 'The detached journalistic professional is still necessary, whether to add all-important context to explain the blogs and the thousands of images, or simply to edit the material so that readers and viewers can speedily absorb what has happened' (Allan 2007).

Any interpretation of media convergence necessarily requires that we now take these new mobile forms into account when we make assessments of our changing mediaspheres.

Conclusion

I began this chapter with a discussion of the conditions of neoliberal communications markets and media convergence. The extent to which media convergence is driven by these wider processes should not be underestimated. My argument has been that basic media and communications industry transformations require contextualizing within the wider dynamics of neoliberalism. Moreover, our interpretations of media convergence benefit from an historical understanding of existing theories of the relations between old and new media, including 'co-evolutionary' accounts. The case studies exemplify how new media distribution practices are dramatically reconfiguring modes of audiovisual product circulation, their exchange value, and consumption in the networked informational economy and society, or at least for those with access to the requisite devices and networks. The building blocks of this new order, network infrastructures, and how cultural usage is materially expressed, including now often in complex mobilities, also now need to be included in our interpretations of the evolving meanings of media convergence. In Chapter 2, we consider how major traditional (or 'legacy') media players have moved into the online space.

Further reading

Goldsmith, J. and Wu, T. (2008) *Who Controls the Internet? Illusions of a Borderless World* (2nd edn). New York: Oxford University Press.

Habermas, J. (1989) *The Structural Transformation of the Public Sphere*. Cambridge: Polity Press.

Hallin, D. and Mancini, P. (2004) *Comparing Media Systems: Three Models of Media and Politics*. Cambridge: Cambridge University Press.

Harvey, D. (2005) *A Brief History of Neoliberalism*. New York: Oxford University Press.

Held, D. (2004) *Global Covenant: The Social Democratic Alternative to the Washington Consensus*. Cambridge: Polity.

Jenkins, H. (2006) *Convergence Culture: Where Old and New Media Collide*. New York: New York University Press.

McLuhan, M. (1962) *The Gutenberg Galaxy: The Making of Typographic Man*. Toronto: University of Toronto Press.

Winston, B. (1998) *Media, Technology and Society: A History from the Telegraph to the Internet*. London: Routledge.

Zittrain, J. (2008) *The Future of the Internet, and How to Stop It*. New Haven, CT: Yale University Press.

2 | TRADITIONAL MEDIA MOVES ONLINE

People are getting used to getting everything on the net for nothing. That's going to have to change.

(Rupert Murdoch 2009)

The responses open to owners of legacy media are becoming more and more restricted as the circulation and advertising revenues decrease. So, either they can reduce costs or they can merge. My sense is that unless there is a striking increase in public intervention in media markets, essentially we are going to see a tightening of the ownership screw.

(Richard Collins 2008)

Introduction

We are witnessing constant, and at times rapid, transformations in media and communications industries brought about by digitization, convergence, interactivity and the general business operations of global media corporations. These developments are reconfiguring personal, local, regional and national media spaces and audiences. The way we use media is changing along with our patterns of living in an Information Economy.

In this chapter it is argued that traditional media corporations are rapidly re-engineering their businesses as multi-platform ones, and increasingly with integrated online outlets. These online platforms are either being built from the ground up, or are being acquired or co-opted, and then adapted to suit the requirements of the particular media corporation. The acquisition of the social networking site MySpace by News Corporation, a case study we will consider shortly, well illustrates this trend. In one sense, the buying up of these online digital media properties is simply 'more of the same': an accumulation strategy that is consistent with the operation of vertically-integrated network conglomerates, and continuing concentration of ownership (Sparks 2004; McChesney et al. 2005; Croteau and Hoynes 2006). After all, they have the deep pockets to invest in any media and communications sectors that they perceive to offer corporate and shareholder benefits. Yet, at another level, these acquisitions represent new content distribution strategies: for large media corporations, the plan is to leverage and cross-promote their branded proprietary content across different audience access platforms. The public sector media are on a similar trajectory, as epitomized by the BBC's cross-platform future.

Next year's model

Year's end in 2008 may well have marked a critical juncture in the transition of news and business models for commercial media. As always, these kinds of transitions represent a cumulative evolution over many years: nonetheless, it was significant when the US Pew Research Center for the People and the Press released its annual trends survey indicating that 'the Internet has now surpassed all other media except for television as the main source for national and international news'. The results showed that Net news had overtaken newspapers in the USA for the first time (Pew Center for the People and the Press 2008). Forty per cent of those surveyed got most of their national and international news from the Internet, with more people claiming they rely mostly on the Internet for news than newspapers (35 per cent), and with television still dominating as the most cited source (70 per cent). The Pew survey noted: 'For young people, however, the Internet now rivals television as a main source of national and international news. Nearly six-in-ten Americans younger than 30 (59%) say they get most of their national and international news online; an identical percentage cites television' (Pew Center 2008). The migration of audiences to the new media for their news diet is clearly accelerating. The Pew 2009 Project for Excellence in Journalism's (PEJ) *State of the News Media* Report notes that: 'The number of Americans who regularly go online for news, by one survey, jumped 19% in the last two years; in 2008 alone traffic to the top 50 news sites rose 27%' (Pew Center 2009).

The UK's House of Lords Select Committee on Communications in their *Ownership of the News* report explain the industry transformations in this way:

> Both here and abroad the newspaper industry is facing severe problems as readership levels fall; young people turn to other sources of news; and advertising moves to the Internet. The newspaper industry is responding to these challenges in a variety of ways including establishing a high profile web presence. However, even when newspapers run successful Internet sites the value of the advertising they sell on these sites does not make up for the value lost. The result of these pressures is that newspaper companies are having to make savings and this is having a particular impact on

investment in news gathering and investigative journalism. The number of foreign news bureaux is decreasing, and there is an increasing reliance on news agency feed and information derived from the public relations industry.

(House of Lords 2008a: 6)

In support of this argument regarding the decline in circulation and readership, the Committee cites a survey undertaken for their inquiry indicating 'that the overall number of adults reading at least one of the top ten national daily newspapers on an average day reduced by 19% between 1992 and 2006 (from 26.7 million to 21.7 million)'. This is further interpreted by the Committee: ·

If the increase in the adult population over this period is taken into account then the data show a 24% decrease in overall population reach (i.e. the proportion of the adult population who read a national daily newspaper has decreased by 24%).

And the data on readership decline among younger people in the UK is even more stark: 'the number of 15–24 year olds reading any one or more of the top ten national newspapers on an average day has declined by 37% and the number of 25–34 years olds doing the same has declined by 40%'. Circulation figures in the UK shows similar trends: 'in 1995 the average daily circulation of the top ten national daily newspapers collectively was 13,189,000; by the first half of 2007 it was 11,137,000 – a reduction of 2% (2008: 12).

The position in the USA reveals a broadly similar trend: the Committee cites empirical research by the US Pew PEJ that in the United States, newspapers ended 2007 with an 8.4 per cent decline in daily circulation and an 11.4 per cent decline in Sunday circulation compared to 2001. The PEJ also note that 'readership is also in decline and this is true for nearly every demographic group, regardless of age, ethnicity, education or income' (Pew Center for the People and the Press 2008).

The flight of advertising to the Internet is a driving factor for the reconfiguring of commercial media and communications industries. The House of Lords Committee reports evidence from the Internet Advertising Bureau that in 2006 online advertising spend overtook national newspaper advertising spend for the first time. The UK spends a bigger share of advertising money online than anywhere else, even the USA: 'In the UK 2006 saw a 41% growth in online advertising spend bringing the online share of the advertising market to 11.4%, compared to a 10.9% share for national newspapers' (House of Lords 2008a: 16).

These trends that show newspaper circulation and readership are in a slow decline, and the shift of advertising to the Internet largely explain why traditional media have been so keen to expand into new online media. But, of course, there are other contributory factors too: TV viewership in general, and news programming in particular, have been on the wane for many years, and people's working patterns and lifestyles have led to changed media consumption patterns (House of Lords 2008a: 15–16; Kung et al. 2008). Advertising, including the 'rivers of gold' classified ads was the model that sustained newspapers in the twentieth century, but it will not do so in the twenty-first. After a gradual build-up of advertising over several years on the Internet, it has now flattening out, and it has become a pattern of 'decoupling of advertising from news' (Pew Center for the People and the Press 2009).

The Pew 2009 PEJ's *State of the News Media* Report identifies six key emerging trends in relation to news media:

1. *The growing public debate over how to finance the news industry may well be focusing on the wrong remedies while other ideas go largely unexplored.* Alternative revenue models include micro-payments; a cable model where a fee to news producers is built into the subscription; building major online retail malls within news sites which could include local search; subscription based on niche consumption; or, collaborative networks to challenge news aggregators like Google and Yahoo!.

2. *Power is shifting to the individual journalist and away, by degrees, from journalistic institutions.* There are some very early signs that through search, email, blogs, social media and more, consumers are gravitating to the work of individual writers and voices, and away somewhat from institutional brand.

3. *On the Web, news organizations are focusing somewhat less on bringing audiences in and more on pushing content out.* The suggestion is that this trend arises from the news industry beginning to more fully understand the viral nature of the Web and the rise of social media. Initially in a few podcasts, RSS feeds and email alerts, the importance of multi-platform distribution including Facebook, Twitter and video-sharing sites like News Corporation and NBC Universal's jointly owned Hulu.com site have been recognized.

4. *The concept of partnership, motivated in part by desperation, is becoming a major focus of news investment and it may offer prospects for the financial future of news.* It is suggested that the general trend to partner by news organizations represents a small step toward individual companies in trouble beginning to pool ideas and resources in a way they traditionally have resisted. This may be a new twist on the legacy media practice of collaboration to offer packaged programming.

5. *Even if cable news does not keep the audience gains of 2008, its rise is accelerating another change – the elevation of the minute-by-minute judgment in political journalism.* 24/7 campaign news may have a shelf life or limited appear, particular in light of the new practice of 'political figures "tweeting" from the Senate and House floor their immediate personal feelings'.

6. *In its campaign coverage, the press was more reactive and passive and less of an enterprising investigator of the candidates than it once was.* The decline of investigative journalism is a result of a complex of broader industry factors. However, the immediate impacts mean that 'smaller newsrooms leave people less time for enterprise'. On the other hand, 'blogs and websites are deep wells of information, but they consume time and attention'. Media management by spin doctors is a key component of this trend.

In everyday living, we can also readily observe changes in the way people organize their own news consumption. People, and especially younger audiences, are increasingly using Google searches or **RSS** (or **Really Simple Syndication**) feeds to tailor news to suit their own tastes. RSS feeds are an easy way to be alerted when content that interests you appears on your favourite Web sites. Instead of visiting a particular Web site to browse for new articles and features, once you set it up, RSS automatically tells you when something new is posted online. But there are many different kinds of news formats and services on the Internet: online news (run by both traditional media outlets and 'new' media owners); web radio news; expert organization websites; expert and opinion blogs; audio and video podcasts; SMS news alerts to mobiles and Personal Digital Assistants (PDAs); web pages for mobiles and social news sites like digg.com or reddit.com. The popularity of the social networking site Twitter continues to grow: Twitter allows people to tune in individuals who update their 'news' to answer 'what are you doing now?', and to 'tweet' on topics, as they feel like it. By using these sources, audiences, and not just news junkies, are making up their own 'daily me' 24/7 by drilling down for more information about an event that they've heard of through word of mouth or from a traditional media source running in the background.

In their move online, legacy media news providers have leveraged their market position to establish a dominant online presence. They have been able to transfer their dominance of the mainstream media to the Internet and in the process attract an ever bigger audience. Yet it's not well understood at this relatively early point in the online migration, or internetization process, that Internet audiences are primarily an extension of the main legacy media brand outlets. And most audiences predominantly use sites that are run by existing news providers, although others are using major US news aggregation sites such as Google News, Yahoo! News, AOL News, and MSN News which tailor the material with nation-specific content. Essentially these breaking news aggregators link to legacy media sources who originate the material. In this sense they are vulture-like in that they have not invested in the costly 'hunting and gathering' required for news production, especially time-intensive investigative material.

We can see that traditional media have evolved to the point where online platforms are now integrated and necessary components of their businesses. This means, for example, that the line between digital broadcasting and the Internet is no longer so clearly demarcated. Arguably the future of broadcast television is one arena where the social and cultural impact of convergence and digitization on traditional media is most obvious. For the last half of the twentieth century, broadcast television was the giant of the media world. It was the medium that we talked about around the mythical 'water cooler'. It was the medium we turned to when an international crisis threatened, and it played a key role in editorializing significant events related to party politics and the public sphere more generally. Broadcast television, whether commercially or nationally funded, particularly in relation to news and current affairs programming, performed a public service role.

It follows, as Nightingale has argued, that the future of television as a public communications system with benefits for audiences is jeopardized by pressure on the television industry from advertising, as much as from the proliferation of interactive and mobile media. The pressure from advertising is linked to that industry's segmentation and targeting practices, which contribute to a situation where little commercial value is attached to broadcast TV's loyal older and very young audiences (Turow 1997; Nightingale 2007). These loyal but vulnerable audiences tend to be under-served: traditional TV's dependence on advertising revenue forces it to provide programming that delivers the audiences advertisers want, while its more dependent and loyal audiences find less and less acceptable viewing that is available (Napoli 2003).

Shifting advertising practices

A consequence of this kind of calculus around loyalty is that one of the most pervasive aspects of the emerging mediaspheres is a significant shift in the relationship between audiences and media service providers. In the past, audiences were packaged and traded alongside the advertising spots or spaces a medium offered, but media content was delivered to audiences at a reduced cost or free, thanks to advertising. The value of advertising spots was directly related to the size and composition of the audiences they could deliver; this trade generated the revenue that funded content production as well as its distribution costs. It also created a situation, now increasingly seen as problematic by media industries, where audiences expect that when they turn on their television or radio, or access the Internet, they should automatically be able to access media services. If audience expectations of free services could be changed, then media companies could offset the increased production costs associated with generating content for the new multi-platform environments and their requirements for diverse content.

The possibility of legacy media organizations using new media revenues to support their existing media operations appears a fading goal. In this regard, the Pew 2009 PEJ *State of the News Media* Report notes:

> It became clearer during the year that newspapers, television and other legacy media are unlikely to ever support their worldwide news gathering with the sale of banners, pop-ups and other display advertising. The real growth online continues to be in search advertising, and no one has figured out a way yet to combine search advertising with news in sufficient volume.
>
> (Pew Center for the People and the Press 2009)

It can be seen that the practice of bringing audiovisual material, targeted advertising and social networking together is being vigorously pursued by Google and many other traditional media corporations. Some of the first evidence of this trend was seen in the announcement of a billion dollar alliance between News Corporation and Google in 2006. The deal was an agreement making Google the exclusive provider of search and keyword-targeted advertising for News Corporation's Fox Interactive Media group, the entity responsible for managing News Corporation's growing international stable of online sites (Shultz 2006). Similarly, the acquisition of YouTube by Google in 2006 for US$1.65 billion in stock positioned the search leader for further advances into the emerging market for video advertising, a market previously dominated by Yahoo! Inc. (Sorkin and Peters 2006).

As a consequence of the rise of powerhouse 'search' businesses like Google, EBay, MSN, Yahoo! and Amazon, the advertising industry has been forced to respond to these altered practices by more strategically matching fragmenting audience consumers to goods and services through specific media providers (Spurgeon 2006). Existing computer giants such as Microsoft, Intel, Cisco, IBM and Apple are an important part of the mosaic of change too. Their vast investment strategies inevitably have an impact on the direction and shape of new media developments as social shaping of technology theorists have argued (Williams 1974; Winston 1998; Sørensen and Williams 2002).

However, the acquisition of MySpace by News Corporation from Intermix Media in 2005 for approximately US$580 million is a case study in how these dynamic relations between audiences, advertisers and vertically integrated media corporations are evolving. The problem for media corporations is one of putting in place the right mix of user-generated and corporately controlled content for an optimized audience experience, and through this to eventually generate shareholder returns. But this is not simply a matter of hitting on the best 'business model': there are many interrelated factors which render this moving target problematic. It's a complex new juggling act, on the one hand, to shape, direct and maintain these vast audience aggregations and to have them working towards a profitable bottom line, while on the other, not to annoy or provoke audience resistance: to interfere with the utility and pleasurable engagements that sites like MySpace offer audiences would be to undermine their popularity.

Against this background of consolidating traditional media ownership and a new generation of high-tech targeted advertising, a process of acquisition, alliances and building new media assets has been a primary objective for media corporations. The corporations involved are usually global players, and in most instances alliances between, and purchases of media assets will have industry and audience ramifications at a number of levels: internationally, nationally, regionally and locally.

Acquiring online assets

There has been a constant stream of acquisitions of online media assets and alliances between traditional and new media corporations in the period 2004–08 (see Table 2.1). In terms of a specific trend, this spike in the acquisition of online sites from approximately 2004 onwards is well beyond the period usually seen as the 'dot-com' boom and bust era, 1995–2001. In other words, there was a resurgence in acquisitions from 2004, even though over a longer time scale, from around the turn of the century, there has been a continuing pattern of both 'old' media and larger Internet corporations investing in 'new' media assets.

The buying up, or partnering with, these 'B2C' (business-to-consumer) and 'lifestyle' content sites are part of an audience aggregation strategy to enhance the attraction of the traditional media's online presence, as seen, for example, in branded portals. They can be interpreted as 'value-adding' to the 'plain vanilla' news, information and other programming brands already available in 'full service' portals, as visitors navigate through their online malls. They are also specifically cross-ownership and cross-promotion strategies to extend brands into other market sectors.

Online classified businesses have been a key category for traditional media to buy into and to extend their own assets. For example, real estate classified sites are reliable cash cows for traditional media: they are businesses built on

Table 2.1 Selected 'convergent' acquisitions or alliances in the USA and the UK, 2004–2008

B2C category	Brand name	Acquiring corporation
Social networking	MySpace	News Corp
Mobile content	Jamba	News Corp
Games	IGN Entertainment	News Corp
Social bookmarking	Del.icio.us	Yahoo!
Image sharing	Flickr	Yahoo!
Popular blogging	Weblogs, Inc	AOL
In-game advertising	Massive	Microsoft
Online content aggregation	AOL (5% stake)	Google
Social networking/content aggregator	YouTube	Google
Financial news	Dow Jones and Co	News Corp
Social networking	Bebo	AOL
Image/video sharing	Photobucket	Fox Interactive Media
Social networking	Friends Reunited	ITV
Content access technology	Nokia	Microsoft
Search and maps	3/Planet3 mobileportal	Google
Social networking	Bebo	Orange
Content distribution	ITV (17.9%)	BSkyB
Mobile and broadband content	The Football League	Virgin Media

enhancing existing print media assets, or in some cases have been acquired outright as a pure investment. This explains the Australian former telecommunications monopolist Telstra Corporation's acquisition of 51 per cent (AUS$342 million) of the Chinese real estate site Soufun. Soufun has a large audience in China – over 40 million users and 400,000 advertisers – with revenues doubling annually (Saarinen 2006). The migration of classified advertising online is a global trend. Respected UK newspaper analyst Roy Greenslade makes this assessment:

> Classifieds have virtually gone online in the States through Craig's List, as Craig's List is in Britain too, but we have our own sites; lots of sites which are not, by the way, owned by big corporations, relatively small and new and inventive. Newspapers have been very bad actually, because we didn't see the future and we thought everything wouldn't change in the way that it has. They weren't good at collecting or starting up classified ads sites,

which would have meant that they could have had that income, although there's very little income to come from it, because with Craig's List, if you want to sell something, you can go to Craig's List and sell it for free. Why are you going to pay somebody for a classified ad when you can find your buyers for nothing on the net?

(Greenslade 2008)

In the past five years, the pattern of online acquisitions is clear. For instance, in the 12 months to July 2006, it was reported that News Corporation had paid AUS$1.5 billion on 'new breed' Internet companies, 'including online communities devoted to gaming, sports and movies, plus a startling eruption of youthful energy known as MySpace' (Reiss 2006). With a total market capitalization of News Corporation of around US$70 billion, this was a small percentage overall. A corporate explanation offered by News at the time was that the 'combined sites will also provide a powerful cross-promotional opportunity for Fox's television and film content and enable the company to more efficiently introduce new products and services using its enhanced web presence' (AAP 2005).

News Corporation also acquired the US Internet games company IGN Entertainment for US$650 million. Under the deal, IGN and its many associated properties, including IGN.com, GameSpy, FilePlanet, Rotten Tomatoes, and TeamXbox, have been folded into News Corporation's Fox Interactive Media division. These acquisitions are indicative of the shift in advertising from traditional media to online media and the decline in engagement with traditional media from the end of the twentieth century. And while overall newspapers and free-to-air TV are expected to continue to have the overall share of total advertising spend dollars until around 2011, after that time their combined clout is predicted to be outpaced by new media. Most of this growth will of course come from the online sector and the global ramifications for classified advertising are even starker. One estimate has it that a quarter of print classified ads will be lost to online media in the next decade. Overall, when considered globally, newspapers claimed 36 per cent of total advertising in 1995 and 30 per cent in 2005, and it's predicted this will fall to around 25 per cent by 2015 (*The Economist* 2006).

During the period 2004–08, there were many mergers, acquisitions and alliances between different media sectors, and between traditional media and new media corporations, often in the online or mobile spaces. Any list will necessarily be incomplete and only a snapshot of the wider canvas, but it is worth looking at a selection of some of the more interesting strategic investments which have a media convergence dimension (Table 2.1).

There is a clear trend for players from historically different parts of the media and communications industries to join forces to take advantage of converging markets. These ranged from straightforward acquisitions, to exclusive partnerships, to the bundling of products and services from different parts of the value chain: content and rights, packaging, distribution, device, navigation and consumption.

These purchases signal both shifting new media industry restructuring and audience usage practices. For example, in adding social bookmarking and tagging site Del.icio.us to its social computing portfolio, Yahoo! was aiming to extend and further cement its connection with new media audiences. The attraction of tagging is that when enough people tag particular sites, then the '**collective intelligence**' of audiences is mobilized – and commodified. For a corporation like Yahoo!, the main advantage is that it can boast to advertisers that its audiences have a richer and more satisfying experience.

Industry, device and network convergence all help account for why media corporations wish to expand into previously adjacent markets. Many deals are between content suppliers, whose bandwidth requirements are increasing, and distribution networks, some of which are now able to carry much more content than they were previously. For example, France Orange has moved into content packaging by launching channels such as Orange Sports TV on its IPTV service, and Virgin Media, in the UK, packages programming for satellite and mobile telephony (Ofcom 2008a). Convergent alliances can also be between network owners and manufacturers, and functions such as video calling or television programming access are now added to what may have been unexpected devices, such as games consoles.

Case study
Fox Interactive Media's MySpace

MySpace is headquartered in Beverly Hills, California, USA, and has over 110 million monthly users (and a much higher number of registered users), with localized sites in more than 20 nations. The Chinese version of MySpace launched in April 2007 with specific censorship-related differences. It is primarily a social networking website with an interactive, user-submitted network of friends, personal profiles, blogs, groups, photos, music, and videos for teenagers and adults internationally. It was reported to have been overtaken by Facebook, in terms of registered users in 2008 (Techtree News Staff 2008).

In an interview for *Wired* magazine about News Corporation's acquisition of MySpace, it was suggested that Rupert Murdoch was betting on 'transforming a free social net-work into a colossal marketing machine' (Reiss 2006). Indeed, News Corporation was quick to tell the market that it would use MySpace to deliver its own branded TV and movie programming on demand. Yet, by its own admission, News was not at the outset entirely clear of the trajectory to that outcome, indicating the fast-paced rate of change in these new media industries.

But how can we best describe MySpace as a new media form? This was how *Business Week* put it not long after its debut:

> With a heavy focus on music, it has become a part of daily life for teenagers and young adults nationwide. Members create highly personalized home pages loaded with message boards, blogs, photos, and streaming music and video. People use it to stay in touch with friends and meet other people. Driven by the expressiveness of its members, the social-networking site has emerged as an important channel for online advertising. TV shows and new music are often debuted on MySpace.
>
> (Rosenbush 2005)

Rosenbush argued that MySpace had succeeded where others 'have generated buzz but then failed' because of its origins in the LA music and club scene, and precisely because it was not 'concocted by Silicon Valley tech types or New York bankers'. He suggests that MySpace set out to be exciting and the early users included actors, models and musicians. It is also the case that bands have become successful through making available their music and video clips for free, without the need for a recording contract. Clearly, it's also explained by Metcalfe's Law – the value of a network increases proportionally with the number of users.

Although Murdoch and others at News Corporation initially insisted they did not know how they would get a return on their investment, or what the precise 'business model' will be, some within the News empire had their own ideas. Jeremy Philips, an executive vice-president for strategy and acquisitions, argued the merits of the MySpace acquisition in terms of a 'two legs' analysis: in his view the MySpace business sits between a leg for content and one for distribution, the traditional areas of the News Corporation business. He suggests it's neither completely one nor the other; rather, it shares aspects of both: it is a media platform (Reiss 2006). In other words, there is a content distribution strategy logic for a large media corporation like News, where they can leverage a multitude of branded proprietary content and their audience platforms. In short, it forms part of an integrated strategy to keep up with the media consumption patterns of young audiences – particularly in the 15–25-year-old demographic. With the benefit of hindsight, Wired's explanation has proven itself to be accurate:

Think of MySpace as an 80 million-screen multiplex where YouTube videos are always showing . . . There may not be a working band or musician left in the English-speaking world who doesn't have a MySpace profile. Ditto comedians, artists, photographers, and anyone else trying to catch the public eye. Why is Disney promoting Pirates of the Caribbean: Dead Man's Chest on a News Corp. site? Because that's where the viewers are. And that's what a platform is: the place you have to be. MySpace is doubly important to an old media armada like News Corp. as it navigates the infinity of distribution channels created by broadband, mobile devices, and search engines.

(Reiss 2006)

The same article quoted a London media consultant who argued that 'MySpace's challenge is to do for branding what Google did for ads – to create a hyperefficient form of interaction.' Or the view of a senior News Corporation executive who apparently hatched the original plan to buy MySpace who argued:

You'll see us morphing from a content company into a marketing company, a youth marketing company especially, because that's where everything starts. No one is going to be able to control the flow of content the way we used to. MySpace gives us the ability to look inside and understand how hits get created – that is, to spot micro-niches, track early breakouts, and identify hot IM buzzwords as they bubble up.

(Reiss 2006)

And it is reported that the site is now a strong advertising performer as well: MySpace is the market leader with 15.9 percent of display-ad spending (ComScore MediaMetrix 2008).

Two years on, the same executive, Peter Levinsohn, was the President of News Corporation's Fox Interactive Media Internet division which oversees MySpace among an expanding online asset portfolio. In a statement reported in the *Los Angeles Times*, Levinsohn announced that News would be launching its long-awaited online advertising network 'to better exploit the online advertising market'. The idea behind the 'FIM Audience Network' was to consolidate its newly developed advertising technologies such as its 'hyper-targeting' tools that tailor advertisements to Web surfers' interests. The claim was that the new advertising technologies would assist in meeting the revised forecast 2008 revenue target of US$900 million instead of the original US$1 billion (*Los Angeles Times*, Business, 2008).

In 1997, Pierre Lévy coined the term 'collective intelligence' to refer to the capability of large audiences to influence media output (1997: 41). The dramatic rise of search engine businesses and social networking only reinforces this pattern. He also proposed that we are living through a technological evolution that will result in diminished dependence on 'molecular' technologies (like mass broadcasting or the Hollywood studio system). For Lévy, this will lead to the replacement of that dependence by user/audience participation in 'molecular' communication environments like Internet-based weblogs and email, in mobile phone-based forms like text messaging or picture phoning, or in game-based environments where system users routinely create new communicative forms in the process of customizing their engagement.

These developments will of course have important implications for how audiences access and participate in new media, and therefore for how political processes occur in society. A new media context where audiences themselves decide what stories will be made and how they will be told increases the possibility that stories that question established interests may gain currency and result in destabilizing social or political action, regardless of whether those stories are true or not. But equally, such contexts could mean that truth claims of established interests are unchallengeable regardless of their reliability. As Castells has argued, with a process where digital media amplify and deepen the pre-existing sociocultural shift from place-based affiliation to 'networked individualism', there are fewer non-digitized public spheres where truth claims can be publicly contested (Castells 2001: 129). The corollary is that established interests hold a much more powerful position than single consumers and citizens.

In the next section I want to turn to some of the specific implications of new media deals, and how they are structured, in a period of global financial crisis and recession, where trillions of dollars have been lost in financial markets.

New media deals and 'taking it private'

In a sense, media corporations can be seen to represent the heartbeat of capitalism. We live in neoliberal times of 'one market under God' where market populism is now often equated with perfect democracy and consumer choice (Frank 2001: 51). But in a period of global financial crisis, the benefits for everyone of unfettered neoliberalism have become even more strained than they have previously been. There are many accounts describing this familiar process that we usually refer to simply as 'capitalist accumulation'. The editorial introduction to the online journal *Fast Capitalism* describes the current period as 'an accelerated, post-Fordist stage of capitalism . . . where people can "office" anywhere, using laptops and cells to stay in touch' (fastcapitalism.com). Schiller's view is that the updated description of 'capitalist accumulation' in the context of intensifying Internet protocol networks and e-commerce is 'digital capitalism' (Schiller 1999). And as Flew (2008) notes, McChesney (1999), Mosco (2004) and Graham (2006) also

> have used this term to argue that new media and the 'Internet revolution' mark the rise of the Entertainment-Communication-Information (ECI) sector to prominence in the global capitalist economy, constituting the core infrastructure of global commerce and the fastest growing sectors of international capitalism.
>
> (2008: 25)

The significance for the broader themes of media convergence is that commodification and digital copyright techniques are the new order of the day for global capitalist relations; such tendencies are scaffolded by the intensifying consolidation of media ownership by large media corporations.

The ECI sector is tightly integrated within the global economy and the operations of the wider financial system. This is therefore an important level at which we need to survey media consolidation for changing patterns in complex schemes of ownership arrangements. There are important implications for how media corporations are run, for media markets, and ultimately for the content the media provide to audiences.

But contrary to first reactions, you don't need to be a deal-structuring corporate lawyer, fund manager, investment banker, venture capitalist or management consultant to observe trends in media consolidation, and more importantly, to consider their implications. Reading the business and media sections of the offline and online newspapers generally provides a great deal of this information. It can be seen that within this wider financial system context there is a new financialization trend in the structuring of media businesses that has attracted the attention of media analysts and commentators from the early years of the turn of the century. So-called **private equity** deals have become more commonplace not only in the ECI sector, but they have been used more generally to financially restructure a range of profitable assets. Noam (2007) describes this new patterning of financing as 'a second wave of media privatisation' following the heady deregulatory days of the 1980s.

Before we consider specific examples of private equity and media deals, we should first briefly consider some apparently related terminology. 'Equity financing' is a method of obtaining funds in return for a share of the ownership and profits of the company. Equity finance can be provided by all sectors of the investment community, from individuals to large companies. The purchase of shares in a company is the most common form of equity financing. By contrast, the term 'equity' as used in the context of 'private equity' deals involving media corporations is somewhat misleading. Most recent private equity financing refers to a debt-funded buyout of a publicly listed company. The *modus operandi* of private equity investors is to take out an enormous loan, buy a controlling interest in a publicly listed corporation and then 'take the company private' for several years. In this process it moves a 'listed' company away from public scrutiny required by stock exchanges. At the same time the principals behind this form of financial engineering reorganize the assets in an attempt to remove lower performing components. The end game is then to refloat the company with a view to selling it back to public ownership at a higher price than when they privatized it. The revenue streams of the company are used to finance the interest payments on their debt (Keen 2008).

Froud and Williams have argued that there is a significant gap between the explicit promise and undisclosed outcome in these arrangements:

> The discursive promise of private equity is about general benefits from the value creation consequent upon a new way of relating finance and management; in our view, private equity represents a rearrangement of ownership claims for value capture which then allows value extraction, particularly for the benefit of the few who are positioned as private equity principals or senior managers in the operating businesses.
>
> (2007: 5)

Froud and Williams (2007: 12) are sceptical of any claimed benefits arguing that 'the extraction of value is pure financial engineering because the operating business acquires liabilities in the form of debt equal to the sum of cash taken out'. The cash then goes into the hands of elite private equity providers and fund managers while the liabilities are passed on with the business.

There are various demands that providers of private equity investors may often require. In addition to board seats they may ask for: regular access to management accounts and detailed budgeting process data; periodic independent review or audit of the company's financial accounts; general discipline and control in respect of decision-making and authority levels; and, the formulation of a strategy to exit from the business, to realize their investment goals at some point in the medium-term future.

In a sense, it's ironic that private equity investors require these higher levels of accountability from the management of media corporations, when their own processes of corporate governance are veiled in non-disclosure in comparison to publicly listed media corporations. Indeed, as Noam argues 'many private equity deals are fuelled by a desire to flee closer regulation and disclosure requirements of public companies' (2007). In other words, a by-product of these kinds of deals is less openness, less transparency and less accountable control. The UK Government financial regulator, the Financial Services Author-ity (FSA), has issued a Discussion Paper warning people to be wary of a broad range of risks associated with private equity investment (2006).

In relation to risk associated with capital markets, the FSA noted:

> The substantial inflows of capital into private equity funds combined with the considerable appetite of the debt market for leveraged finance products is fuelling a significant expansion of the private equity market. The quality, size and depth of the public markets may be damaged by the expansion of the private equity market. An increasing proportion of companies with growth potential are being taken private and fewer private companies are going public (as a consequence of the development of the secondary private equity market).
>
> (FSA 2006: 8)

Froud and Williams' view is that the formula of loading an operating business with debt enables the traditional assets to shore up that side of the business. In short, it is not 'a new form of capitalism'. They suggest 'this general formula then defines the field of operation of private equity and its preference for activ-ities like infrastructure, utilities, retailing and media' (2007: 11). While the conjunction of easily accessible and cheap debt has created a boom in private equity from the mid-2000s, the problem is that when the economy turns down and interest rates climb, 'it will all end badly' (2007: 13).

So who and what are these private equity fund players and how do they operate? There are many international private equity fund players investing in the media industry space: Kravis Kohlberg Kravis (KKR), Bain Capital, Carlyle Group, CVC, Hellman and Friedman, Merrill Lynch Private Equity, Newbridge-TPG, Texas Pacific Group, Thomas H. Lee Partners are some of the well-known global private equity firms. Usually these private equity firms have raised money largely from superannuation savings, they look at publicly listed com-panies and ask 'Where is their value over and above what we see in the current share price?' Typically they see unresolved issues or problems that they believe they can solve in a short timeframe and sell the asset for solid profits. In the case of traditional media corporations the funds sense pressures and problems, yet see stable or slowly declining revenues, which is their main attraction (Sorkin and Peters 2006).

Recent examples of private equity restructurings in the entertainment, com-munications and IT sectors include:

- Australian TV networks Seven Media and PBL Media
- German TV network and satellite operator ProSeibenSat
- Dutch market research and publishing company VNU

- National telecom carriers Eircom and TDC in Ireland and Denmark
- UK music industry major EMI
- US satellite operator PanAmSat
- US film studio MGM
- US producer Warner Music
- US broadcaster Clear Channel Communications (radio and TV assets)
- Spanish language TV network Univision

Noam (2007) notes that 'other companies, such as Vivendi, EMI and parts of the Tribune Company, have been circled by private equity firms'. Nasdaq-listed Virgin Media (formerly NTL-Telewest) was on the growing list of stalked targets with an offer of £5 billion from the US private equity group, Carlyle. Since Noam made these comments, the UK music business EMI Group has agreed to be bought by a private equity firm Terra Firma for £3.2bn including debt (BBC 2007).

For Noam, the critical issue is also one of transparency for corporations which hold government-granted licences. He uses the example of Thomas H. Lee Partners:

> a US$20bn Boston private equity firm that has acquired singly or in partnerships the media companies Clear Channel, Univision, VNU, Houghton Mifflin and Warner Music, does not appear to maintain a website. Small investors and activists have no public shareholder meeting to probe management information is available to the press. Securities analysts stop following the stock. Governments cannot evaluate the soundness of companies that may provide essential national infrastructure.
>
> (Noam 2007)

The key issue regarding what we can refer to as the 'financialization' of media assets, and in particular 'private equity' financing, must be what the implications are for serious news, current affairs and other informational genres. These kinds of content are the lifeblood of democracies. Private equity investors are notoriously conservative and they aim to make savings through cost cutting, (usually meaning laying-off production or journalist staff), and by not paying for more expensive, or innovative content, or research-intensive and critical content. Many people regard the role of media as being precisely connected with these public sphere aims of information provision, and illuminating matters of public interest. Private equity investment may change all these assumptions. Their main agenda is usually short to medium-term 'value extraction', focused on the search for expanded cash flows to meet debt payments, and positioning the company for resale.

In the wake of the 2008 global financial crises, governments and their regulatory agencies will no doubt be more wary of the consequences of these kinds of financial structuring on audience engagements media and communications products and services. Unfortunately, we are already seeing the damage caused by the wider financial downturn, with many job losses, and fewer people required to produce more content across multiple platforms. In the next section we consider news and information content practices in online media.

Online news and diversity

Behind new developments in delivering audiovisual content to audiences over the Internet are important questions in relation to the availability of diverse, meaningful sources of information, which remain critical in a healthy democracy. Even though the technological characteristics of media provision and consumption are changing, few would dispute that news and information are privileged genres and that they remain the responsibility of our parliaments, corporations and civil society groups. Dessauer has reviewed the growth of Internet use in the USA (faster than any previous medium) and the increasing use of news on the Internet (2004: 121–36). These early findings note that benefits include the broadening of the definition of 'news' and formats, mobility and news provision, and news delivered in a 24-hour cycle. But there are also detriments, mainly arising from increased repurposing of news brands originating from traditional media outlets. A key question for twenty-first-century citizenship is whether new information and communication technologies are leading to a splintering of civic discourse or revitalizing public sphere communication by allowing new forms of information provision. In this context of changing business models and methods of audiovisual delivery, matching the regulatory frameworks governing network ownership and content provision structures with audience needs requires a new perspective. Arguably this issue is even more acute in rural, regional and remote communities, who traditionally have less service options than metropolitan areas, and where concentration of ownership can be more consequential (Dwyer et al. 2006). While some commentators suggest that Internet diversity constitutes an alternative to existing media power, others argue that claims about the diversity of opinion in new media are greatly overstated. In fact, a number of studies have shown that most news content on the Internet is repurposed or supplied by traditional media sources (Doyle 2002; Calabrese and Sparks 2004; Bolton 2006; Downie and Macintosh 2006). This should be a matter of concern for governments and civil society groups wishing to promote diversity of opinions and viewpoints in new media. Yet debates over the implications of online news formats are dividing expert commentators. Turner has argued that online journalism (of the personal blog-ging kind) remains an elite, individualistic pursuit, lacking sufficient audience reach or the pro-social objectives of public service broadcasting (2005: 135–47). By contrast, Dennis argues that 'the Internet has greatly benefited journalism by allowing for the development of new media, whether websites, cable outlets, or so-called web TV alongside traditional media that have cautiously used it as a platform' (Dennis and Merrill 2006: 165). Allan's interpretation of the algo-rithmic 'neutrality' of Internet news aggregators is instructive, focusing as it does on the 'weakest links' of their 'diversity' claims:

> Given that objectivity is very much in the eye of the beholder, though, this principle will be realized in practice to the extent that the user compares and contrasts various renderings of a news event from a sufficiently diverse range of linked sources.
>
> (2006: 177)

If it is the case that younger audiences' media consumption is shifting dramat-ically, then this is a major concern for all democracies (Carnegie 2005). In particular, it gives rise to concerns about the power and influence of new online media and the functioning of contemporary plural nation-states. The Carnegie Foundation's study 'Abandoning the news' provided forceful data for advocates of media liberalization. Data from the study show how younger US audiences (18–34-year-olds) are using media today, arguing that this cohort will soon have a much greater influence on media industries. The Carnegie study presented data showing these audiences (more than 50 per cent of this age cohort) are access-ing Internet portals (for example, Yahoo! and MSN) more frequently than network or cable TV websites, traditional newspapers, cable TV general news programmes, national TV network newscasts, newspaper websites or local TV station websites. In light of these trends in media consolidation and globalizing, entertainment-driven consumption habits, we can reasonably wonder, where will young people be kept informed about a range of political, social, health, education and international news?

Over the longer term, we need to track how changing media delivery modes will affect the important policy settings of universality, equitable access and service provision to diverse publics. Traditionally, the model of professional news interpreters/makers (journalists) has dominated both commercial and public-service news media provision. Now, hybrid forms delivered over broad-band Internet networks that mix those earlier forms with netizen/blogger modes of practice are creating new audiences. The implications of these devel-opments for the provision of news and information content in democracies are potentially far-reaching. The complexity for regulatory agencies arises from the wide variety of news formats and services on the Internet, and their different levels of mediation and general 'trustworthiness' (Allan 2006: 26–9, 83–7; Collins 2009, 61–86); as I discussed earlier in this chapter, there are now many species of online news with a spectrum of editorial approaches. In the public sphere, the provision of 'trustworthy' news has historically been an important issue for democratic governments, policy-makers and regulators. And changing categories of news raise a series of issues, including: Will policy and regulation be able to apply this notion to these different Internet formats and technologies? Indeed, what important roles do news and information formats have in this fragmentary public-sphere space? And, what is the future of community and alternative media within new mediaspheres?

There is no doubt that the rise of the Internet has changed how news and current affairs information are accessed. Yet that access needs to be considered in light of the evidence in relation to ownership of the most-used new online media. The major incumbent media operators (in broadcast and print) are also the owners of the most-frequented websites and portals. As Sparks notes, 'offline media across the spectrum from print to broadcasting have strong online presences' (Calabrese and Sparks 2004: 310). Opinion polling continues to show that a majority of people who regularly use the Internet to obtain news and current affairs rely on websites controlled by or associated with traditional media sources.

Conclusion

In this chapter I have discussed transformations in our media and communications industries, suggesting there is a need to have a critical alertness to the bigger picture where digitization and convergence are being used by media corporations to redesign the terms of people's engagements with the media. In this process, place-based audience formations like publics and communities are being supplemented with, and in some cases replaced by, Internet-based global consumerist alternatives, virtual communities and social networks, often linked to services, brands and product flows (Lury 2004).

As the discussion has shown, there is a resurgent trend for traditional media corporations that had a dominant role in the last century, including for use by advertisers, to expand their businesses into online space. The account presented here concerns a familiar process that we usually refer to in shorthand as 'capitalist accumulation'. The updated description in the context of intensifying Internet protocol networks and e-commerce is 'digital capitalism' (Schiller 1999). In this period of lurching and crisis-prone neoliberalism, corporations in communications media markets are exploring new ways of amassing audiences for the purposes of building and maintaining profitable consumer media cultures. Marketization of access and use and 'networked individualism' are the hallmarks of these developments.

And it is evident that there is both uncertainty and innovation in the way that convergence and digitization are being used by media corporations to redesign the terms of people's engagements with the media. Facebook, MySpace, Google Video, YouTube, Twitter and the full range of interactive e-commerce sites that people engage with suggest an ongoing tension between the 'segmenting' and the 'society-making' tendencies in media industries (Turow 1997; Turow and Tsui 2008). Equally, access to news and information forms is undergoing related transformations linked with audiences' changing usage of new media technologies.

The implications of traditional media more intensively integrating with online media are not all good news for an informed, mainstream citizen audience. As traditional commercial media corporations reconfigure themselves as digital and convergent business operations, and build their online consumer malls, the bottom-line demands of global private-equity capital are unlikely to allow much scope for thoughtful news journalism, or other forms of more questioning information programming. In these circumstances, the policy response by governments and their regulatory agencies needs to be underwritten by an evidence-based approach in the public interest; recognizing that media consolidation will have adverse effects on democracy-maintaining news and information genres, on localism, and on diversity in general. Therefore, the onus must fall on our legislators to develop public-interest legal frameworks in consultation with the wider community. This is a theme we explore in the next chapter.

Further reading

Allan, S. (2006) *Online News: Journalism and the Internet*. Maidenhead: Open University Press.

Calabrese, A. and Sparks, C. (eds) (2004) *Toward a Political Economy of Culture: Capitalism and Communication in the Twenty-First Century*. Lanham, MD: Rowman & Littlefield.

Collins, R. (2009) 'Trust and trustworthiness in fourth and fifth estates', *International Journal of Communication* 2: 61–86.

McChesney, R., Newman, R. and Scott, B. (eds) (2005) *The Future of Media: Resistance and Reform in the 21st Century*. New York: Seven Stories Press, pp. 117–25.

Schiller, D. (1999) *Digital Capitalism: Networking the Global Market System*. Cambridge, MA: MIT Press.

Turow, J. and Tsui, L. (2008) *The Hyperlinked Society: Questioning Connections in the Digital Age (The New Media World)*. Ann Arbor, MI: University of Michigan Press.

MEDIA OWNERSHIP AND THE NATION-STATE

I see a lot of challenges ahead. Am I worried? Of course, we should all be worried. Powerful economic forces that favor consolidation are converging with regulatory policies that pave the way. They could yet carry the day. But I also see opportunity and the good news is that we still have a chance to avoid all this.

(Michael J. Copps 2005)

Introduction

The ownership of media corporations, and how they are controlled and operated, matter a great deal. A US Federal District Court, which sentenced disgraced press baron, Conrad Black to 6.5 years in prison in late 2007, made a similar assessment (Balogh 2007). Black, who gave up his Canadian citizenship in 2000 to become a British Lord, was formerly a major shareholder of Hollinger International, and had previously presided over a media empire that included ownership of newspapers in the UK, the USA, Canada and Australia. Black and three co-accused Hollinger lieutenants were convicted of fraud and obstruction of justice, relating to theft of fees from the sale of community newspapers, which instead of paying to shareholders, they pocketed themselves as tax-free bonuses. How could a person like Black be expected to act as a responsible media owner and observe laws and regulations in place for the benefit of wider publics?

Regulatory mechanisms for the protection and promotion of local, national content (as opposed to foreign-produced material), regional diversity and diversity of viewpoints are common to most western democratic countries. And yet some people might expect that in an era of intensifying neoliberal globalization, complete abandonment by liberal-democratic nation-states of laws, policies and regulations that restrict media ownership would be the order of the day. In certain nations such as New Zealand, this has been the case. But New Zealand is the exception to the rule; in all other broadly comparable nations there are varying restrictions on domestic and foreign media ownership consolidation. The maintenance of ownership restrictions is a stark reminder that the governance of traditional and new media remains a matter for national governments, as shaped by specific national cultural priorities (Goldsmith and Wu 2008).

This chapter outlines the current state of play in regulatory regimes for media ownership in Australia, Canada, New Zealand, the United Kingdom, and the United States, and then considers the extent to which their unique cultural expressions of media ownership regulation can inform generalizations for future policy development. However, before considering the application of ownership policy, law and regulation in individual nation-states, we should first examine the underlying concepts behind these cultural and economic policy mechanisms.

Rationales of pluralism and diversity

A key issue that arises with media convergence is the implication of ongoing consolidation for the policy rationales of **pluralism** and **diversity**, and the available range of viewpoints in our emerging **mediaspheres**. Both terms have emerged as underlying principles in contemporary debates in media policy. In the European context Karpinnen (2007) has argued: 'Notions of pluralism and diversity today seem to invoke a particularly affective resonance; to an extent that these permeate much of the argumentation in current European media policy debates.' Media commentators agree that although there is ambiguity in their use, and the terms tend to be used somewhat interchangeably in a range of social, political, cultural and economic discourses, as Doyle (2002) points out, there's a great deal more consequential to media ownership concentration than simply questions of market efficiencies and the economics of providing content to audiences. In industries strongly characterized by economies of scale and scope, and the general tendency towards oligopoly, the knee-jerk position is often to suggest that it is all a matter of balancing the inefficiencies of diverse ownership and the efficiencies of sustaining effective levels of competition. In Doyle's view, 'Special policies to deal with ownership of the media owe their existence, in the first place, to concerns about *pluralism*, not economics' (2002: 42). Notwithstanding this point of departure, economic discourses ('the bottom line') have become more prevalent in recent decades of media deregulation and as they have circulated more widely under ascendant **neoliberalism**. And while the USA and the UK diverge in relation to specific regulatory practices, as Freedman notes, 'Policy objectives concerning media diversity and media pluralism may be expressed differently in the USA and the UK but they are both converging around the rhetoric of competition and choice' (2008: 77). However, although economic discourses are not figured exclusively in such debates, they tend to dominate them in the contemporary political milieu.

In Hitchens' view, the way to maintain a plurality and diversity in our changing mediaspheres is to adopt a different approach that relies on Habermas' (2006) conceptualizations of a **public sphere**. She argues such an approach is a much more satisfactory normative measure for regulatory reforms in changing media environments (Habermas 1989). For example, in the context of a discussion of structural regulation to promote broadcasting pluralism, she writes: 'If the public sphere is to function adequately, then it is important that as much diversity can be introduced into the market as possible – diversity in structure, in funding, and in programming (Hitchens 2006: 134).

Hitchens' discussion of the potential contribution of the public sphere concept for revitalizing the design of media systems draws on the work of a range of scholars who have refined Habermas' original theoretical framework – including Habermas' own rejoinders to these debates. The result is a practical toolkit for modelling how the media may participate in a more democratic public sphere, one that 'values and promotes pluralism and diversity' (Hitchens 2006: 49–60).

In contradistinction to normative Habermasian accounts of pluralism in media policy, Karpinnen advocates a radical-pluralist position recognizing the limits to pluralism. For Karpinnen (2008), the radical-pluralist position recognizes that democratic mediaspheres are structured through political and economic power in perpetual conflict. Karpinnen argues that radical-pluralism is an untapped source to inform policy making:

> The problem seems to be that while the Habermasian public sphere approach has long been mobilised as a normative backbone in debates on media structure and policy, for instance in defence of public service broadcasting, the implications of radical pluralist perspectives for the media have been less debated. In fact, it seems that a lack of institutional proposals or of interest in concrete political questions is a widespread feature of postmodern theories of radical difference and pluralism . . . these perspectives have been used more as oppositional discourses or critical tools in questioning various monism's of media studies and political economy, and not as coherent normative theories that would pertain to questions of media structure and policy.
>
> (2008: 35)

So his suggestion is that radical pluralism and postmodern theories tend to get lumped together as being ineffectual and relativist when if comes to making contributions to normative media policy. Railing against a naivety in pluralistic media debates, Karpinnen's work draws on the antagonistic pluralism of Mouffe (2000) to argue for revitalized engagement that actively sets agendas for media structures and policy.

In spite of these divergent theoretical accounts, it is a widely accepted proposition in debates relating to ownership and control that the objects of policies for 'pluralism' and 'diversity' can at best be targeted in a diffuse, even indirect way, by somewhat 'blunt' legal instruments. That is, the link between ownership and different voices is not necessarily an accurate science. As Baker (2007) argues, the policy assumption is that a plurality of owners will be a proxy for a plurality and diversity of voices. Collins and Murroni in their influential study of these policy objectives in the mid-1990s in the United Kingdom saw the value of using several different kinds of policy tools too, but they also considered that the focus ought to be on 'behaviour, not structure' (Collins and Murroni 1996: 73). Like Hitchens, they saw the importance of structural ownership regulation, more fine-grained ownership controls, and competition policy all deployed to foster diversity of voice in the media. They considered that the goals of diversity of opinion and accurate reporting needed a multi-levered approach because 'the behaviour of journalists and editors cannot be "read-off" from the structure and ownership of firms' (Collins and Murroni 1996: 73).

Collins and Murroni make the point that 'cross-ownership is in itself not significant; what counts is concentration of ownership'. Undoubtedly true in a wider sense, their solution was to explore mechanisms for editorial independence in addition to the internationally accepted policy approaches, including competition policy and sector specific and cross-media limits. The at times seemingly diffuse links between ownership and voice can be explained by its multiple determinations including the commercial context and financial structuring of an outlet; the owner-content link; the question of where power resides more generally; and in terms of relations to the political system in question (Hallin and Mancini 2004). The foundational argument that is often made in these debates is that while it is not always possible to establish with certainty the specific impact separately controlled broadcasting outlets have on content and views aired, compared with monopoly provision, this has not been a sufficient reason to abandon such regulation. Instead, it calls for an intuitive and cautious response, to favour regulation over no regulation (Baker, cited in Hitchens 2006). The failure of regulation in the global financial industries crisis in 2008 is a recent non-media (but interrelated) illustration of this argument.

The key point is that although there may not always be a conscious projection of voice, 'the absence of a diversity of owners in the market may constrain voice':

if the resources and outlets are under monopoly control, then there may be much less scope for different voices and ideas to be heard, even within an outlet, simply because there may be less incentive to explore other perspectives. Monopoly control is likely also to have a chilling effect on journalistic and editorial voices, because they will have few alternative employment opportunities. A diversity of outlets, even those all firmly placed within the commercial context, simply because they will utilise a different blend of resources and media professionals, will have the potential to throw up at least different shades of a voice.

(Baker, cited in Hitchens 2006: 135)

Naturally, a rationale of this kind invites the attention of neoliberal governments and their regulatory agencies. It's a soft target when the calculus is animated by rhetorics which privilege economic efficiencies over societal priorities: in this sense, the policy objects of diversity and pluralism tend to get spun off to the outer limits of contemporary regulatory purview. They run in 'background mode', waiting to be called on to justify specific policy interventions, which inevitably tend to be liberalizing. In a perverse and yet probably predictable twist, even the chief proselytizers of market liberalization, such as Rupert Murdoch, appear to sing the praises of pluralism and diversity. But as Freedman observes, in this process, when media diversity and pluralism are conceptualized as only about consumer choice and competition, there is a 'danger of neutering expansive concepts of diversity through neoliberal reforms' (2008: 77). The challenge for policy-makers is to maintain the link of these concepts to their original objectives: ideas that promote the open ability of groups to maximize expression of divergent viewpoints and values, and the ability of citizens to have equitable access to these informational resources.

Public interest discourses and citizenship

Pursuing these interconnected rationales and their consequences, Lunt and Livingstone have explored how the new breed of 'convergent' media regulators, such as Ofcom, might ensure that updated ideas of the 'public interest' are repositioned at the heart of regulatory processes (2007: 2). In their view, a regulatory struggle is yet to resolve the balance of consumer and industry, and consumer and citizen interests, in the reformulation of the public interest. They see a primary tension in this regard between, on the one hand, the need to regulate a market so that it is 'competitive and delivers good value to consumers', and, on the other, 'the need to protect citizens from risk and detriment' (2007: 2).

Indeed, they describe other ongoing tensions between the needs of individual consumers and broader public policy objectives, and consumer protections and consumer awareness-raising policies. Yet, for the big picture, Lunt and Livingstone note that regulation in the public interest is embedded within discourses of more media-literate consumers, where regulators act with a 'light touch', guided by claims to 'evidence-based' rationales (2007: 2).

By contrast, in his analysis of the establishment of Ofcom, Feintuck writes that despite the recommendations of the Puttnam Committee, which scrutinized the legislation setting up Ofcom for 'the long term interests of all citizens', these are not necessarily well represented in the practical realities of modern media regulation (Feintuck 2004: 94, 114–25; Feintuck and Varney 2006). And when the Communications Act 2003 was enacted, his observation is that the 'vulnerability of broad public interests in media regulation has not been satisfactorily remedied by the Act' (Feintuck and Varney 2006: 115).

In Feintuck's view, the contemporary UK regulatory focus can be characterized in this way:

> In the context of ongoing trends of technological development and convergence, and corporate conglomeration in the media industries, the previously dominant 'public service' tradition in British broadcasting has been replaced by a model in which regulators must justify their interventions in relation primarily to the economics of the market. From a citizen-oriented vision embodied in the public service tradition, regulation has turned its focus to an agenda derived from perceptions of consumer interests, contributing to and reconfirming the commodification of the media within an increasingly producer-led, free-market media economy.
>
> (Feintuck 2004: 94–5)

His argument is that these conditions, which are by no means unique to the media industries, have developed historically from the deregulatory *Zeitgeist* of the Thatcher/Regan era; they downplay the key 'public sphere' role of the media, and have replaced it with a consumerist market-driven framework. This kind of analysis is well known, and Feintuck cites Keane's critique that 'communications media . . . should aim to empower a plurality of citizens who are governed neither by undemocratic states nor by undemocratic market forces' (Keane 1991: 11, cited in Feintuck 2004: 95).

Feintuck's view is that public interest values have historically been integrated into the process of media regulation for several reasons. Importantly for the concerns of this chapter, he suggests that it is only when these foundational rationales for intervention have been considered, is it then possible to justify their ongoing application. There have been four main categories of classification into which these rationales may be placed: (1) effective communication; (2)

diversity; (3) economic justifications; and (4) public service (Feintuck 2004: 95). For Feintuck, 'The democratic significance of the media is unquestioned, and permits substantial public interest claims, in terms of collective values which . . . go far beyond the consumerist expectations of choice.' These public interest claims are embedded in the structures in which expressions of pluralism take place (2004: 40). Sorauf's understanding of the public interest provides guidance: 'the complex procedures of political adjustment and compromise which the democratic polity employs to represent and accommodate the demands made upon its policy-making instruments' – as seeming to 'capture a potential relationship with pluralism' (Sorauf, F. J. (1957) The Public Interest Reconsidered *The Journal of Politics*, 19(4): 616–39).

Yet, in the end, this framing remains somewhat limited since it 'risks failing to take the concept's function beyond that of a contested arena within which the pluralist fray may take place' (Feintuck 2004: 40). In developing his 'democratic vision of the public interest', Feintuck advocates traditional constructions of the public interest which include connections with ideas of community, human rights and dignity, general welfare and the 'maintenance of conditions that permit an ongoing social order'. However, overlain on these concerns he argues, the concept should also go beyond specific interest groups in pluralistic societies, and incorporate the interests of future members of society (2004: 41).

Essentially, then, Feintuck is critical of understandings of the public interest which reduce it to a 'spoils' system of democracy. In his opinion, such hegemonic views of particular social groups define 'public interests' in line with their own political and economic power. But equally, definitions of public interest which rely on market-based understandings fail to incorporate a wider set of democratic values. Notions of equality of citizenship that have justified in the past, and may continue to justify and inform, media regulation, offer the best prospect for public interest interventions. At their best, such understandings have the capacity to combine a collective element with what he sees as the ascendancy of an 'individualistic version of citizenship' (2004: 46), and may in so doing, better fulfil 'the immanent promises of the liberal-democratic settlement' (2004: 58).

His case study of Ofcom is instructive for how concepts of the public interest are (or more accurately, are not) being applied in convergent communications media policies, and for looking at the operation of mechanisms for dealing with media merger situations. These consolidation situations have been important for some decades because of 'the relationship between concentration of ownership of media outlets and control over what is communicated through them, and ultimately the range of views in circulation in society' (2004: 113). He discusses how the 'Public Interest Test' (also referred to as a 'plurality' or 'media mergers' test) operates conjunctively with communications and com-petition or fair trading laws, noting how it was introduced late in the parlia-mentary process 'as something of a concession in the Lords' arising from citizen (rather than consumer) concerns. Feintuck argues that the mechanism itself is open to political pressures, since the intervention test powers 'will be engaged only at the instigation of the Secretary of State, allowing the possibility of party political influence and hence inconsistency in their application' (Feintuck and Varney 2006: 115).

Under this intervention process, Ofcom uses criteria to adjudicate when the public interest may be harmed through consolidation between newspapers and broadcasters, or within these sectors. There are different public interest criteria for these sectors. For newspapers, the criteria relate to accuracy in the presentation of news, free expression and a plurality of opinions, whereas for broadcasters the criteria cover 'plurality of persons with control' in relation to specific audiences, the range and quality of programming, and commitment to standards (including accuracy, impartiality, harm, offence, fairness and privacy) (2006: 114).

The House of Lords in their *Ownership of the News* report proposed changes to the mergers test to 'ensure that the system is as independent, robust and streamlined as possible' (2008a: 68). Their suggestion was that the current mergers test is unnecessarily complex and drawn out: the application of the Public Interest Test is currently a five- or six-stage process:

1. The Secretary of State issues an Intervention Notice.
2. Ofcom and the OFT report back to the Secretary of State.
3. The Secretary of State decides whether to refer the case to the Competition Commission (if s/he decides not to, then the process stops here).
4. The Competition Commission reports back to the Secretary of State.
5. The Secretary of State makes a final decision.
6. Interested parties can appeal case to the Competition Appeals Tribunal.

Importantly, their recommendations include a new requirement to establish that a merger will not adversely affect professional news-gathering and investigative journalism. Since media consolidation will often mean a reduced investment in this critically important genre, the Committee reasoned that such a requirement was now required in the public interest.

The Lords saw a significant difference between the way the mergers test was working for newspapers and broadcasting. Noting that Ofcom has the critical responsibility of advising the Secretary of State about whether a newspaper merger is likely to harm the public interest, and whether or not there is a case for referring the merger to the Competition Commission on public interest grounds, the Lords in their report recommended that Ofcom undertake a review of the merger test for newspapers. Presenting the *Ownership of News* report to the Parliament, the Chairman of the Communications Select Committee, Lord Fowler, made the comment that when designed by Lord Puttnam, the purpose of the Public Interest Test was 'to ensure that no single voice becomes too powerful'.

In evidence to the inquiry, the Guardian Media Group (GMG) argued that 'under current competition rules, a Google acquisition of a major UK media asset might not automatically trigger an investigation'. Yet such an event would, they argued, raise clear 'public interest' concerns. In an interesting attempt to weigh up the relativities of media influence, GMG argued that Google's share of voice in the online world could be seen reaching levels similar to that of the analogue terrestrial broadcasters on television (House of Lords 2008: 72). Other specific recommendations in the Lords report for the Public Interest Test were that:

* The Government should be more flexible and adopt a case-by-case approach when considering which media mergers the Public Interest Test should apply to. We believe that it would be essential to apply the test if a major international Internet company bought a stake in a UK news provider.
* Ofcom should be given the power to initiate the Public Interest Test. This would sit more comfortably with Ofcom's duty to promote the interests of the citizen. We do not believe that the power to trigger a Public Interest Test should be taken away from Ministers. Along with Ofcom, Ministers should retain the power in the event that they consider there is a risk to the public interest that Ofcom has not fully recognized. Therefore, the power to issue an Intervention Notice should be held by both Ofcom and the Secretary of State.

The only use to date of the Public Interest Test has been the high profile case of BSkyB's purchase of a 17.9 per cent stake in ITV. BSkyB, the highly popular UK satellite broadcaster, is owned by News Corporation, the owner of four of the UK's national newspapers amounting to a third of total circulation, MySpace and a vast number of other global media interests (Freedman 2008). After its investigation, Ofcom concluded that if the acquisition went ahead, 'There may not be a sufficient plurality of persons with control of the media enterprises serving the UK cross-media audience for national news and the UK TV audience for national news.' The House of Lords Select Committee expressed their strong concern that the Competition Commission reached an entirely different view on the question of plurality. The Commission had argued they: 'did not expect BSkyB's ability materially to influence ITV to have an adverse effect on plurality of news' and 'the acquisition would not materially affect the sufficiency of plurality of persons with control of media enterprises servicing audiences for news (2008a: 78). To remedy this contradictory outcome (even though the conclusions reached by Ofcom and the Competition Commission in the BSkyB/ITV transaction were ultimately the same), the Lords recommended that legislation should be amended so that Ofcom investigates the mergers only on the basis of the public interest criteria, and the Competition Commission considers only the competition aspects of a merger. The Secretary of State would then have the final responsibility for accepting or rejecting Ofcom's recommendations and remedies, as they relate to the public interest criteria.

Not surprisingly, the formal responses by Ofcom (2008b) and the government (Department of Culture, Sport and Media) were consistently opposed to the Lords' recommendations. The government's overall response was that it was 'considering the future of ownership regulation, and how it will be challenged by the changes in communications technologies, services, platforms and consumption that come with convergence'. The government and Ofcom both thought the existing processes adequate, and the roles of the Secretary of State, Competition Commission and Ofcom satisfactory in their existing form.

The citizen/consumer policy dichotomy is discussed in the Lords report. They make the point that although the word 'consumer' (or 'consumerism') is mentioned 79 times, the word 'citizen' is mentioned only three times. In fact, they interpret Ofcom's role in the merger test as relating primarily to citizen interests. In this regard they recommend that 'when Ofcom considers the public interest considerations of a media merger it should be required to put the needs of the citizen ahead of the needs of the consumer' (House of Lords 2008a: 78).

Writing some years before the Lords' *Ownership of the News* report, Feintuck found there was still some cause for limited optimism:

> The range of public interest criteria established under section 375 and subsequent sections do outline some key factors which might usefully form the basis of a meaningful version of the concept . . . and which may establish a framework against which decisions must be justified.
>
> (2004: 115)

Against this optimism, Feintuck is fully aware of the 'serious technical-legal' difficulties arising from the application of diversity and competition rules in relation to media markets. These include problems of market definition and measuring the actual market and audience shares. His arguments seem to have pre-figured the Lords' recommendations, and in Feintuck's view, it is doubtful whether the Public Interest Test measures 'go any significant way towards resolving the overall lack of clarity' in the operation of concepts of public interest in the context of media regulation (Feintuck and Varney 2006: 115). This essentially was the position of the Lords in their report. Freedman's view is that 'Without a fundamentally different attitude by government towards media concentration, the Public Interest Test is doomed to be a lightweight tool in the face of aggressive liberalisation' (2008: 120). For him, the future of ownership policies is not a pretty picture:

> The liberalisation of ownership rules is likely to contribute to a situation marked not by heterogeneity and diversity, but by restricted competition, oligopolistic markets and political consensus. Media ownership is by no means the sole explanatory factor of media performance and the existence of media ownership rules are not at all sufficient to ensure genuine competition and diversity, but they are an important first step in challenging concentrated and unaccountable formations of media power.
>
> (2008: 122)

In line with Lunt and Livingstone's analysis, Feintuck sees too much tension between divergent commercial and democratic values, with few clear guidelines to resolve conflicts when they do arise. For him, this conflict is embodied in the notion of a 'citizen-consumer' invoked in the legislation, and 'even the most deft use of a hyphen' is unlikely to assuage the range of expectations in this merged concept. In this argument the citizenship intentions of the Puttnam Committee, and therefore a sophisticated contemporary articulation of the public interest have, in effect, been defeated in their practical regulatory expression in the Communications Act 2003. Watered-down variants of citizenship may only exist in the policies of so-called 'public service communications', the updated version of the public service broadcasting tradition.

International developments

Evaluating the similarities and differences in media ownership law, policies and regulation between Australia, New Zealand, the United Kingdom, Canada and the United States is an exercise which highlights the very specific evolution in these nations' media systems. Their histories and cultures are unique, and they illustrate the interaction of law and policy with particular corporate players and cultural expectations, and ultimately how they have shaped the range and diversity of available media. However, as Anglophone nations occupying a broadly aligned set of political and cultural norms, they can be categorized in Hallin and Mancini's terms as belonging to the Liberal or North Atlantic model (Hallin and Mancini 2004). We shall return to these points of comparison following the discussion of these media systems.

Australia

In their efforts to ameliorate the potentially more detrimental effects of increased media ownership concentration, successive Australian governments have balanced different and, at times, conflicting policy outcomes. On the one hand, the interest in maintaining a diversified and locally relevant media has led to various combinations of ownership restrictions on what have been traditionally the most influential forms of media. On the other hand, media proprietors and media companies, like other businesses, are always keen to expand their media and other interests, consolidate their operations, and become more competitive in an increasingly globalized marketplace.

Australian Governments have also attempted in the past (and not necessarily successfully) to ensure strong, diverse and independent regional media voices in the face of aggregation, networking and increased syndication across commonly held media outlets. There is evidence of concern about media ownership in regional communities, and in particular the important place it plays in local media in regional areas, and recognition of the relationships between local media and the powerful or influential local elites (Dwyer et al. 2006). These issues of local power, as much as anything else, seem to fly in the face of recent changes to media ownership regulation, and earlier priorities to maintain diversity in regional media.

New media ownership laws in Australia, enacted as the *Broadcasting Services Amendment (Media Ownership) Act 2006* (BSA), took effect from 4 April 2007. The Act repealed foreign control rules, amended cross-media rules and introduced a number of key concepts relating to media ownership including prohibitions and specific tests for 'unacceptable media diversity situations' and 'unacceptable three-way control situations'. There has been some commentary in the broadsheet press to the effect that the dismantling of cross-media and foreign ownership rules will undoubtedly, over time, lead to industry consolidation through mergers and acquisitions, and that this does not augur well for media diversity in Australia. But media ownership is yet to strike the kind of popular chord in Australia that it did in the USA in 2004/2005 (when the repeal of cross-media rules was attempted unsuccessfully by the FCC). The strong support by civil society activist groups at the 2008 National Conference for Media Reform in Minneapolis, organized by the Free Press, is testament to the vitality of a more grassroots media ownership debate in the USA.

With the 20-year-old cross-media limits now lifted, Australia is in a context of contracting media diversity. This can only add to its reputation as having 'perhaps the greatest degree of media concentration in the world' (Hoffman-Reim 1996). Nonetheless, it can be seen as being consistent with an international neoliberal trend to relax ownership rules, and Australia now has gone further than other comparable nations. For example, in the UK, cross-sector limits remain at the local, regional and national levels; while in the USA, new FCC rules (from December 2007) allow newspaper/broadcast combinations in the 20 biggest markets only, subject to certain conditions, but these are under a cloud following opposition in the US Congress (discussed further shortly).

Australia's Rudd Government, coming to power after the new rules were introduced, has indicated that it will not repeal them. However, the Communications Minister, Senator Conroy, has said that the government, who were opposed to the changes, would work on 'additional media ownership safeguards' during its first term (Steffens 2008).

The first impacts in the wake of the changes to the cross-media and foreign media reforms in Australia were not the awaited media merger and acquisition feeding frenzy. Instead the key moves were characterized by opportunistic debt refinancing based on the share price bubble, courtesy of the previous (Howard) government's 'telegraphed' legislative package. Predictably, when the share prices rose in the wake of the passage of the new laws, Australia's largest media corporations were able to take advantage of the situation, and go ahead with their business strategies based on cash windfalls, allowing them to make new acquisitions – for both media and non-media assets.

In essence, the new laws removed the main cross-media ownership restrictions, now allowing TV/newspaper/radio mergers with a 'two out of three' (of these) media sector limit, and introducing metropolitan and rural/regional voice limits – under the so-called '5/4 voices test'. Under the new media ownership laws, a 'voice' refers to a 'media group', or a group of two or more traditional media operations (a commercial radio broadcasting licence, an associated newspaper or a commercial television broadcasting licence). The new *Broadcasting Services Amendment (Media Ownership) Act 2006* amends the previous cross-media ownership restrictions subject to there remaining a minimum number of separately controlled media groups in city (five) or rural/regional areas (four). A new section 61AB of the BSA establishes a new concept of an 'unacceptable media diversity situation'. Where transactions occur in breach of these limits, so-called 'unacceptable media diversity situations' are said to exist.

In fact, there have been a number of media asset transactions which all amount to a significant reduction in the diversity in Australia's media ownership, and that signal important implications as test-beds for cross-owned, digital media corporations.

The coming into force of amendments to media ownership laws triggered a major private equity refinancing of free-to-air television, effectively taking much of the network ownership offshore into private institutional ownership. This was the dramatic and largely unanticipated impact of removing foreign ownership restrictions. At the same time, liberalization of the cross-media rules has allowed consolidation by existing traditional media players, further concentrating media ownership into fewer hands, with implications for both audiences and employment practices. Overall, then, there has been significant consolidation in the print, radio and television sectors.

Television

The national commercial free-to-air TV networks, Seven and Nine, both sold 50 per cent of their media assets in US private equity arrangements (first, Nine with CVC Asia Pacific and then Seven with Kravis Kohlberg Roberts), using the cash from the sales to position themselves for expansion into other media and non-media assets. The Packer family-controlled media interests (via Consolidated Media Holdings) have since sold down at first a further 25 per cent of PBL Media (Nine Network) to the CVC Asia Pacific, and there has been further dilution of their interests, taking the private equity group's stake to almost 100 per cent of PBL Media (Shoebridge 2008). These refinancing manoeuvres were read by some analysts as the coming to fruition of the Packer family's long-awaited withdrawal from traditional media assets. Consolidated Media Holdings still has significant investments in Foxtel Pay TV, Fox Sports, Seek, the market-leading online job classified company and ACP magazines, the main competitor to News Corporation's magazine interests.

Kerry Stokes' Seven Network bought a strategic 5 per cent in Consolidated Media Holdings which was worth about $100 million in July 2008. Remaining TV sector limits (of two stations per market) prevent Seven Network from controlling the Nine Network stations in markets where they already run television stations. The purchase by Stokes of this stake came several months after parties led by James Packer and Lachlan Murdoch attempted to privatize CMH in a AU$3.3 billion deal. However, the deal eventually collapsed after a US private equity investor withdrew its support. Stokes' Seven Network took his stake in CMH to almost 20% in July 2009, eyeing off CMH's coveted pay TV assets.

Australia's other commercial network, Network Ten, was already over 50 per cent foreign-owned by the Canadian CanWest group. (This was permissible under the previous laws through the use of creative corporate structuring, based on economic instruments that were distinguishable from direct voting control interests in the licensee company.) In the wake of the recent changes, the group moved into a more formalized position of control of the network. Further, there has been speculation that the CanWest group itself is about to be 'taken private', through private equity financing, as a result of a dangerously high level of debt, and inability to meet scheduled repayments.

Newspapers

The cashed-up Seven Media Group (SMG includes the Seven Network) initially bought up 14.9 per cent of West Australian Newspapers (WAN) and then to approximately 22 per cent (well over the statutory controlling position of 15 per cent under Australian broadcasting laws). But it is now lawful to have broadcast/newspaper combinations like this under the new laws. In the Perth market, this means that the highest rating, most watched free-to-air TV network, has control of the highest circulation daily newspaper and the second most popular online news site associated with that paper (TheWest.com.au). Control was sealed when Stokes eventually won the two WAN board seats in his home city that he had desperately wanted for so long. Shortly after this he succeeded in becoming chairman of WAN. News Corporation's 'PerthNow' is the frontrunner in this online news market, and Fairfax Media have now launched WAtoday.com. Fairfax Media, who together with News Corporation own around 70 per cent of Australia's newspaper market, explained to the market that their move was about creating a national news and advertising footprint. Some commentators have predicted that Stokes' SMG will steadily increase Seven's stake in WAN. Undoubtedly this was a significant cross-media development, and not surprisingly at least attracted the attention of the competition regulator (ACCC 2008).

In a climate of buoyant share prices in the period leading up to the 20-year cross-media changes Fairfax Media made a pre-emptive defensive move and initiated a merger with the Rural Press group, creating Australia's largest (in net value terms) media group. The total deal was valued at that time at around AUS$9 billion (including $2.3 billion in debt). At the time of the merger, the group held more than 240 regional, rural and community publications, 9 radio stations and the leading NZ internet site TradeMe (discussed in New Zealand below), as well as 20 agricultural titles in the USA. Fairfax Media claimed it would have 'over 5 million visitors each month to websites including smh.com.au, theage.com.au, farmonline.com.au, canberratimes.com.au and yourguide.com.au'.

> This merger positions the group tremendously for internet expansion. Combining the local content and connections of the Rural Press titles with the national reach of Fairfax Media's online brands and technology will accelerate growth in online classified revenue, and enable the development of local news and information sites and a world-class rural services online business.
>
> (Fairfax/Rural Press MR 2006)

The business case was that the merger would boost Internet revenue growth and new online business development for national classifieds, regional news and information services, regional and rural trade and services, cross-promotion through regional print and radio. In addition, for the traditional print operations, there would be 'printing optimisation and expansion'. Overall, the pitch to the market was that the combined companies would be converting to a digital media company that would continue to integrate 'news gathering and story management for multiple media' that would further develop the 'capacity to distribute across multiple platforms'.

Few have explicitly linked the merger of the Fairfax and Rural Press in the wake of changes to the cross-media rules, to the unprecedented layoff of over 550 journalists and other production staff. Yet despite rather muted commentary, it is clear that the post-merger rationalizations were symptomatic of a seachange at the *The Sydney Morning Herald* and *The Age*, mastheads of Fairfax Media, and signpost wider processes of digitization and convergence. These kinds of newspaper staff retrenchments are occurring in all the countries reviewed in this section; they can be read as connected with global reconfigurations in media business models as discussed in Chapter 2.

In the event that the Murdoch family-controlled News Corporation (or Seven Media Group for that matter) were ever permitted to acquire this group, the consequences would be quite stark in terms of market dominance in Australia. While unrelated to the ownership law changes in the sense that they were within the same sector not across it (magazines have never been included in the cross-media restrictions), News Corporation finalized their acquisition of the Federal Publishing Company's magazine and community newspapers interests (13 community newspapers, 2 commuter papers, 25 magazines and 6 online properties). The deal was approved by the competition regulator, the ACCC (Australian Competition and Consumer Commission). The wider significance of this transaction is that it added to their existing dominance of the metropolitan, regional and community newspaper markets; it represents unprecedented concentration of print media ownership and circulation.

Radio

The largest radio network, owned by the Macquarie Media Group (owned by the investment bank that specializes in infrastructure projects) took a strategic 14.9 per cent AU$170 million positioning stake in Southern Cross Broadcasting (a networked radio and TV operation). Shortly after the Fairfax/Rural Press merger, a three-way deal involving Fairfax Media/Macquarie Media/Southern Cross Broadcasting was launched. This merger was the first major cross-media implementation under the new rules in Australia.

The Fairfax/Macquarie Media Group/Southern Cross deal was a complex deal requiring both ACMA and ACCC oversight. MMG agreed to pay AU$1.35

billion for SCB, which adds regional TV interests (approx. 14 stations) to its 87 regional radio stations in 45 markets. The trouble was:

> By combining radio and TV assets, MMG has breached diversity levels in 13 markets and has been forced to offer 15 stations for sale in a process now under way. It also on-sold SCB's metropolitan radio stations – 4BC and 4BH Brisbane, 2UE Sydney, 3AW and Magic Melbourne and 6PR and 96FM Perth – to Fairfax Media for $520 million in a deal completed in November 2007. In turn, MMG agreed to buy nine regional stations acquired by Fairfax when it merged with Rural Press earlier in 2007.
>
> (ACMA media release 23/2008)

The deal also delivered to Fairfax Media the nation's biggest independent television and video production company Southern Star, co-producer (with Endemol) of *Big Brother*. There has been some speculation that Fairfax Media are now looking for a buyer for Southern Star, with the apparent attractiveness of being a convergent media 'value-add' perhaps not enough incentive to stem general losses, including from the waning *Big Brother* franchise. Media ownership limits are still working to the extent that Macquarie Media Group (MMG) divested 12 regional radio licences in accordance with an enforceable undertaking accepted by the ACMA (ACMA media release 23/2008).

Academic legal commentators in Australia have noted the irony of proponents of cross-media liberalization, asserting that the advent of new forms of media justified their repeal, when these platforms have not been included in the new diversity tests. Indeed, neither national newspapers, free local papers, the public broadcasters ABC and SBS, nor narrowcasting, subscription, community broadcasting or online media, constitute a 'voice' in the new diversity tests. Nor do the new rules take into account the relative influence/market share of different outlets (Butler and Rodrick 2007: 642).

Voices, content sharing and ownership disclosure

Interestingly, though, the new rules do figure ownership issues in ways that they previously have not been used, or with a different twist. First, the new rules monitor 'unacceptable media diversity situations' in relation to content sharing between commercial television stations only – however, not between *other* media platforms (BSA, s. 61AE). Content sharing in this context constitutes, in effect, a grandfathering mechanism that expressly allows the same content to be used, as a way of accommodating existing joint control of two or three existing television licences in a media group; together the stations may only count as one 'voice'. Yet content sharing within a single media sector is probably not the kind of arrangement that many people would envisage when they contemplate the impacts of cross-media liberalization, as this quote from a very comprehensive investigation into the broadcasting industry in 2000 indicates:

> There are mixed views within the sector as to the source of other benefits from cross-media reform. Industry respondents to the PC Inquiry nominated content sharing as one, but not the only, advantage of cross-controlled companies. Cross-selling of advertising, cross-promotion of products and services, and sharing of administrative and corporate functions, such as marketing, have also been anticipated. However, the actual extent of the benefits remain unclear.
>
> (BSA, Explanatory Memorandum, Para [31] 20)

Arguably this type of content sharing mechanism and ACMA's role in relation to it are under-utilized in an era of convergent media. The implications of content sharing will be an increasingly important area of analysis for those interested in media diversity. In particular, the sharing of news content within and across platforms is an area of intensified focus in media consolidation by media corporations themselves. And clearly the reduction of diversity in news voice through mergers and acquisitions raises important issues of pluralism for citizen audiences. To take one obvious example, (discussed above in relation to WAN), it is noteworthy that Australia's largest circulation newspapers also control the most widely read online newspaper sites, and this situation falls outside the scope of existing regulatory mechanisms for diversity (and this applies to the other jurisdictions in this chapter).

Second, the *Broadcasting Services Amendment (Media Ownership) Act 2006* introduces new provisions for the disclosure of cross-media relationships into the *Broadcasting Services Act 1992*. They require commercial television broadcasting licensees, commercial radio broadcasting licensees and newspaper publishers to publicly disclose cross-media relationships if they broadcast or publish matter about the business affairs of another party in a set of media operations (ACMA media release 2008c).

These provisions were added later in the parliamentary debates as an olive branch to political parties who did not support such extensive liberalization of the cross-media rules. The mechanism echoes disclosure standards imposed on Australia's commercial radio licensees, following several high profile scandals arising from the excesses of the unrestrained 'commercial speech' of 'shock jocks' in the early 2000s. But as a regulatory measure they appear to be an 'after the fact' or reactive solution to more obvious structural arrangements to promote diversity of voices across media platforms.

There is a strong argument to be made that both the content sharing and cross-media disclosure provisions represent concepts that could be usefully subject to further development, in the context of regulating convergent media in the public interest. There is already evidence of a high level of sharing (or syndication) of news programming within radio and television networks in Australia to the detriment of audiences at a local level (Dwyer et al. 2006). This was already a clear trend under the previous regime of cross-media restrictions; this kind of news content sharing will continue, and that sharing between platforms – in both old and new media – is likely to increase if the stated corporate objectives of consolidating media companies are successfully implemented.

Canada

Canada has both significant concentration of media ownership and high levels of cross-media ownership. While there is undoubted concern in Canada regarding the effects of increased concentration of ownership, especially from journalists and people in regional areas, debate is tempered by the presence of many of the world's largest media conglomerates just south of the border. Canadian cultural policy generally has historically been 'inward-looking', developing ways to protect Canadians from overwhelming US cultural influence, while supporting Canadian cultural producers (Maule 2003: 12). In its 2001 submission to a major Canadian House of Commons review of Canadian broadcasting, the independent public interest group Friends of Canadian Broadcasting argued that: 'from the dawn of the audiovisual age eight decades ago, the major challenge facing the [Canadian] English-language system has been the overwhelming influence of United States programming' (Friends of Canadian Broadcasting, Submission, 2001). This desire to maintain a Canadian media identity, through ensuring continued production of Canadian content, has led to policy decisions that have generally accepted consolidation of the Canadian media industry in order to finance substantial production funds for Canadian content, and build corporations with the strength to compete against the American giants of Disney, Time-Warner (AOL), and Viacom.

Canadian media ownership regulation allows the Canadian media regulator a flexible and discretionary role. With the exception of a short period between 1982 and 1985, there has been no direct regulatory restriction on cross-media ownership. Foreign ownership in Canadian media (and telecommunications) *is* restricted by legislation, and there are some policy restrictions on ownership concentration in commercial radio or television. The Canadian communications regulator, the Canadian Radio-television and Telecommunications Commission (CRTC) has tended to examine media mergers within its area of responsibility (television, radio, pay television) on a case-by-case basis. Newspapers are not within its jurisdiction, although the Commission has taken into account newspaper holdings in its merger/takeover decisions.

The proliferation of cable, satellite and other alternative distribution platforms has meant that Canadian broadcasting policy has been dealing with issues of audience fragmentation for many years. As with the United States, cable distribution in Canada began in the early 1950s as a community-based, non-profit means to deliver television to areas with poor reception (Townsend 1999: 253). The early importance of cable has been reflected by the imposition of 'must-carry' requirements for cable providers, initially in relation to provincially-produced educational channels, then later to ensure local and regional stations. Pay television – that is, the provision of specialized services on a fee-paying basis on top of the basic broadcasting service – was introduced in 1982 (Townsend 1999: 65). Satellite delivery was a priority for the more remote areas, with cable distribution prominent in urban areas. Most Canadian homes have at least the basic cable or satellite service, while pay and specialty services account for nearly half the audience share in English-speaking markets, and less than this in French-speaking markets. Arguably, this has meant that concern over the concentration of ownership in traditional media is tempered by the greater range of news, information and entertainment services available.

The *Canadian Bill of Rights* guarantees freedom of speech and of the press, while the *Charter of Rights and Freedoms* guarantees freedom of thought, belief, opinion and expression, including the freedom of the press and media and communication. While Canadian newspaper proprietors have used these free speech guarantees to argue against the regulation of newspaper ownership (in fact, any regulation of newspapers generally), the guarantees can also be used to justify regulation of media ownership in terms of preserving and promoting diversity (Farbstein 2001).

Canadian broadcasting regulation

The broadcasting policy of Canada, as provided for in the *Broadcasting Act 1991* (Can), provides that the Canadian broadcasting system:

• shall be effectively owned and controlled by Canadians;
• shall operate primarily in the English and French languages and comprise public, private and community elements, and provide, through its programming, a public service essential to the maintenance and enhancement of national identity and cultural sovereignty;
• should:
  ◦ serve to safeguard, enrich and strengthen the cultural, political, social and economic fabric of Canada;
  ◦ encourage the development of Canadian expression by providing a wide range of programming that reflects Canadian attitudes, opinions,

ideas, values and artistic creativity, by displaying Canadian talent in entertainment programming and by offering information and analysis concerning Canada and other countries from a Canadian point of view;

o   reflect the circumstances and aspirations of Canadian men, women and children, including equal rights, the linguistic duality and multi-cultural and multiracial nature of Canadian society and the special place of aboriginal peoples within that society; and

o   be adaptable to scientific and technological change.

Canadian broadcasting regulation provides the CRTC with a wide scope in its determination as to the best way to achieve the goals of the Act, with the Act and supporting statutory instruments evidencing a less prescriptive regulatory framework than its Australian equivalent. The Regulations specify the level of annual licence fees, and set specific requirements for Canadian content for both free-to-air television and distribution networks (whether cable, satellite or wireless). Apart from occasional government directions, and those areas specified in the Regulations, the CRTC is allowed a flexible and substantially independent role within the statutory framework to determine both generic licence standards and (more commonly) specific licence conditions on a case-by-case basis. The report in 2003 by the Canadian Standing Committee for Canadian Heritage suggested that the lack of clear governmental guidance had the potential to create uncertainty over the appropriate scope of the Commission's role, and its relationship to other relevant regulators such as the Competition Bureau.

Cross-media and media concentration

With the exception of the period 1982–85, Canadian broadcasting legislation has not had any formal rules regarding cross-media ownership. The CRTC has, however, developed specific policies in relation to concentrated ownership in television and radio. It generally permits ownership of no more than one terrestrial broadcasting television station in one language in a given market. The Commission argues this policy 'ensures the diversity of voices in a given market, and helps to maintain competition in each market' (CRTC 1997). In the case of radio, the CRTC permits ownership or control of as many as three stations operating in a given language (including up to two in any one frequency band) in markets with less than eight commercial radio stations. In larger radio markets, a person may be permitted to own or control as many as two AM and two FM commercial stations in a given language (CRTC 1997).

Mergers and acquisitions of terrestrial broadcasting entities are considered by the CRTC on a case-by-case basis, with the Commission setting licence conditions in relation to the market and media environment in which they operate. In the case of vertical integration between an independent producer and a broadcast licensee, the Commission expects companies involved to develop appropriate safeguards for competition and diversity concerns, and they may include additional such safeguards as part of the licence conditions of the broadcaster. Until 2001, cable companies were generally not allowed to purchase interests in analogue pay and speciality programming services. However, in June 2001, the CRTC overturned the general rule, allowing the renewal of the licences of CTV and Global but stipulating that no more than 25 per cent of their Canadian content in prime time could come from production companies they owned (CRTC 2001). While the CRTC has included consideration of newspaper holdings as part licence renewal procedures, the legal authority for the CRTC to consider newspapers has been clearly defined (Townsend 1984).

At present, the policy objective that the Canadian broadcasting system 'shall be effectively owned and controlled by Canadians' is enforced by a direction from the Government to the CRTC requiring 80 per cent Canadian ownership and control for all broadcasting licences, and 66.6 per cent for holding companies (Canadian Parliament). The *Investment Canada Act 1985*, like its predecessor the *Foreign Investment Review Act 1973*, screens all major foreign investments in Canada. Several industries considered especially important, such as banking, broadcasting and telecommunications, are subject to specific provisions in relation to foreign ownership.

Winseck has argued that as early as the 1970s the Canadian mediascape was being envisioned as a convergent one, combining the telecommunications, broadcasting, publishing and computing sectors. Indeed, since a broadband cable-driven networked future was also seen as the goal from the 1980s:

> The current revival of media reconvergence has been driven by changes in government and corporate policies that have gone from *preventing* to *promoting* convergence and concerted efforts to transform information/communication into the pivotal commodities of the 'new economy' and 'information societies' . . . the shift from *preventing* to *promoting* convergence also entailed greater tolerance of ownership concentration and a new hierarchy of values that privileged the expansion of information and media markets over concerns about freedom of expression and the role of communication in a democratic society.
>
> (Winseck 2002: 796, emphasis in the original)

Given this officially sanctioned expectation of convergent change involving legacy and new media, it was in many ways a self-fulfilling prophesy that the Canadian media would undergo continuous consolidation.

Media mergers and acquisitions in Canada are subject to general competition regulation, and may be scrutinized by the competition regulator, the Competition Bureau. The Bureau regards the advertising market as the general point of reference in relation to competition regulation in the media sector, and has tended to regard newspaper, television and radio advertising as operating in distinct markets. As such, it has not appeared too concerned about the proliferation of cross-media mergers, and is generally satisfied that adequate competition still exists in specific sectorial markets.

With the CRTC as the primary broadcasting and telecommunications regulator, this regulatory overlap has, at times, led to conflicting regulatory processes for Canadian media. Like the different regulatory remits operating in agencies in the UK and Australia, the Bureau has taken the view that the CRTC should not concern itself with competition issues and concentrate only on cultural issues in relation to media mergers and acquisitions, such as diversity. The view of the CRTC has been that its broad mandate under the *Broadcasting Act* to ensure diversity requires it to examine issues of economic viability of media organizations. While a memorandum of understanding was signed between the two regulators in 1999 in attempt to clarify their roles in respect to media and telecommunications, a degree of tension remains – perhaps understandably, given the contrasting objectives of each regulator (Senate of Canada 2004: 86–7).

Media ownership consolidation

Since 1970, the various inquiries into media have expressed concern over levels of ownership concentration. Newspaper ownership in Canada has gradually become more concentrated: by 1981, two newspaper chains – Southam and Thomson – controlled 60 per cent of daily circulation. The Southam newspapers were later sold to Hollinger (controlled by Conrad Black). With newspaper concentration reaching such oligopoly levels, vertical and diagonal mergers and acquisitions became the only realistic options for expansion. The period from 2000 onwards has seen ownership concentration across television, radio and newspapers at unprecedented levels. Three major media mergers occurred in Canada in the first two years of the new millennium:

• *BCE* (Canada's largest telecommunications company) acquiring CTV (at the time, Canada's largest television network) and *The Globe and Mail* (one of Canada's leading national dailies).
• *CanWest Global*, taking control of most of Hollinger's newspaper, Internet and magazine assets (previously owned by Conrad Black).
• *Quebecor* (a major newspaper publisher), acquiring Videotron (telecommunications and cable broadcasting) and TVA (television).

As a result, BCE-CTV and CanWest Global control over half of Canada's commercial free-to-air television stations, while over 60 per cent of the population get their local newspaper daily from the same company that owns one or more of their local television stations (Zerbisias 2001). CanWest Global now has a potential audience reach of almost all of the English television market. In the Vancouver/Victoria area, CanWest Global operates two television stations as well as three daily newspapers. In both Montreal and Quebec City, Quebecor owns the most popular daily newspaper and the most viewed television station (Senate of Canada 2004).

The CRTC has, on occasion, refused media merger requests where it determined that the risk to diversity by greater concentration outweighed any benefits that might accrue. For instance, in 2002, the Commission rejected an application by Quebecor, already the major media player in television and newspapers in Quebec, to purchase a number of AM radio stations in the same market. However, there is a general trend by the CRTC (and the government) of acceptance of the notion that Canada needs large and integrated media organizations to achieve the economies of scale required to compete effectively with the US media giants, and to ensure a viable production industry for Canadian content. This sentiment is reflected in the CRTC's 1997 Television Policy statement, which argued that ownership consolidation

> has resulted in efficiencies and synergies which should provide increased investment in Canadian programming and a greater likelihood of the export of that programming. The Commission expects the consolidation of broadcasting, production and communication companies will continue, to the benefit of Canadian audiences, the Canadian broadcasting system and the public interest.
>
> (CRTC 1997)

CanWest Global expressed similar views during the Cultural Heritage Committee hearings into broadcasting:

> Cross-media ownership is about adding value and improving quality, to ensure there are Canadian voices in an increasingly borderless media market. If we artificially chop the Canadian media market into uneconomic pieces, then Canadian media will not be able to compete with media from everywhere that will be coming into Canada, and that will ultimately lead to a reduced ability to tell Canadian stories to Canadians and the world.
>
> (Goldstein 2002)

In evidence to the Senate Committee on Transport and Communications, the CRTC argued that, while issues of cross-ownership and concentration are of concern, in some cases these concerns may be outweighed by 'offsetting advantages' such as stronger broadcasting companies with the capacity to ensure continued production of Canadian content (Senate of Canada 2004). Cross-promotion conducted through different media organs of the one company is not necessary a bad thing, either, according to the then CRTC Chairman, particularly if what is being promoted in a newspaper is a Canadian-made television programme on that company's station.

Diversity and ownership

The CRTC has used three broad policy approaches in an attempt to ameliorate negative effects of cross-media ownership and media concentration: (1) operational/editorial separation of newspaper and electronic media newsrooms; (2) obtaining commitments to preserving local news and information programming; and (3) ensuring Canadian programming through substantial financial support for the production industry and detailed Canadian content requirements. While these interrelated measures may have ensured substantial investment in Canadian content production and broadcasting and communications infrastructure, they have not necessarily led to an increased audience for Canadian material in Canada.

To some extent this approach represents a media ownership policy that encourages (if not relies on) media industry consolidation to achieve public interest objectives. Policies can be seen as 'trading-off' diversity in ownership for the greater good of Canadian content production, or as one commentator has observed, a trade-off between diversity of voice within Canada versus diversity of voice in a North American context (Stursberg, cited in Barron 2002: 996).

In 2008, the CRTC announced new media ownership rules including:

- a person or company will only be permitted to control two media outlets such as newspapers, radio and television stations in the same market;
- one person or company does not control more than 45 per cent of the total television audience share as a result of a merger or acquisition; and
- the CRTC said it would not approve transactions between cable or satellite companies that would result in one person effectively controlling the delivery of programming in a market (city or region).

Predictably, critics noted that the changes 'come too late, on the heels of consolidation in the Canadian broadcasting and newspaper industry that led to the emergence of media behemoths CanWest Global, CTVglobemedia and Quebeco', and were in effect 'legalizing the status quo' (AFP 2008).

New Zealand

Regulation of the media in New Zealand remains minimalist in comparison to Australia, Canada, the UK or the USA. There are no comparable rules for limitations of ownership, foreign ownership, cross-media restrictions or audience reach limits to those currently existing in Australia, the UK, or the USA. Laws operate, as for print media, in the area of general competition, consumer protection legislation and censorship (Cheer 2003).

Writing in 2000 about cultural diversity and local content in the New Zealand (NZ) television industry, Lealand observed that the deregulation of that broadcasting system 'is probably without peer in the rest of the world' (2000: 77). Cheer cites one commentator who describes the outcome of policies of market liberalism as a situation where: 'every major company in the private sector in New Zealand was at that time (2001) foreign-owned, a situation without parallel in the Western World, which no doubt flows from the fact that there are no legal restrictions' (Norris, cited in Cheer 2003: 36).

Little has changed in the intervening few years. The extent of this foreign dominance in media is laid bare by Rosenberg:

> Four companies, all overseas owned, dominate the New Zealand news media. There is a near duopoly in two of the three main media – print and radio – a monopoly in pay television, and only three significant competitors in free-to-air television including the state-owned channels. Each daily newspaper has a near monopoly in its main circulation areas.
>
> (Rosenberg 2008)

In print, two Australian companies, John Fairfax Holdings Ltd and APN News and Media (ANM) between them own 86.9 per cent of audited daily press circulation of the provincial newspapers and 92.2 per cent of the metropolitan readership. The commercial radio duopoly consists of ANM and MediaWorks; the former controlled by Irish Independent News and Media (INM), controlled by the O'Reilly family, while the latter is owned by Australian private equity corporation, Ironbridge Capital (formerly Canadian CanWest Global Communications). Until June 2007, MediaWorks was 70 per cent owned by CanWest, but is now 100 per cent owned by Ironbridge. MediaWorks also owns the next two largest radio networks, and two television channels. Its competitors in television are state-owned television, plus the News Corporation-controlled Sky Television, which has a monopoly on pay television and also owns Prime Television (Rosenberg 2008). A relatively recent development in the print sector is the role of Australia's national news agency, Australian Associated Press (AAP) in providing subediting and other outsourced production for ANM's NZ titles. Through its Pagemaster production subsidiary,

AAP have been producing various sections and providing subediting for approximately two years. AAP is 94 per cent owned by News Ltd (Australia) and Fairfax Media. Pagemaster is in a steep growth phase with the downturn in the global newspaper sector, and has contracts with Fairfax Media for their Australian broadsheets *The Sydney Morning Herald* and *The Age*, and with the UK's *Telegraph* (Steffens 2009).

Fairfax Holdings bought its New Zealand empire in June 2003 for NZ$1.188 billion from Independent Newspapers Ltd (INL, controlled by Rupert Murdoch's News Corporation with a 45 per cent shareholding at the time). As part of its online business strategy in 2006, Fairfax bought the market leading online auction trading site, Trade Me, for NZ$700 million. In 2004, INL took a majority (78 per cent) shareholding in Sky Network Television (and approximately 8 per cent is held by the Australian Commonwealth Bank). Sky and its majority shareholder INL merged in 2005 (Sky Network News Release 2005) with its pay-TV services quickly reaching more than 40 per cent of New Zealand households. In what is, after all, a relatively small market as at mid-2008, Sky had about 20 per cent of the television market and had 748,576 subscribers, representing approximately 46.0 per cent of homes (Sky TV 2008).

In terms of free-to-air television, in addition to the main free-to-air channels of the public service broadcaster TVNZ's ('a crown-owned company') TV One and TV2, there is TV3 (owned by Ironbridge Capital as MediaWorks NZ) and TV4 (now remodelled as the music video channel C4) and Prime (the Australian-owned regional broadcaster) which made a strong push from 2005 onwards to capture a larger audience share by drawing on a joint venture arrangement with Publishing and Broadcasting Limited.

In February 2006, Sky TV bought Prime Television New Zealand Ltd for NZ$30.26 million, giving Sky 'the opportunity to showcase its channels and programmes whilst ensuring that New Zealand consumers can view delayed free-to-air sports programmes such as rugby, rugby league and cricket in prime-time' (cited in Rosenberg 2008: 13). Consistent with the use of sporting rights elsewhere in the News empire, Rosenberg argues that 'The primary motive was clearly to give Murdoch-controlled Sky a free-to-air outlet to increase its bargaining power for selling sports programmes to other free-to-air channels.' The implications of concentrated ownership of subscription and free-to-air were not lost on a range of industry actors and media commentators. State broadcaster TVNZ accused Sky of anti-competitive behaviour and called for Sky's network operations to be split from its broadcasting activities; MediaWorks called for Sky to be divested of Prime (Rosenberg 2008: 14).

In May 2007, ANM minority shareholders rejected a AUS$3 billion offer from a consortium comprising INM (35 per cent), Providence Equity Partners (37.5 per cent) and The Carlyle Group (27.5 per cent). INM currently holds its

39.16 per cent shareholding in ANM partly (26.89 per cent) through an Australian subsidiary Independent News & Media (Australia) Limited and partly (12.27 per cent) through News and Media NZ Limited (NMNZ).

In the commercial radio sector, Cheer notes that there are two foreign-owned groups: RadioWorks (owned by CanWest), and the Radio Network (a subsidiary of Australia's ARN network, a joint venture between APN News and Media and Clear Channel International, the main US radio player). There are also a number of independent, non-profit and community access broadcasters (Cheer 2003). The situation on the ground in a deregulated media system in 2004 has been described by Radio New Zealand chief executive, Peter Cavanagh as 'deregulation gone mad', with 'more radio stations per head of population than most other countries' (Rosenberg 2008: 22).

The limited amount of local content that gets to air in New Zealand can be accounted for in terms of a number of regulatory agencies which fund local content, including content specifically for Māori people, New Zealand's indigenous citizens. Were it not for these mechanisms, there would be even less local content. For instance, in relation to Prime, Rosenberg notes:

> Other than the one news bulletin and sport there is not much to show it is a New Zealand channel. According to local content funding agency New Zealand On Air's monitoring, it has easily the lowest proportion of New Zealand content – 12% in 2007, compared to 24% for TV3, 23% for C4, 57% for TV One, 18% for TV2, and 80% for Māori TV.

'Māori TV' is clearly the success story in these local content figures: *The Independent* was reporting that Māori Television is proving early critics wrong as audience numbers rise and advertising revenue is predicted to double this financial year. Two-thirds of its audience was non-Māori, and the audience had grown strongly, with a monthly average of 1.4 million individual viewers, according to surveys by AGB and Nielsen in 2008 (2008: 15).

However, the content of New Zealand's media can be seen to be directly related to its ownership and financing. Linked to this proposition is a view that demands for New Zealand programming may be difficult to sustain in the longer term, due to the financial imperatives of its foreign media owners. And, in general, the point should also be made that the state of media in New Zealand needs to be considered in a wider frame of the general decline of free-to-air audiences whose market share is being undermined by expansion in the pay sector and new media. Developments in digital media (it has a 'Freeview' platform comparable to the UK and Australia) and in online media, including the IPTV space, will also eventually restructure these media markets and patterns of access. For example, it is reported that TVNZ has done deals to provide high-speed access to its video-on-demand services involving internet service provider Orcon, telecommunications giant Vodafone (Keown 2008). This is consistent with trends in TV markets internationally.

The United Kingdom

There have been two key periods of media ownership deregulation in the UK since the mid-1990s. The first of these occurred in 1996, and the second in 2003. The UK's *Broadcasting Act 1996* ushered in a raft of liberalizing provisions for media ownership. Importantly, the Act introduced a new overall ceiling for single media ownership (Doyle 2002: 100). The new common ceiling became 15 per cent of audience time, at a national level, with BBC audiences being included. In addition, restrictions applied to terrestrial TV including that no single owner may own two ITV licences in the same area, and an ITV licence holder may not hold a C5 (Channel 5) licence.

In terms of cross-media ownership, the 1996 Act significantly liberalized the existing framework for terrestrial TV, radio and newspapers at the national and regional levels. Before these changes were introduced, media companies were only permitted to hold minority interests in different media. After the 1996 Act took effect, individual media companies were allowed to hold:

*   up to 15 per cent in the radio sector (excluding BBC audiences) but no more than one national radio licence;
*   up to 15 per cent of the TV sector (including BBC audiences) but not more than one national ITV or C5 licence;
*   up to 20 per cent of national daily newspaper circulations.

Doyle argues that these differences in limits between radio and television were strikingly anomalous with the result that 'commercial TV operators effectively are allowed to have a market share twice as large as commercial radio operators', arising from the inclusion of BBC audiences. In her view:

> Given that the BBC enjoys a share of almost one half of total UK audiences both in TV and radio, the decision about whether to include or exclude those audiences when computing any other individual organisation's market share is of immense significance. The effect of including BBC audiences with the total television market is to almost double the size of that market and thus to double the audience share a commercial television broadcaster may serve, in comparison with what is allowed for commercial radio.
>
> (Doyle 2002: 111)

Doyle considers that there does not appear to be 'any logical justification' for having a tighter control over radio than television, when 'many people would regard television as a more powerful medium'. She suggests that it is therefore difficult to form another conclusion other than regarding this kind of anomaly as a reflection of 'the political clout on the part of media owners' (2002: 111).

This 20 per cent newspaper ceiling applied only in the context of cross-media expansion scenarios. Cross-media restrictions no longer applied between newspaper and cable or satellite broadcasters, as was previously the case under the UK's 1990 legislation.

At the local or regional level, cross-ownership of terrestrial television and radio licences with the same licence areas continued to be prohibited. However, cross-ownership between local broadcasters and *newspapers* was deregulated by the 1996 law.

The 1996 Act allowed:

- local newspaper owners to hold regional TV licences (unless there is a circulation share of more than 20 per cent in the takeover target's transmission area);
- local newspaper owners to acquire radio licences if the market share is less than 50 per cent of the target's transmission area – unless there is at least one other radio service of the same category transmitting in the same locality.

The 1996 Act introduced a specific Public Interest Test to give regulators (then the Independent Television Commission and Radio Authority) a discretionary power to block mergers at the national or regional level deemed to be against the public interest. This involved the regulator taking into account plurality, diversity, any potential economic benefits arising and the effects on the operation of the affected newspaper and broadcasting markets.

These reforms under the 1996 Act were described as a 'sweeping shift in UK media ownership policy' attributable to the success of ' "economic" arguments submitted to the DHN by large media firms, and the Government's receptiveness to these arguments' (Doyle 2002: 102). Doyle argues that potential cost savings through consolidation were to some extent limited by the obligation under the 1996 Act for licensees to maintain 'regional programming activities and investment in associated resources, irrespective of any ownership changes'. In this respect, regulatory authorities were able to place a condition on a regional ITV licence if they considered there would be negative effects following an ownership change. The economic benefits were limited as a result of ITV licensees already participating in a number of cost-saving arrangements in connection to network program syndication, transmission and advertising sales (2002: 115).

In Doyle's view, although there is evidence that there are significant savings arising from single media consolidation, she found there was little compelling evidence in a UK context to suggest that increased cross-ownership between television and newspaper businesses, now allowed if certain market share thresholds are not breached, would lead to greater economic efficiencies. In essence, her argument on this point flows from an analysis which sees the skills required in the broadcasting and newspaper industries as being quite different. She does, however, distinguish this from the advantages of cross-promotion which can arise from common broadcast and newspaper business ownership (2002: 116). For Doyle, this begs the question: why then do newspaper proprietors invest so much in trying to effect liberalization of the cross-media laws? Her answer is that they do so in order to change laws which would allow them to diversify into the very profitable terrestrial television sector, and thereby focus less on the stagnant business of newspapers. In other words, it was the 'veneer of an economic case' of industry convergence that provided a more respectable public policy argument for the use of newspaper proprietors (2002: 117).

The main impact of the 'first wave' of deregulation ushered in by the 1996 Act was changes allowing significant cross-media ownership between television, radio and newspapers, and higher levels of terrestrial television ownership than was previously allowed. In rebuttal of the stereotypical pro-liberalization defence, Doyle argues that the only change from previous restrictions which is 'unambiguously supported by the potential for additional economic efficiency gains is the relaxation of monomedia restrictions' affecting these main traditional media industries. Indeed,

> There is little or no economic evidence to support a case for liberalizing cross-media restrictions affecting television, radio or newspapers. This is because, on the whole, the economic performance of television, radio and newspaper firms does point to clearly identifiable benefits arising from expansion *within* each of these individual sectors of activity. On the other hand, diagonal cross-media expansion *across*, say, newspapers and television appears *not* to be well-supported by any specific economies of scope or inherent cross-synergies.
>
> (Doyle 2002: 114)

The standard explanation for these expansionary moves is that they deliver consolidation of back-office functions of finance and administration, as well as specific cost savings in relation to shared programming costs, transmission operations and airtime sales. Clearly, Doyle is not persuaded by the economic efficiencies that may arise between television *and* newspaper operations. But she recognizes that in diversified media organizations such as Pearsons, the benefits of cross-media synergies have been evident: 'The combinations of cross-ownership that yield the most significant efficiency gains are those that allow either specialized content or a distribution infrastructure to be shared across different sectors or product markets' (2002: 115). On the basis of this analysis of how the policies and legal framework actually interact with UK media organizations, it appears that there is a significant shortfall between the policy justifications put forward for deregulating cross-ownership between newspaper publishing and television broadcasting and the operational realities of editorial, production and distribution processes in these legacy media.

The Communications Act of 2003

The changes that the *Communications Act of 2003* were intended to introduce reflected a view that, after a relatively short period of time, the ownership restrictions contained in the 1996 *Broadcasting Act* were already past their 'use-by' date. There is also the argument that the decision to take action in 'reforming' legislation comes against a background of almost continuous corporate activity across the media and communications industries, both in the UK and internationally.

The key features of the *Communications Act 2003* were that:

- The Act removes the disqualifications on ownership of *Broadcasting Act* licences by non-European Union persons.
- The Act lifts the ban on local authorities holding licences so as to allow them to broadcast information about their services or the services of bodies with similar functions.
- The Act repeals the two rules which prevent the joint ownership of Channel 3. These were the rules limiting ITV licence holders to no more than 15 per cent of the TV audience, and which prevented the same company from holding the two London licences. Basically, it cleared the way for a single ITV, subject to the competition authorities being satisfied that a merger was not anti-competitive.
- The Act removes all ownership rules for Channel 5, which could now attract investment from any company.
- For television, the existence of the BBC and Channel 4 requires at least three separate free-to-air broadcasters, plus other platforms.
- Local radio ownership rules ensure that wherever there is a well-developed choice of radio services, there will be at least two separate owners of local commercial radio services, in addition to the BBC.
- The Act prohibits one person from owning more than one local digital multiplex in any area (most areas will only have one or two).
- The Act removes the Channel 3 nominated news provider system and most

of the ownership rules for the Channel 3 news provider, while maintaining the quality obligations.

- The Act allows the Secretary of State to introduce an appointed news provider system for Channel 5 if that channel's share of the audience for television broadcasting services is broadly equivalent to that of the services comprising Channel 3.

Cross-media ownership rules

- The Act introduces a national '20 per cent' cap rule:
  - no one controlling more than 20 per cent of the national newspaper market may hold any licence for Channel 3;
  - no one controlling more than 20 per cent of the national newspaper market may hold more than a 20 per cent stake in any Channel 3 service;
  - a company may not own more than a 20 per cent share in such a service if more than 20 per cent of its stock is in turn owned by a national newspaper proprietor with more than 20 per cent of the market.
- There is a parallel, regional '20 per cent' rule: no one owning a regional Channel 3 licence may own more than 20 per cent of the local/regional newspaper market in the same region.
- Rules on local radio ownership ensure there are at least three local/regional commercial media voices (in TV, radio and newspapers) in addition to the BBC in developed markets.

The Lords' *Ownership of the News* report recommends

> [a] significant relaxation in present regulation concerning local cross-media ownership. We see no reason why they should not be able to take over local radio stations. Subject to public interest considerations, we saw no need for specific cross-media ownership restrictions at the local level.
>
> (House of Lords 2008b)

As discussed at the beginning of this chapter, the Communications Act introduced a new Public Interest Test to allow the Secretary of State to intervene in media mergers which raise public interest considerations. The Act provides that Ofcom will be required to review all media ownership rules at least every three years, and then to make any recommendations for further reform to the Secretary of State, who will be able to amend or remove rules by secondary legislation. Both Ofcom and the Government in their responses to this recommendation saw no need to change the process for the application of the Public Interest Test – locally, regionally or nationally (Ofcom 2008c; DCMS 2008).

Regional television consolidation

There was consolidation within the ITV sector soon after the laws were liberalized in 1996 (Doyle 2002). Carlton TV took over Westcountry TV in December 1996 while Scottish Television acquired Grampian Television in 1997.

By 1999, a succession of corporate manoeuvres had resulted in three major ITV players – Carlton, Granada and United News & Media (UN&M) – plus, in Scotland, Scottish Media Group (SMG). Only Ulster TV and Border – two of the smallest companies in the ITV network – were overlooked in the consolidation process. In general, the UK's Competition Commission has cleared these mergers with few qualifications. The two key areas of concern for the Commission were in relation to the potential of air-time sales breaching an agreed total net national advertising revenue (NAR) limit of 25 per cent of the total advertising, and the potential for abuse of market power in programme supply. Yet the main players were spared adverse public interest findings for both issues.

Deregulatory measures introduced by the *Communications Act of 2003* have resulted in further consolidation. With the removal of the rules that limited ITV licence holders to no more than 15 per cent of the TV audience, and which prevented the same company from holding the two London licences, the ITV network is now largely owned by one player – ITV plc – created through the merger of Granada and Carlton. BSkyB's purchase of a 17.9 per cent stake in ITV was a clear indication of the value of the ITV network from the perspective of the Murdoch-controlled News.

Ownership of the news

One of the more important media policy debates to occur in recent times in the UK has been the House of Lords Select Committee on Communications reporting on their inquiry into media ownership and the news (House of Lords 2008a). The Committee examined evidence on changes in news agendas, how people access the news, changes in the way news is gathered and provided, and how concentrated media ownership affects the balance and diversity of news in a democracy. In relation to the public interest dimensions of their investigation, the Committee sifted through evidence focusing on the concentration of media ownership, on cross-media ownership and on the regulation of media ownership.

We have already discussed some of the evidence and arguments before the committee. However, in terms of media ownership reforms the Committee made some important findings and recommendations including:

> We do not accept that the increase of news sources invalidates the case for
> special treatment of the media through ownership regulation. We believe

that there is still a danger that if media ownership becomes too concentrated the diversity of voices available could be diminished.

> The public interest considerations for newspaper mergers and broadcasting and cross-media mergers are amended to refer specifically to a need to establish whether a merger will impact adversely on news gathering.
>
> (House of Lords 2008a)

The pressures on the cross-media rules will obviously continue as the media and communication industries evolve. The recognition of a continuing need for specific media ownership policy and law from such a well-informed parliamentary committee was an important moment in these debates. The recommendation that Ofcom's remit for its Public Interest Test be amended so that newspaper mergers are assessed for their impact on the *quality* of news is also a milestone for convergent regulation. Similarly, the suggestion that it would be 'essential to apply' the Public Interest Test 'if a major international Internet company bought a stake in a UK news provider' (e.g. Google) is also prescient for convergence policies. In their report advising against the 17.9 per cent share acquisition of ITV by BSkyB, Ofcom made the point that it could lead to a single news provider spanning ITN, Sky News and newspapers owned by News Corporation (News International Plc). (News Corporation owns *The Times* and *The Sun*, and approximately 39.1 per cent of the satellite broadcaster BSkyB.) Yet, perhaps surprisingly, it was not the satellite TV service, Sky, which ran up against the UK's cross-media rules. Rather, it was the rule providing that a national newspaper is prohibited from holding more than 20 per cent of an ITV (Channel Three) licence. And for future instances of industry convergence and consolidation, it was a significant precedent when the Office of Fair Trading formed the view that Sky's 17.9 per cent stake in ITV was enough to qualify as a merger of the two companies.

The United States of America

The United States of America (USA) also has highly concentrated levels of media ownership and high levels of cross-media ownership. This has enormous consequences for all other national media markets, not just the Anglophone ones, when it is considered that the USA is the largest media market in the world; its corporations operate extensive global networks exporting content well beyond US borders.

In the USA, the FCC's December 2007 broadcast/newspaper rule liberalization is under ongoing scrutiny by Congress. In May 2008, the Senate voted to repeal the FCC's loosening of the ban on newspaper-broadcast cross-ownership in the country's 20 largest media markets, the pressure was on the House of

Representatives to do the same. Former Senator Barack Obama urged the House to follow the Senate's lead and pass a resolution of disapproval (used effectively against FCC rules in 2003, see below), an unusual legislative step that would invalidate the FCC's vote to deregulate the broadcast/newspaper rule. It was reported that President Bush's advisers were urging him to veto the measure should it pass the House. In the event, in June 2008 the House Appropriations Financial Services Subcommittee voted to block new FCC media ownership rules that would allow newspaper-broadcast outlet cross-ownership. The provision was part of a spending bill that provides funds to the FCC and would deny the agency any funding to implement the rule. Commentators suggest that the action in the House Appropriations Financial Services Subcommittee achieve virtually the same result at the Senate's vote. It was reported that Subcommittee Chairman Jose Serrano (a Democrat for New York) said that in his opinion the loosening of the media consolidation rules by the FCC 'is detrimental to the goals of diversity in ownership and viewpoints'. The step, although a boost for groundswell of opinion against the FCC's lifting of the newspaper-broadcast outlet cross-ownership, is somewhat indirect. Another more direct option would be that at any point in the process, lawmakers could remove the FCC provision; a more likely scenario with Barack Obama as President (Benton Foundation 2008).

Consolidation in context

Lessig has provided the following snapshot based on FCC data as given by Senator John McCain at a Senate FCC oversight hearing into the state of US media ownership:

- five companies control 85 per cent of media sources;
- the five recording labels of Universal Music Group, BMG, Sony Music Entertainment, Warner Music Group, and EMI control 84.8 per cent of the US Music market;
- the five largest cable companies pipe programming to 74 per cent of the cable subscribers nationwide;
- two companies control 74 per cent of the revenue in the radio market.

(Lessig 2004: 161–8)

Although there are several variations of these market concentration figures, the high levels of concentration are indisputable. Interpretation of the data is also critical. For Hesmondhalgh, the more important issue is the material size and scope of these corporations and the general consequences of this for cultural consumption (Hesmondhalgh 2007). Lessig, on the other hand, is unequivocal about the overall effects of concentration:

If a handful of companies control access to the media, and that handful of companies gets to decide which political positions it will allow to be promoted on its channels, then in an obvious and important way, concentration matters. You might like the positions the handful of companies selects. But you should not like a world in which a mere few get to decide which issues the rest of us get to know about.

(Lessig 2004: 168)

In his view, it is also an argument about innovation in content. In *Free Culture*, he uses the example of how previously some television productions have been blocked, resulting in an overall reduction of independent companies due to network and conglomerate control. He attributes this in large measure to the repeal in the mid-1990s of FCC rules that prohibited major network (ABC, NBC, CBS) production and control of syndicated prime-time content.

Bettig and Hall paint a picture of diminishing public discussion over media concentration even as concentration has steadily increased since the 1980s. For them, this has occurred at the same time as the media themselves 'conveniently ignore it' (Bettig and Hall 2003: 27). It is argued that the 'inherent logic' of vertical integration in 'Big Media' is to continue to seek to reproduce a captive audience – whether in older media or new media – and this is confirmed by the 'historical record':

Each new medium is introduced with high hopes and expectations of increasing diversity and communications democracy. However, existing economic and political forces always seem to undermine these promises . . . there is no reason to believe that the future of the Internet will be any different.

(Bettig and Hall 2003: 29)

It may be surprising to those unfamiliar with the history of the US media scene that it has from the outset been guided by principles intended to protect the public interest. Federal Communications Commissioner Michael Copps observed:

To fulfil our public-interest obligation, for decades we have promoted the goals of localism, diversity and competition – all building blocks for a healthy and dynamic media environment. These things aren't luxuries, nice things to have if we can afford them. They are necessities for a thriving American society, and we can't afford *not* to have them. And we need them across our entire media landscape.

(Copps, cited in McChesney et al. 2005: 118)

As the first-mover communications deregulator, the USA began its now well-documented sweeping deregulatory process of political and economic reform from the 1980s. In that context, licence renewals for broadcasters, traditionally an opportunity for allowing governments and the public to see how the 'public interest' is being served, have become less frequent and more perfunctory. Deregulatory changes to ownership were introduced incrementally from that period.

Legislative and regulatory framework

Media ownership regulation in the USA dates from the Radio Act of 1927. But it was only in recent times, under the previous FCC Chairmanship of Republican Party-aligned Michael Powell, that concentration in ownership became an issue of 'broad general concern'. That context of concern in 2003/ 2004 was the culmination of a deregulatory process set in train in 1996 with legislation that 'led to the greatest wave of media consolidation in history' (Schwartzman et al. 2005: 149).

The major changes began with the Telecommunications Act 1996; a rewrite of the Communications Act 1934, particularly insofar as telecommunications was concerned. The main purpose of this Act was to 'provide a way for telephone companies to compete for local phones', but it also made some 'serious changes to media ownership' (Dunbar 2005: 129).

The key reforms to media ownership at that time were:

- removal of a national cap on radio station ownership;
- introduction of a mandate that the FCC review ownership policies every two years.

It is reported that by 2000 the removal of the radio ownership cap had given rise to broadcasting giants such as Clear Channel Communications Inc., who expanded their network to 1,200 plus stations, in an industry now dominated by three operators (Dunbar 2005). In 1995, prior to this rule change, there were 75 independently operating corporations in the radio industry sector (Croteau and Hoynes 2006: 92). At the same time, the mandatory FCC review gave broadcasting lobbyists the opportunity to throw their extensive resources into persuading Members of Congress to further liberalize market rules, every two years. In January 2004, President Bush signed into law an Appropriations Bill which extended the review period to a quadrennial rather then biennial requirement.

In terms of cross-media ownership, under the previous so-called 'duopoly rule' the FCC did not permit the granting of a licence to anyone already holding a licence for the same type of TV outlet in the same community. By 1999, the

1996 legislation had allowed the FCC to introduce a rule for common owner-ship of two stations in the same market if eight independently owned and operated TV stations remain in the market post merger – provided one of the merged stations is not among the top four ranked stations in a designated market area. Other conditions did apply – for example, a 'failing' station could now be used to justify multiple station ownership. TV duopolies became commonplace. Another change to FCC rules allowed a single company to own two TV stations and six radio stations in a market if there are at least 20 competitors among all media outlets: cable, newspapers, and other broadcast stations (Croteau and Hoynes 2006).

The numerous deals arising from these regulatory changes resulted in exten-sive industry consolidation. Less than a month after the 1999 FCC changes, Viacom and CBS announced their plans to merge. It was a huge deal leading to a $US38 bn merger which was bigger at that time than any previous deal between media companies. CBS's television network of 15 TV stations, more than 160 radio stations and Internet sites combined with Viacom's well-known cable channel brands (e.g. MTV, Nickelodeon, Showtime, TNN), 19 TV stations, movie and television production (Paramount Pictures, UPN), publishing (Simon & Schuster), theme parks, among other assets (Croteau and Hoynes 2006: 85). It was the first of even larger mergers that were to follow, including the AOL-Time-Warner $US166 bn merger in 2000.

The Viacom-CBS merger put it in breach of existing ownership rules: it now owned both the CBS network and a 50 per cent stake in the UPN network, and the combined networks could reach nearly 40 per cent of US households, when the FCC cap was 35 per cent. In response, the FCC proposed new consolidation-friendly rules.

FCC Order and Appeals Court response

The immediate past history of ownership policy formulation in the USA is very relevant to contemporary debates. In June 2003, the Federal Communications Commission (FCC) made an order on media ownership that would have recast the US regulatory scene irreversibly. That decision, subsequently overturned on appeal to a DC Third Circuit Appeals Court, did not lead to the anticipated 'big bang' of mergers and acquisitions which would certainly have occurred had the FCC's original decision been permitted by the Court to stand.

The FCC's 2003 proposed changes included:

- Raising the 35 per cent national audience cap to 45 per cent.
- Not allowing a single company to own *any two* of the top four networks (effectively exempting Viacom's ownership of the UPN network).

- Lifting a ban on cross-ownership, thus allowing a single company to own both a TV station and a daily newspaper in the same market, as long as the market had at least three stations.
- Easing restrictions on TV station ownership to allow one company to own two stations in mid-sized markets and three stations in the largest markets.
- Recalibrating radio ownership rules so that a single company could own up to eight stations in the largest markets with at least 45 stations, seven stations in markets with 30–44 stations, six stations in markets with 15–29 stations, and three stations in markets with 14 or fewer stations (see http://www.fcc.gov/ownership).

It is reported that during the public comment period in the wake of these proposals, the FCC was

> flooded with hundreds of thousands of emails and letters, nearly all opposing the changes. The outpouring constituted the greatest number of comments received on any issue in the FCC's history and was so great that it overwhelmed both the agency's voice comment phone line system and its Internet server.

Croteau and Hoynes note that as with the 1996 Telecommunications Act, 'the mainstream news media gave scant coverage to the proposed changes or opposition to it' (2006: 95).

The opposition to the FCC's proposed changes also came from diverse organized civil society organizations. Although the FCC and the Bush Administration held firm, the US Senate, using a rarely used procedure, passed a 'resolution of disapproval' with the effect of repealing all the FCC changes. The move did not, however, overcome a threatened Presidential veto. In a compromise, Congress rolled back the national audience cap from 45 per cent to 39 per cent, which was enough to allow the Viacom and News Corporation (whose Fox Network had reached 39 per cent of households) to avoid divestiture of stations.

In late 2004, the US Court of Appeals for the Third Circuit reversed the Commission's decision in its 2002 'Biennial Regulatory Review pursuant to Section 202 of the Telecommunications Act of 1996', ruling in favour of the 'Prometheus Radio Project' [*Prometheus Radio Project v. FCC*], in a suit led by the Media Access Project (a non-profit, public interest telecommunications law firm), against the FCC changes. In brief, the court invalidated many of the reasons cited by the FCC for its actions, including the rationale underpinning its so-called 'diversity index', ordering the FCC to reconsider the 2003 rule changes.

The battle over media ownership continues in the USA. In 2006, an alliance of public interest groups filed their submission to the Federal Communications

Commission's Review of the Commission's Broadcast Ownership Rules. Specifically, the alliance filed comments in relation to three main rule-making areas: on the Cross-Ownership of Broadcast Stations and Newspapers; Rules and Policies Concerning Multiple Ownership of Radio Broadcast Stations in Local Markets; and on the Definition of Radio Markets. These organizations argued that, jointly, they were dedicated to 'increasing the diversity of voices in the media' and saw their role as being to 'promote a free and vibrant media, full of diverse and competing voices, which is the lifeblood of America's democracy and culture, as well as the engine of growth for its economy' (Media Access Project 2006: 2).

The Prometheus case held that the FCC had erred in its review of ownership regulations because it had applied a presumption in favour of eliminating or relaxing the rules. The Prometheus submitters argued that it was the FCC's role to undertake reasoned analysis, not to simply consider competition effects but to examine 'whether the public is actually being served by a diversity of voices and whether the current rules at least help to maintain those voices' (Media Access Project 2006: 3). The mechanism for built-in legislative review periods (now every four years) has ensured that the deregulatory pressure will be maintained in future years by pro-liberalization lobby groups.

Who will be the last media giant left standing?

What began as a hostile takeover bid for Dow Jones Inc, the publisher of the influential *Wall Street Journal* (WSJ) business paper, became a protracted battle, then ended up as a cordial agreement between News and the Bancroft family to sell for around $US5.3 bn. Initially the Bancroft family who had held a controlling stake in Dow Jones for 105 years, totally rejected the bid. At the time various media commentators noted the adverse potential that a successful takeover would have for US news and information consumers. Others thought it a direct attack on one of the much-respected pillars of the old-school, independent journalism establishment. One commentator with a (vested) family interest of 6.2 per cent supervoting shares in Dow Jones issued a statement observing:

> Rupert Murdoch comes from a very different tradition of Australian-British media ownership and editorial practice in which he has for a long time expressed his personal, political, and business biases through his newspapers and television channels. We see this every day here in America in his *New York Post* which regularly runs biased news stories and headlines supporting his friends, political candidates and public policies, and attacks people he personally opposes.
>
> (Ottaway, in Crikey.com 2007)

Within days of completion of the take-over in December 2007, News Corporation had installed Robert Thompson, editor of the *The Times* as its own publisher, and Les Hinton, executive chairman of the British papers of the News Corporation, as head of Dow Jones, and had taken out full page ads trumpeting the deal in major broadsheets including *The Times* and the *New York Times*. The version appearing in *The Times* took up three full pages, and it was an exposition of neoliberal ideology writ large: 'Free people/Free markets/Free thinking', comments which the *New York Times* noted was 'a tweaking of the Journal editorial page's guiding philosophy, "Free markets, free people" ' (Perez-Pena 2007).

In the period following the take-over, News has already made good use of the prestige WSJ brand throughout the News empire. Mastheads in the USA, Britain, Australia and New Zealand share and re-use WSJ copy in their financial pages, arguably lifting the quality stakes in these papers. Other major consolidations have been far more drawn out and without the gloss (or apparent success) of the Dow Jones and News Corporation merger. Among these we should include the controversial Sirius-XM Satellite radio merger and Sam Zell's failed acquisition of the Tribune papers. The former merger was ultimately approved by the FCC in July 2008 against the objections of two of the Democrat-appointed Commissioners, Michael Copps and Jonathan Adelstein, who warned about allowing further consolidation of ownership of the media, and creating a satellite radio monopolist. The latter situation, although given the green light by the FCC for Tribune to be sold to Zell and its own employees for $US8.2 bn, was based on waivers to override newspaper/broadcast cross-ownership breaches in five markets and had other non-regulatory problems. The privatized, highly leveraged Tribune Company has now filed for bankruptcy, its inability to meet vast debt repayments was the cause of the company's collapse, resulting in employees losing their jobs (Sorkin 2008).

But, of course, there has been incessant restructuring consolidation in US media markets, despite high levels of debt and a great deal more caution in the wake of the ongoing financial meltdown. One firm specializing in the analysis of media publishing merger and acquisitions, the Jordan, Edmiston Group (JEGI) asserted in a 2008 year-end report that the 'centre of gravity' had shifted in media M&A, with deals moving from larger traditional media deals to mid-sized digital and data deals. They claimed that 'only 12 percent of the dollars spent on media industry deals came from traditional media'. The firm tracked 758 media deals in 2008, down from 13.1 per cent from 872 in 2007. The report noted: 'Deal values last year, however, dropped 68.1 percent to $33.3 billion, down from $104.4 billion in 2007.' JEGI identified four growth sectors in 2008: database and information, business-to-business online media, consumer online media and interactive marketing services (Fell 2009).

An article in *Businessweek* ('Who will be the last media giant left standing?') makes an argument that the financial doldrums in US media markets, and in particular a forecast by Barclays Capital (BCS) of a 10 per cent decline in US ad expenditures over 2009, 'the worst since the Great Depression', will be the quiet before the media consolidation storm. Declining revenues and heavy debt loads are placing major traditional media corporations like Univision, Clear Channel, and the now-bankrupt Tribune Co. under severe pressure. But the suggestion is that, this may allow the deep-pocketed News Corporation, Comcast or Time-Warner to make their moves (Fine 2009).

Nation-states compared

Any comparative analysis of media ownership between these democracies must at the end of the day be an understanding of how national laws allow international cooperation and recognize cultural differences. Legal academics Goldsmith and Wu draw a similar conclusion in their assessment of the 'bordered Internet'. In their analysis of the differences in how US and Australian law has dealt with reputations in online defamation in the *Gutnick* case they argue: 'It reflects deeper disagreements between the United States and Australia about the processes that best secure truth, and about the relative values of robust speech versus reputation and uninhibited debate versus order.' But, more importantly for the comparisons in this chapter: 'These examples show that deeply held differences in values, even among democracies, lie behind conflicts of laws. A bordered Internet is valuable precisely because it permits people of different value systems to coexist on the same planet' (Goldsmith and Wu 2008: 152).

The point of selecting these western democracies for a comparison of media ownership laws is precisely because of their systemic proximity *not* because of their vast diffences. As I noted earlier, as Anglophone nations occupying a broadly aligned set of political and cultural norms, they can be categorized in Hallin and Mancini's terms as belonging to the Liberal or North Atlantic model. For Hallin and Mancini, their market-driven priorities means they can be distinguished from the 'Democratic-Corporatist' and 'Polarized' media system models prevalent in Scandinavian and Southern European nations. The explanatory power of Hallin and Mancini's comparative framework is that it conjunctively reviews global media systems in terms of the relationships between the state, business and media and their institutional and regulatory expression. Conversely, as Lund notes, these comparative models are useful to avoid 'reproduction of prejudices and unwarranted generalizations, [and] media researchers must pay close attention not only to media convergence, but also to divergence in terms of the political economy that constitutes the national framework surrounding media corporations and media regulators' (2007: 121).

Importantly, too, all of these nations have in the past two decades responded to the pressures of neoliberal market policies now pervading the global economy. In this respect, Gillian Doyle has argued industrial or 'economic' arguments favouring a more liberal approach towards concentrations of ownership have become more influential in determining media ownership policies since the early 1990s.

At the same time, it is clear that national debates on media regulation are increasingly occurring within, on the one hand, the wider global context of transformations in social-cultural and technological conditions, and on the other hand, the ongoing liberalization of capital and cultural markets. This new regulatory environment includes the increasing prominence of free-wheeling financial corporations, international economic organizations, media corporations, and free trade agreements (Given 2003).

Although there are strong pressures to further liberalize ownership policies where they are retained, and on top of already significant dilution in all the nations reviewed, they have kept some core components of their ownership regimes (especially in the UK), and less so in Australia and the USA. Canada is the only country to counter this trend in recent years. The UK has made continuous changes to cross-media and foreign ownership and now Australia has passed more radically deregulatory media ownership rules, allowing the merging of traditional media. The lack of foreign ownership restrictions in New Zealand has resulted in all major media in private hands being held by foreign corporations. This is a very different situation to the UK, the USA or Australia. Canada's cultural relationship with the USA means that Canadian ownership of Canadian media is still regarded as an important safeguard. Foreign investment in US media has been constrained by the size and scale of their conglomerates.

The lack of cross-media regulation in New Zealand leaves it exposed to ongoing reconfigurations in what is after all, a relatively small media market. In issues concerning maintaining local culture, this makes it more significant. Changes to ownership laws in Australia have had flow-on impacts in New Zealand, where Australian companies own a large proportion of their media assets. Two of the larger Australian players, Fairfax Media and APN News and Media, both now have extensive New Zealand interests that bridge these neighbouring nations, already linked in numerous social, cultural and economic ways. This is facilitated by their bilateral free trade agreement. The maintenance of local content funding, including for Māori content (and subsidy for its production at a regional level), indicates its perceived importance to New

Zealanders, at a time when their media is still recovering from the ravages of deregulatory policies.

In the UK, the 2003 Act continued the steady liberalization of media ownership. Yet the British Government has retained key restrictions on cross-media ownership, with caps of 20 per cent on national and regional television and newspaper cross-ownership. Radio ownership rules provide for a default setting of a minimum of 'three voices' (television, radio, newspapers), and provide that there will be at least two local radio stations in addition to the BBC. The House of Lords (2008a) report, surprisingly to many observers, has recommended further deregulation at a local level, while continuing to adamantly reject concentrated ownership at the national level.

The UK established a Public Interest Test in the 2003 legislation, but the ability of this mechanism to prevent mergers deemed to be against the public interest, has only been put into effect once with the blocking of News' Corporations ambitions for a greater stake in ITV. And as discussed earlier in this chapter, there is considerable scepticism regarding its ability to prevent further consolidation. On the face of it, deregulation of their regional television ownership has dramatically concentrated ownership with a single dominant regional television network provider, ITV plc – in effect, allowing a monopoly. On the other hand, the strength of the public service requirements now regulated by Ofcom is that there is an obligation to comply with programming quotas in key genres such as news and current affairs. In this regard, rules for regional television production and programming, and independent production quotas, effectively ensure safety net levels of production.

The recent Public Service Review conducted by Ofcom demonstrated a commitment to the importance of local content in regional output, and an awareness of the potential influence of new digital television and broadband distribution technologies on local content provision. Yet it also indicated a commensurate inability of the legacy commercial PSBs to fund important genres like news and current affairs at the level it previously has done so. The debate in relation to 'top-slicing' BBC coffers is yet to be settled.

In Canada, broadcasting regulators have taken the 'pragmatic' approach that, to ensure an appropriate level of Canadian content is maintained on television and radio, and is not overrun by less expensive (and generally more popular) programming from the United States, Canada's media need to be allowed to consolidate into larger corporations that can compete with their American rivals. As a counterbalance to increased media ownership concentration and cross-media ownership, recent developments such as Canada's 'transaction tax' on media mergers have provided a significant windfall for the Canadian content production industry.

Yet, until 2008, the lack of legislated cross-media ownership and media ownership limits, and the flexibility the CRTC is afforded in its regulation of broadcasting licences, have enabled the growth of large conglomerates such as CanWest with interests in television, radio, subscription broadcasting, newspapers and the Internet. (The 'global' in CanWest Global Communications' corporate branding, clearly has more than token significance.) It has also meant, however, that decisions regarding media mergers are not in the hands of politicians but an independent regulator which has the authority to extract significant benefits for Canadian content production and undertakings in relation to regional content and editorial separation when deciding on proposed media mergers involving the broadcasting sector.

The widespread accessibility of a range of cable, satellite and other non free-to-air broadcasting services in Canada, even in most regional areas, to some extent mitigates questions of content diversity that arise in Australia or New Zealand, where there is substantially less competition in (and from) subscription television and non-terrestrial broadcasting. However, what can be drawn from the Canadian experience is that, despite the best intentions of regulators, it is difficult to avoid increased centralization of news and current affairs production (and consequent reduction in regional programming) from media companies with significant nationwide cross-media interests, precisely because it is the economies of scale and scope that can be achieved through rationalizing operations that makes such mergers attractive.

In the USA, the largest of national media markets, proposed FCC changes in 2003 included increasing the national audience cap from 35 per cent national audience cap to 45 per cent; allowing single companies to own multiple networks; lifting a ban on cross-ownership, thus allowing a single company to own both a TV station and a daily newspaper in the same market, and easing restrictions on TV station ownership. They have all been rejected for the time being. More recently, in 2007, the FCC attempted to all but remove the newspaper/broadcast ban, it remains to be seen whether, like the 2003 changes, they are unambiguously reversed by Congress and the appeal courts.

Although Congress and appeal courts disallowed the 2003 proposed rule changes, significantly, the national audience cap was been increased to 39 per cent, up from the previous level of 35 per cent. These compromises indicate the 'always-on' power of media corporations to have their way on Capitol Hill. The provision in the 1996 Telecommunications Act, requiring periodic reviews of ownership rules, has ensured that the deregulatory pressure will be maintained in future years.

Conclusion

In this chapter, I have argued that at this stage in the evolution of global media it is reasonable to conclude that news and information delivered by free-to-air TV, radio and newspapers are still the most popular sources for the majority of audiences, and therefore justify continued ownership restrictions in some form. The evidence is that the removal of the former rules and the consolidation of existing owners across multiple platforms will further concentrate cross-media ownership, reducing the diversity of news sources available to audiences. However, it also clear that in this period of transition from mass use of traditional media to the popular take-up of online media, and in particular, news and information formats, new rules for achieving objectives for pluralism and diversity will be needed for the maintenance of democratic states. The origins of these rules no doubt lie in the existing rules, but will require innovation and development. These will include more sophisticated rules in relation to content sharing and syndication across platforms.

As news organizations are rapidly changing their approaches to content sharing, repurposing and reuse, this has inevitable consequences for news workers and news users. Since the 1980s, knowledge industries have been subject to the impact of informationalization: the combined effects of digitalization, Internetworking and market liberalization (Lash 2002; Murdock 2007). News organizations, as core media content producers, have been engaged in ongoing and often radical restructuring during this process (Paterson and Domingo 2008). This can be seen in the widespread adoption of Internetworked production systems and the alteration of their news cycle to supply 24-hour channels. News organizations now repurpose single stories for multiple channels and, as a result, are integrating previously separate production areas. To support technological development and increasing production costs, they have sought to exploit both their own information rights, through content licensing arrangements, and the creative potential of their audiences, via user commentary and content generation.

As a rhetorical construct, media convergence tends to obscure important shifts in work practices, editorial processes and publishing strategies that may affect the construction of news diversity. At the same time, changes to national news production and distribution must be appraised in relation to wider regulatory conditions; we have seen in this chapter that globally media ownership laws are in a very dynamic phase. News media industry changes to news production, distribution and use that will impact international governance include:

- changes in news agendas;
- changes in the way news is gathered and provided;

- changes in how people access the news on various screen devices;
- how concentrated media ownership affects the balance and diversity of news in a democracy;
- how news producers are adapting their operations to address the economics of online and multi-channel distribution;
- how news users will be affected as old news media morph into new media, moving online and to mobile technologies.

The key question for governments and their media regulatory agencies is, how will the old diversity rules (media policies, law and regulation) be applied to new media industries? For the past 50 years, there has been substantial international support for the proposition that plurality in ownership is the best way to promote diversity of opinions. The assumption by legislators and policy-makers was that concentrated ownership confers undemocratic power on owners to sway governments and advance their own private interests. Structural limits on the number of media outlets owned by one proprietor have been regarded as a precondition for achieving plurality of viewpoints. These assumptions in convergent, online news market are now being reassessed by all shades of neoliberal governments.

As traditional media corporations expand their new digital media offerings, usually on the back of talk of 'media convergence', the pressure for further liberalization of rules created for traditional media can only increase. In my view, continuing media consolidation will therefore require innovative public policy, laws and regulation for promoting and maintaining democratic values of diversity and pluralism for the media and communications industries. In the next chapter, we consider the ways that media businesses imagine their audience engagement strategies in social networking new digital media contexts, and reflect on the consequences of those developments.

Further reading

Croteau, D. and Hoynes, W. (2006) *The Business of Media: Corporate Media and the Public Interest* (2nd edn). Pine Forge Press, CA: Sage.

Doyle, G. (2002) *Media Ownership: The Economics and Politics of Convergence and Concentration in the UK and European Media*. London: Sage.

Feintuck, M. and Varney, M. (2006) *Media Regulation, Public Interest and the Law* (2nd edn). Edinburgh: Edinburgh University Press.

Freedman, D. (2008) *The Politics of Media Policy*. Cambridge: Polity.

Hitchens, L. (2006) *Broadcasting Pluralism and Diversity: A Comparative Study of Policy and Regulation*. Oxford: Hart Publishing.

House of Lords (2008a) *The Ownership of the News*, Vol. 1: report HL paper 122–1,

House of Lords, Select Committee on Communications, UK Parliament. London: The Stationery Office.

Karpinnen, K. (2007) 'Making a difference to media pluralism: a critique of the pluralistic consensus in European media policy', in B. Cammaerts and N. Carpentier (eds) *Reclaiming the Media: Communication Rights and Democratic Media Roles*. Bristol: Intellect.

Winseck, D. (2002) 'Netscapes of power: convergence, consolidation and power in the Canadian mediascape', *Media, Culture & Society*, 24: 795–819.

AUDIENCES OF NEOLIBERAL IMAGINARIES

The collapse of the mid-twentieth-century media system, and its replacement by a media system clearly dominated by market forces, took place in the context of a broader social and political transformation in which key institutions of the political field, particularly the organized social groups that made up the political public sphere, lost their centrality to people's lives and commitments. This transformation began before the rise of neoliberal ideology in the 1980s and 1990s, and is clearly crucial to understanding the latter.

(Hallin 2008: 47)

Introduction

In this chapter, a key argument is that commercial media corporations are closely implicated in the performance of neoliberal ideologies, and that emerging audience engagement strategies can be seen as imagined responses to the 'segmenting tendency' in media industries. Such developments signal a further shift away from 'society-making' of traditional mass media forms to the social networking in new digital media usage (Turow 1997; Turow and Tsui 2008). At the same time, the 'networked individualism' of digital media has divergent ramifications for audiences as citizens and consumers. Hybridized genres and convergent usage modes are modifying audience relations with communications media, and this has significant consequences for any potentially unified public sphere polities.

The transformations that Hallin is describing in the epigraph constitute the historical backdrop to the emergence of some of the audience engagement strategies I want to explore in this chapter. For Hallin, understandably, it is not possible to evaluate the implications of neoliberal ideologies, and the media's role in relation to them, without exploring *how* and *why* they arose in the first place. In his account of the 'shift to neoliberalism in media systems', Hallin is concerned to explain the trajectory of mass audience aggregation media and their connection with a political public sphere beginning with Johannes Gutenberg's press in the fifteenth century, through to the mass circulation press in the twentieth century and beyond.

Early print capitalism eventually segued into mass circulation newspapers, with their 'marketplace logic counterbalanced and modified' by ties between the media and organized social groups making up the public sphere. For Hallin, drawing on Bourdieu's field theory, political groupings of political parties, trade unions and churches acted as a counterbalance to the economic fields inherent to mass-produced and consumed media. When these balanced relations were restructured by 'purely commercial media', and by a changing journalistic professionalism from the mid-twentieth century, neoliberalism began its steep ascendancy (2008: 45). Broadcasting, though, had its own trajectories. In Europe, it was governed by various combinations of 'political logics and logics of journalistic professionalism' basically outside commerce, while in the US context, despite being predominantly commercial, their media operated on a 'trusteeship model' until that faded out in the 1970s.

The 'why' part of the shift to neoliberalism equation is for Hallin an open question. However, the incorporation of the bulk of the post-war populations into an affluent consumer society with a stable welfare state must be a large part of any explanation. People no longer felt the dependencies on the organized political groups to the extent they once had. The neoliberal shift generally wound back the collectivist political cultures that had prevailed earlier in the twentieth century.

Benedict Anderson's influence on theoretical reflections in relation to how media audiences are 'imagined' continues to provide valuable signposts for media and communications researchers. For Anderson, print capitalism was responsible for constructing the 'imagined communities' of nation-states. Newspapers, in particular, informed a collective understanding that there was a 'steady, anonymous, simultaneous experience' of a community of newspaper readers (Anderson 1983: 31). But the rise of social networking in new digital media usage problematizes Anderson's spatially and temporally inflected notions of 'community' and 'simultaneity'. The audience imaginings of transnational media corporations within discourses of neoliberalism infer both aggregation strategies, as various categories of new media virtual communities (of interest, subculture, geography), and the potential to generate 'networked individualism'.

Networked individualism

Internet media characterized by P2P architectures and social networking software has complicated the transformations in the political and economic and cultural fields of communications media. For example, democratic social movements using Internet media are evidence of non-commodified, or gift economy forms, largely outside of the reach of market structures. The anti-globalization or fair trade movements illustrate these kinds of activist uses of Internet media. However, we need to be aware that in such arguments there is a strong possibility of setting up a binary of consumerist market-shaped media supportive of a neoliberalist project on the one hand, and a citizenship-oriented activism arising from new forms of Internet media attempting to wind it back, on the other. Hallin cautions against such an oversimplified reading: 'Neoliberalism, moreover, has been very effective in creating political ideologies that can co-opt and incorporate rhetorics of empowerment and liberation and popular critiques of authority into legitimations of the market' (2008: 52). He makes the point that commercialization in media cultures is not the only force shaping social change. To it we can add, the legacies of 'critical professionalism in journalism' and a 'more populist political culture where social movements and ordinary citizens demand and often get a public hearing' (2008: 55).

The idea of the Internet being a layered, fragmented, often individualized domain of hyperlinked sites and portals that is subject to concentration and enclosure along with (and by) traditional media is critically important for these debates too. 'Individualization', 'networked individualism' and 'mass self-communication' are all terms with critical currency for arguments about neoliberal media 'audiencing' (McGuigan 2004; Castells 2007; Nightingale 2007b). Nightingale has argued that 'emergence' is another useful theoretical perspective we can use for understanding rapidly evolving Internet media systems and audience formations. The study of self-organizing systems or 'morphogenesis' has informed a field of engineering that produces systems of 'artificial emergence' and these kinds of systems are already a feature of every-day life in cyberspace. What occurs, Nightingale suggests, is that 'Software, modeled on the interactive skills of its creators, enters into dialogue with human users and creates a site-based response environment where the software predicts the user's intentions based on current and past choice patterns' (2007: 295). However, one of the main concerns in applying ideas of emergence or self-organization to Internet media is the tendency to equate these with autonomy in what are, after all, new contexts for media commodification and consumption. For Nightingale, this indicates:

The better the software is at predicting the user's intentions, the more satisfying the use of the site is felt to be. This type of software specialises in making better use of collective intelligence and user-generated content. The technology gurus talk about the ways this type of software is changing the nature of business practices online. In broad terms, Web 1.0 was about establishing websites and encouraging search (the Microsoft era); Web 2.0 discovered user-generated content and financed the cost of collecting it with advertising (the Google era); Web 3.0 will complement use-generated content with data-sharing options and finance these expensive services by linking the choices of individual users to the automatic generation of market research data.

(2007b: 295)

Human agency, then, plays an important role in participative web architectures: adaptive responses are forging a patterning of interactivity as seen, for example, in the ranked viewing of YouTube videos or book purchasing recommendations on Amazon. But it is predominantly about a selling machine: commercializa- tion and commodification are the *raison d'être* for the way these sites are structured. Were they primarily about linking people together for the purposes of social capital building, their architectures of participation would have an entirely different look and feel. These business logics envision a particular set of relations since:

> the more information and transactions a customer delivers to a brand or e-commerce site, the better online service they should receive . . . emergent systems allow Internet sites to respond to past user action by anticipating future interests or intentions, provided users keep feeding information into the system.
>
> (Nightingale 2007b: 296)

In this context of changing media usage patterns, will news and information genres retain their privileged place? The general erosion of boundaries between 'hard' and 'soft' news formats is bound up with the reconfiguring of public and private communications, and larger transformations in the polity. Media corporations have developed new ways of amassing audiences for the purposes of building and maintaining profitable consumer media cultures. The boundar- ies between editorial and advertising functions of commercial media organiza- tions are constantly redrawn as the industries change, including how they are correlated with changes in the previously clear demarcations between information and entertainment genres (Thussu 2009). It is clear that in the late twentieth and early twenty-first centuries, traditional media corporations have rapidly re-engineered their businesses as multi-platform ones with inte- grated online outlets, for the milieu of digital capitalism. As we've discussed in chapter 3, Internet protocol networks and e-commerce underpin the rise of online platforms. These platforms have either been built from the ground up, or are acquired and then adapted to suit the requirements of the particular media corporation. It can be argued that the resulting adaptations by media corporations have been summonsed up by the hegemonic demands of the neoliberalization project in a global marketplace. Neoliberalism requires the technologies of information, including the massive interactive databases of social networking websites, to provide adaptive responses to the market. The acquisitions of the social networking site MySpace by News Corporation (see Chapter 2), Google's YouTube, or the awaited buy-up of Facebook illustrates this trend. Such acquisitions are both capitalist accumulation and new media content distribution strategies: for media corporations they allow leveraging and cross-promotion of branded proprietary content across multiple audience access platforms.

The announcement of a partnership between Google's YouTube and the Universal Music Group (UMG) to launch a stand-alone online music video site based on Vevo.com is a business model for packaging higher quality videos from UMG's catalogue linked with targeted advertising (Harvey 2009). The site will offer merchandising and concert tickets to mainstream music/fan publics. This development is a way of side-stepping some of the fractious copyright issues which have plagued YouTube in the past, and a method to drive traffic and revenue with an extended range of advertising features. In a sense it's an old media story involving the most popular online video site and a major legacy media player; commodification in this context means strategies for increasing audience consumption of online music videos and boosting revenue in that process.

The rise of 'Web 2.0' new 'hyper-targeting' technologies using 'ad-serving platforms' constitute a new turn in the evolution of commercial speech for media conglomerates. The 'hyper-targeting' tools, as the industry itself refers to the practice, now tailor advertisements and stalk Web surfers' interests in this cross-platform future. Turow and Tsui in *The Hyperlinked Society* (2008: 163) argue that the cross-platform audiences will be increasingly exposed to content tie-ins and 'inter-woven storylines' following non-linear content distribution logics. Jenkins' notion of 'transmedia story-telling' embraces related ideas of branded content strategies, concerned with flow over multiple platforms and devices, where corporations aim for the advertising media equivalent of 'carpet bombing' (Jenkins 2006). Advertising models and strategies will both follow and lead innovations in the communications and media industries. Turow and Tsui argue that this is a powerful development in advertising because it addresses specific individuals and is 'less intrusive'. The efficiency is based on knowledge of past interests as evidenced in searches and sites visited, and therefore a built-up profile of preferences, interests and media consumption habits. 'Those interests can be segmented out and compared with advertiser goals. Then the ads can be delivered to the right person across all media' (2008: 163).

MySpace's parent, News Corporation is continuously diversifying into and actively shaping this online media space. They now have a specific division, Fox Interactive Media (FIM) that oversees many of these online commercial activities. It is possible to get a sense of News Corporations' audience aggregation strategies for FIM from this description by online analytics firm ComScore:

> FIM is a portfolio of leading social networking, entertainment, sports and information sites that offer a platform and tools for consumers to express themselves, communicate with each other, and engage with media. The company's worldwide network includes such category leaders as MySpace, Photobucket, IGN Entertainment, FOXSports.com, RottenTomatoes, AskMen, Flektor and more that together comprise one of the largest audiences on the Web.
>
> (ComScore Media Metrix 2008)

In 2008, FIM established an advertising network they call their 'Fox Interactive Media Audience Network' to service leading web brands. The financial and trade press reported that 'The new unit's charter will be to optimize monetization across FIM's content network and for third-party publishers leveraging both the company's industry-leading hyper-targeting technology and ad-serving platform' (Reuters 2008). The setting up of this audience network was the outcome of the 2007 acquisition of Strategic Data Corporation (SDC) by News Corporation's FIM, and this was consolidated to form 'the basis of FIM's monetization platform'. These developments exemplify the new media way of corralling and engaging with audiences, in the 'mass self-communication' contexts of Internet social media. It is a reasonable assumption to make that neoliberal market systems will become increasingly dependent on these kinds of decentred Internetworked processes. Another example of the trend can be seen in the acquisition of DoubleClick in 2007 by Google; the online ad serving company uses similar audience hunting and gathering logics to FIM, and is testimony to online being the fastest growing advertising sector (Rampell and Ahrens 2007). By combining their respective technologies, Google is able to more precisely target display and video advertising to those customers who are the best prospects for products. It has also perfected the commercial behaviours of traditional media companies by driving traffic to its own sites too. But all these decisions are informed and made possible by massive data storage that Google routinely collects as Internet users travel around the net for their entertainment and e-commerce purposes. Not surprisingly, privacy advocates are very concerned about these developments and their potential to infringe people's privacy rights. The market power to abuse personal information aggregated through usage is unprecedented; it represents the long held dream of directly threading together the production, distribution and consumption of goods and services.

On occasions, the presumed advantages of new social media for 'linking people up' are put under the microscope in a very public backlash. This was the case when Facebook, the brash start-up, and now a very large new media company, introduced a new selling feature called 'Beacon'. The purpose of Beacon was mostly about advertising, even though it had a veneer of 'social networking' attraction for its audience users. Free to advertisers, the Beacon feature was not restricted to e-commerce: people getting a high score on an online game can be posted as news for friends on the network.

Introduced in 2007, the idea was that Facebook users' purchases from an affiliated group of more than 40 external websites, were then broadcast to other members. But it went off the rails when Sean Lane's supposedly surprise purchase for his wife of a diamond ring became a Beacon news headline on Facebook: 'Sean Lane bought 14k White Gold 1/5 ct Diamond Eternity Flower Ring from overstock.com' (Nakashima 2007). *The Washington Post* reported: 'Without Lane's knowledge, the headline was visible to everyone in his online network, including 500 classmates from Columbia University and 220 other friends, co-workers and acquaintances.' A social networking feature conceived of as a 'word of mouth' promotion tool, was actually a new way of marketing that was highly invasive of people's privacy. However, in a dramatic show of grassroots resistance 50,000 other users signed a petition calling on Facebook to stop the unauthorized use of members' data. Facebook quickly backed down, and implemented an active 'opt-in' mechanism for members who agreed with the process. It was clear that Beacon was a vivid instance of social networking sites introducing more sophisticated advertising businesses that are relying on the buying preferences of its membership. My point here is that, as with legacy media, corporate advertisers are again writing the rules of the Internet: as one commentator has noted, advertising is 'the essence of Facebook's business; it's the great and shining hope of that company and social media in general' (Fuchs 2009).

Privacy and surveillance are frequently connected in some way, and this can be seen in any number of convergent new media devices. For example, the Google phone is a web-enabled wireless device that gives Google access to all users' data as they travel around using it. That includes access to email, instant messages, contact lists, web search history and geographic location. Since it has all this data relating to those using it, social networks and where users are moving around, Google exploits this to send highly context specific advertisements. These data are incredibly accurate, and explain both its commercial value and the concern of privacy advocates who are conscious of the fact that advertising is also shifting to follow those people using the mobile web (Cauley 2009). With estimates of the worldwide users of the mobile web now being around the 4 billion mark, the mobile net is undoubtedly going to continue to shape the audience/user and content nexus. The industry association GSMA (Global Standard for Mobiles Association) is forecasting further growth to 6 billion by 2013 (Mika 2009). This will have ongoing consequences for how mobile audience users are imagined in this primarily e-commerce space.

The kind of exponential growth we have seen in the mobile communications sector requires facilitation by a controlled market system on an enormous scale. Therefore, theoretical tools to explain this kind of coordinated industry expansion are also necessary. In the next section we revisit a well-known model that, with a few adjustments, remains highly relevant for the analysis of developments in media and communications.

Propaganda revisited

When it was first introduced in 1988, Herman and Chomsky's **propaganda model** of the media was seen to be groundbreaking in its explanatory force (1994). Elements of their model have become increasingly relevant to the persuasive new commercialized role of Internetworked media. Their ideas of the 'propagandistic' role of media in producing a consensus in the way people were informed of events in the news, was premised on the role of certain 'filters'. These filters related to ownership structures, the role of advertising, reliance on routine sources of information and agents of power, the role of 'flak' in disciplining media, and anti-communist ideologies. The model proposed that news and information in general is distilled through these filters, and the available 'residue' serves the interests of ruling elites. But the model was seen to have wider application than simply 'news', and extended to the dominant ideas of the day in market societies.

Herman and Chomsky's model (1988), with some reinterpretation for new digital Internet media contexts, can make an important contribution to how we explain the role of commercialized new media forms in neoliberal reorganization. There is a populist tendency to dismiss the relevance of trends to media concentration in online contexts. My argument is that, on the contrary, in spite of the prevailing myopic discourses of technological determinism that uncritically celebrate Internet media, such talk is akin to populist assessments of a 'revolution' in media and communications. At a global level, such assessments benefit particular political and economic relations, and depoliticize the roles and affectivity of the structural preferences embedded in media systems. News and information in democracy are primarily resources for social engagement. In this sense Herman and Chomsky's formulations regarding the filters of 'ownership' and 'advertising' in market systems remain important and useful categories for a revivified application of the model. New media industry developments, especially an intensified commodification process that continues to 'manufacture consent' in powerful ideological ways call for their model to be updated primarily in relation to these filter categories.

Concentrated media ownership is consolidating into the online media, just as the press diversified into broadcast and cable media in the twentieth century, with implications for the way these corporations enter into profitable relations with audiences (see Chapter 2). Many of the arguments in *Manufacturing Consent* have ongoing purchase in relation to the way that concentrated ownership diminishes the pool of news sources, particularly within consolidated media empires, as news becomes shared and re-used between a number of outlets (1994: 3–14). Structured corporate relations through mergers and acquisitions, interlinked directorships, revolving doors between industry and regulatory agencies, and links with government policy and political elites, were all regarded as having the ability to filter and shape media outputs.

Similarly, the 'advertising filter' of the model continues to have heuristic value in the way that it provides an account of the shaping force of advertising (1994: 14–18). The 'hyper-targeting' that now characterizes Internet advertising and marketing strategies is having a potent systemic role in the evolution of the Internet media, as I've discussed. The best advertising models were not at all clear when the Internet was in its first phase of development through to the Nasdaq tech crash period. Banner advertising was often obstrusive and ill-suited to the interactivity of particular sites. The emergence of Web 2.0 online advertising has taken several years of fine-tuning to get to the hyper-targeting stage. Reports about the ability of Search Engine Optimization (SEO) strategies to influence how news journalism is being constructed, for the sake of increasing traffic and therefore advertising revenue, and now more commonplace (Martin 2008). Google and other search engines now refer many viewers to the sites of news organizations through **organic** rather than **paid listings**. Advertisers continue to shape the content that becomes available, as they have in legacy media contexts. And as media outlets and producers of the broadcast era intensely watched the rise and fall of ratings, since audience size and affluence directly correlate with advertising revenue, so it is with Internet media. Measures of 'unique browsers' and 'page impressions' have comparable influence on where advertising expenditures are flowing to, especially content of wide appeal for specific market segments.

The value of the Herman and Chomsky model can be seen to emerge from a wide interpretation of the term *propaganda*. Some 15 years after it was first published, Herman reviewed the model in these terms

> In short, the propaganda model describes a decentralized and nonconspiratorial market system of control and processing, although at times the government or one or more private actors may take initiatives and mobilize coordinated elite handling of an issue. We never claimed that the propaganda model explained everything or that it shows media omnipotence and complete effectiveness in manufacturing consent. It is a model of media behavior and performance, not of media effects.
>
> (Herman 2003)

Herman argues that there is an 'enhanced relevance' in applying the model:

> Some argue that the Internet and the new communication technologies are breaking the corporate stranglehold on journalism and opening an unprecedented era of interactive democratic media. There is little evidence to support this view as regards mainstream journalism and mass communication. In fact, one could argue that the new technologies are exacerbating the problem. They permit media firms to shrink staff even as they achieve greater outputs, and they make possible global distribution systems that reduce the number of media entities. Although new Internet media technologies have great potential for democratic communication, there is little reason to expect the Internet to serve democratic ends if it is left to the market.
>
> (Herman and McChesney 1997: 117–35, cited in Herman 2003)

I agree with this argument – for example, one needs only to look at the search engine market to see oligopoly structures characteristic of earlier capitalist media industries. As Herman persuasively suggests:

> The competition for advertisers has become more intense and the boundaries between editorial and advertising departments have weakened further.
>
> The dramatic changes in the economy, the communications industries, and politics over the past dozen years have tended on balance to enhance the applicability of the propaganda model. The first two filters – ownership and advertising – have become ever more important.
>
> (Herman 2003)

Herman's argument, then, suggests that the model is a framework of analysis for analysing complex and interrelated sets of media events. The scale of the propaganda is clearly important for its operation as well: 'it offers insight in numerous important cases that have large effects and cumulative ideological force, it is arguably serviceable unless a better model is provided' (Herman

2003). Criticized by some for being too functionalist, and by others for being too 'conspiratorial', supporters of the model see ongoing merits in their critical political economy frameworks. I would argue that large-scale, structured and systemic features of Internet media, then, validate Herman's rejoinder to various commentaries (Herman 2003). In the next section we consider how digital media are restructuring audiences relations within a predominantly, consumerist and on-demand framework.

Multichannelism, 'the long tail', interactivity

In the context of the rollout of digital terrestrial television broadcasting (DTTB) in the UK, Starks has suggested that traditional broadcasting has been transformed by a greater choice of content supplied to audiences by multichannelling, access to archived programming, and interactive features (Starks 2007: 185). In addition to these changes, he argues, we need to add improved quality (HDTV, better sound), greater convenience (time-shifting, easier remote controls, mobility) and greater personalization (self-scheduling) to the new digital experience. All these developments have made important contributions to changes in the way we 'watch television'. It is really this new common-sense understanding of television that has tended to work cooperatively with neoliberal ideologies to convey an unquestioning view of advancement or progress. Of course, many of these improvements are obvious and make our television viewing lives better. Yet the problem with these kinds of 'progress' arguments is that we tend to uncritically accept changes without thinking through what some of the implications might be. Starks is not encouraging such a reading. Indeed, he explicitly makes the point that 'there is no technological determinism driving us away from acting collectively as citizens', and he holds out a hope that a licence fee may continue to sustain public service broadcasting. However, there has been a perceptible 'shift in relationships', and he refers to comments made by Ed Richards from Ofcom, who characterizes the changing position of audiences as:

> a gentle, gradual, evolving, historic act of liberation – the liberation of consumers, viewers, listeners, to determine their own viewing, their own listening, their own schedule, their own compilations, their own content and even their own services. What is going on here . . . is a gradual transfer of power from broadcaster, distributor and supplier, to viewer, listener and consumer.
>
> (Richards 2005, in Starks 2007: 188)

The trend identified by Richards is on one level fairly uncontroversial, and in the few years since he has made these comments, there is considerable evidence to support the broader trends he points to. Chris Anderson has dubbed access to an archive of programming 'the long tail', where although there is 'demassification' and segmentation of markets, there is simultaneously a deeper historical store of mostly payment-for-use content (2006). But there is a need to qualify these arguments and add a caveat that it is choice from a limited palette of offerings from specific sources and genres: that it is a very specific kind of *consumerist* 'liberation' available in commercial media markets. 'Liberation' also happens to mean spending increasing amounts of income on 'triple' or 'quadruple' play bundling of mobile, broadband, DTTB or premium tier subscriptions, and fixed telephony. Perhaps there will sometimes be savings to be made by people in these packaged offerings. Often it will mean more money going into the coffers of convergent media corporations.

An 'insider' account by Barry Cox provides another uncritical example of how neoliberalism imagines digital broadcast audiences, in a mediasphere where broadcasting and broadband have converged:

> In the digital world all broadcasters and producers should be free to choose how they get their programmes to us, and we should be free to choose how we want to receive them – in particular how we want to pay for them . . . Let's say you subscribe to 20 channels, half of them premium standalone services, the rest a bundle of cheaper channels that you buy en bloc. Your PVR has auto access to these, plus all the free advertising-funded channels. Before you go to work you tell it the two films or programmes you want it to record. It might, of its own accord, also record a couple of hours of other programmes it thinks you will like. There are all kinds of variation on that model, but I trust you get the idea. It is what the combination of PVRs, broadband distribution and micro-payment systems can do.
>
> (Cox, in Starks 2007: 186–7)

In fairness, Cox acknowledges that taxation and subsidy systems could potentially be used to ensure universal coverage. However, his market-driven predictions are representative of a neoliberal vision of how digital services within convergent Internet provision structures may unfold for audiences.

Voices in neoliberal media markets

As we discussed in Chapter 3, the idea of 'voices' first began to be used in traditional media policy of the broadcast era, in discursive constructions which made the assumption that ownership diversity is able to produce voice diversity (see Price and Weinberg 1996). The other general departure point for engaging with the concept of 'voices' in media policy is an assertion, quite rightly, that multiperspectivalism arising from a range of societal voices or representations is necessary in democratic media systems. At the same time, the rise of Internet media has played into a parallel discourse under neoliberal policy regimes that has asserted that online access to a burgeoning range of sources of information would weaken the case for these earlier regulatory justifications.

I would argue that these kinds of discourses have complemented existing regulatory measures for the support of diversity of voices through media pluralism. In this context Karpinnen provides a persuasive critique of what he refers to as 'naïve pluralism' in media policy discourses (see Chapter 3). Too often the term 'pluralism' is used in an inexact way to invoke heterogeneity and content choice diversity in media. The trouble with these conceptions is that they echo 'the postmodern antipathy towards all kinds of social centralism and planning and leads to a more general critique of all kinds of "cultural policing" ' (2008: 36). Such postmodern renderings, as many others have noted, convey an antipaternalistic stance that then is reread as praising individualist cultural autonomy and choice. The upshot for Karpinnen is that it is little wonder

> if the current stress on popular consumption, active audiences and individual creation of meaning is mistaken for the neoliberal idea of consumer sovereignty. It can be argued that the discussion of pluralism in media studies and media policy has often taken a form of naïve celebration of all multiplicity, which all too easily converges with the neoliberal illusion of free choice.
>
> (2008: 36)

This 'naïve celebration' of multiplicity is consonant with not only *laissez-faire* notions of consumer sovereignty and their 'power', but also with celebrations of a digital (Internet) smorgasbord that is so often imagined, and relied on to legitimate, deregulatory media policy discourses.

Karpinnen argues that the alternative is to apply a radical-pluralist democratic theory drawing on the work of, for example, Mouffe (2000) where pluralism and constructions of difference are based on antagonistic understandings of the limits of pluralism. By recognizing the role of economic and political power in structuring hegemonic order, democratizing any institutions, including media, becomes a political task. The corollary of this explanation is that invocations of 'choice' or 'DIY' media are usually a distraction from first principle discussions of planning democratic media systems.

To rely on notions of 'voice' in media policy development, therefore, is to recognize the role of economic and political power in structuring media markets. Accordingly, in contradistinction to liberal pluralist understandings of the 'free marketplace of ideas' and freedom to choose, radical pluralists contend 'that spaces in which differences may constitute themselves as contending identities are today most efficiently established by political means' (Karpinnen 2008: 37). For policy-makers and media regulation in general, this can be interpreted to mean that choices (in outlets, programmes, genres) must represent existing social differences, and that resources are made available to sustain them. The laws, policies and regulations which govern how media institutions are planned and designed lie at the heart of audience access to these resources. In the following section, we explore some of the shifting relations in the circuit of media content production, distribution and consumption.

User content and 'audiencing'

A study by Van Der Wurff has found that, on average, around 70 per cent of the content of the major online news stories is identical to the original story in the offline version (2005: 79). The exception to the rule is that what little new content there is in the online versions of newspapers is to be found in User Generated or User Created Content. Traditional media outlets of broadcast TV and radio are using audience content to innovate and extend their public service remits. Research by Flew et al. on the way that Australia's multicultural broadcaster the Special Broadcasting Service (SBS) is experimenting with and developing its audiences and content provision offers considerable promise for how future media organizations organize themselves (Flew et al. 2008).

Recent accounts of the changing dynamics of content production, distribution and consumption have analysed shifting relations between producers and consumers. For instance, Rosen has referred to 'the people formerly known as the audience' (Rosen 2008) to underscore the new autonomy of citizens in participatory media, who are creatively using online media tools to produce and distribute stories and information, and to make contributions to discussions in the mediasphere. The Organization for Economic Co-operation and Development (OECD) in its report on the *Participative Web: User-Created Content* (OECD 2007) identified six major socio-economic points of impact of the rise of user-created content that are shaking up traditional media provision:

1. decentralized creativity;
2. new forms of competition for audience time, advertising revenue and content sources, as well as audiences/users who will demand 'any time, any place, any device' content;
3. 'pro-am' (i.e pro-amateur) content producers;
4. participation, re-use and remediation become core aspects of the consumption experience;

5. 'long tail' economics (Anderson 2006);
6. open platform media.

Flew et al. (2008) suggest, drawing on Leadbeater's argument, what we are witnessing with user generated/created content is that 'the irresistible force of collaborative mass innovation meets the immovable force of entrenched corporate organisation' (Leadbeater 2008).

There is a great deal of merit in these perspectives, and it is particularly applicable in public service media organizations. Yet it remains a problematic account for large aggregations of individuals assembled for the purposes of capital/commodified engagements. Paradoxically, at the very time that corporations wish to aggregate or assemble the largest possible number of people ('unique users' or 'page impressions'), *content* is being offered in a disaggregated or personalized way. Thus my argument is that the term 'audience' continues to be a meaningful and important way we can account for the relationships with the 'entrenched corporate organisation'. This will remain the case until after such time that there is a very significant tilting of the balance between these two ways of supplying content and the underlying power symmetries. At present we need to recognize that a great deal of the design and access regimes of the participatory context continues to be underwritten by large multiplatform media corporations.

Conclusion

In this chapter we have seen that media businesses are closely implicated in the performance of neoliberalist ideologies and strategies for audience engagement. In an ongoing contest between commercialized proprietary media content and more participatory structures of social networking and user-created content provision, old and new prophets make forecasts about what Bill Gates once famously called 'the road ahead'. Tim Berners-Lee one of the founding fathers of the Internet, told an assembled conference audience that it was time to 'reimagine' the web. Berners-Lee was advocating what he calls 'linked data' or 'raw data', which he promises will go beyond hypertext and 'make readily accessible digital information stored in any format from any source' (Crovitz 2009). Others call these developments 'Web 3.0' or 'the **semantic web**', where more meaningful, instantly useful content can be brought together. He imagines that distress in financial markets might be ameliorated if fast access 'to better information' were available.

My argument in this chapter has been that powerful stakeholders in a position to shape relations with audience users are constantly promoting ways to imagine communications media. In the neoliberal era, unpaid labour in participatory content provision is restructuring media organizations in ways that are yet to be fully understood. And it remains to be seen whether people find this restructuring emancipatory, or ultimately, just another adaptive set of relations, where the rules of engagement are being set by those who find it profitable to embed some level of ambiguity in the balance of power of our media systems. In Chapter 5 we consider the vital new economic, social and cultural roles of broadband communications media, and how universal service provision now requires rethinking.

Further reading

Anderson, B. (1983) *Imagined Communities: Reflections on the Origin and Spread of Nationalism*. London: Verso.

Anderson, C. (2006) *The Long Tail: Why the Future of Business Is Selling Less of More*. New York: Random House.

Fuchs, C. (2009) 'Social networking sites and the surveillance society' paper presented at Salzburg/Vienna, Austria. Forschungsgruppe 'Unified Theory of Information' – Verein zur Förderung der Integration der Informationswissenschaften. Available at: http://fuchs.icts.sbg.ac.at/SNS_Surveillance_Fuchs.pdf.

Hallin, D. (2008) 'Neoliberalism, social movements and change', in D. Hesmondhalgh and J. Toynbee (eds) *The Media and Social Theory*. London: Routledge.

Herman, E. and Chomsky, N. (1994) *Manufacturing Consent*. London: Vintage.

McGuigan, J. (2004) *Rethinking Cultural Policy*. Maidenhead: Open University Press.

Mouffe, C. (2000) *Democratic Paradox*. London: Verso.

Thussu, D. (2009) *News as Entertainment: The Rise of Global Infotainment*. London: Sage.

5 | LIVING AT THE NETWORK EDGE

The leaders of the nation's largest cable and telephone companies are telling lawmakers something familiar. New national policies are required to connect everyone to what they call a 'superbroadband' Internet highway . . . they claim that the emergence of the Internet has set the stage to remove most of the public policies and safeguards that now govern media and communications – everything from limits on media ownership, to rules governing equal time for political candidates, to requirements that communities receive public-service programming. Competition, we are assured, will address any problem once handled by law or regulation, and also bring us the promised digital cornucopia.

(Chester 2007: 182)

Introduction

Jeff Chester of the Center for Digital Democracy in his book *Digital Destiny* provides a disturbing account of the inexorable trend to concentration in media industries, and the creation of 'supermedia monopolies'. Chester's argument is that the lobbying strength and ongoing liberalization of media restrictions have allowed the US cable and telephony giants to 'gain greater leverage over broadband Internet' (2007: 184). In the USA, Chester argues, successive Republican-controlled Federal Communication Commissions (FCC) have facilitated the growth of corporations such as Comcast, Verizon and AT&T, by allowing them to forge near-monopoly status as broadband providers in individual local markets. The criticism of the capture of the FCC by 'big media', and this includes powerful telco and cable corporations, is one that has been expressed repeatedly for over a decade in the USA (McChesney et al. 2005). Under these circumstances, as it was to be expected, the Obama Administration has marshalled its resources, including taking a broom to the FCC, which is now Democrat-controlled.

In this chapter, we examine how policies for broadband by national governments have assumed centre-stage position, and are increasingly important elements in twenty-first-century infrastructure projects; they are now usually embedded in wider political rhetorics of 'nation-building' and strategic industry policy in globally competitive markets. Accordingly, soon after the inauguration of President Obama, in the context of an ongoing crisis in financial markets, talk of rolling out high-speed broadband networks was high on the new administration's list of priorities. The need to kick-start an ailing economy through a programme of concerted government spending was reminiscent of the 'New Deal' in the 1930s in the USA. Australia's Prime Minister Rudd had been in power for just over a year, and his government's economic 'stimulatory' measures included building a national broadband network with access for all. But the approaches taken by the two governments were quite different, largely the result of their nation's unique political and institutional histories. The centrepiece of the Rudd Government's election promise of a high-speed national broadband network was that a contracted network-builder receive A\$4.7 bn of government funds as the basis of a public–private partnership model. An important element of a parliamentary review process in 2008 was to establish the terms of the tender documents, which were to call for offers to build a new high-speed network.

By mid-2008, the Australian Senate had launched a review of broadband regulation, and began to consult widely about the establishment of an appropriate National Broadband Network (NBN) model and the mode of its rollout (Senate 2008). Seventy public submissions were received from a range of domestic and international stakeholders: ISPs, telcos, local councils, state governments. Google thought that the future provider of the network ought not be permitted to operate both the network, and the retail broadband business (Hart 2008). No doubt the ironies of this suggestion were not lost on some readers of their submission who would have thought their argument rather Janus-faced, given the dominant position of Google in the search engine market. Google had argued that the new network should: 'offer services on a wholesale basis to retail competitors on non-discriminatory and equivalent terms as it offers them to its own retail operations, from the perspective of both price and non-price terms and conditions' (Hart 2008).

They were far from being alone in this suggestion. British Telecom also supported such a **structural/functional separation** model. Trenchantly opposed to this argument was the former monopoly provider Telstra Corporation who argued in their submission: 'All that presently stands between Australia and world-class broadband infrastructure is the current regulatory regime' (Hart 2008). In reply, Telstra's critics put the case that Telstra was one of the world's most highly integrated telecommunications companies: that its structure gives it both the incentive and ability (reinforced by a very favourable access regime) to impede competition and slow the release of new technologies/ products. Critics, quite rightly, noted that it was vertically integrated, owning both network and retail businesses. And that it was also horizontally integrated, owning various networks – including copper (ADSL), Hybrid Fibre Coaxial (HFC), 3G mobile and satellite – distribution platforms which all generate broadband products. Their argument was that maximizing shareholder value for Telstra means minimizing retail sales cannibalization by refusing rivals access to its network or stalling and charging the highest access prices possible.

In the USA, President Obama also pledged a large sum – approximately US$790 billion would be set aside under the Congress' 'New Deal'-like 'stimulatory package'. Of this amount, Congress targeted approximately US$7 billion to wire rural America with Internet service. Not long after his inauguration in early 2009, President Obama argued in Congressional debates for the stimulus funding for broadband Internet in underserved areas to create new jobs while also providing better economic, educational and health-care opportunities (Kang 2009). The way those funds will be invested in broadband is an emerging, and highly politicized debate. For example, local planning and development agencies strenuously argue against any allocation to allow incumbent cable and telephone corporations such as AT&T or Verizon to build these networks. Wally Bowen in the *Daily Yonder* blog writes:

> Here in the mountains of North Carolina, Verizon, AT&T and Charter control more than 90 percent of the landlines to homes and businesses. Yet local politicians and economic development officials – and the state's broadband authority – gave up years ago trying to cajole or bribe the big carriers into deploying broadband to underserved neighborhoods and rural areas. The idea that these carriers might suddenly produce plans for 'shovel-ready' broadband projects in our rural mountains is more magical thinking than pragmatic logic. Instead, we are far more likely to find 'shovel-ready' projects on the drawing boards of local planning agencies and state broadband initiatives like the N.C. Rural Internet Access Authority, now known as the e-NC Authority.

It is interesting to note that this particular US local area has around 600 miles of fibre networks run by four not-for-profit organizations, and a public–private partnership managed by the Eastern Band of the Cherokee. As the executive director of a local Internet service provider based in Asheville, North Carolina, Bowen is hardly a disinterested observer. Yet his view is that although this is a good start and has its merit, he makes the point that the communities' needs are much higher, and after a connectivity mapping exercise 'we easily identified $US26 million in shovel-ready projects to recommend to the Obama transition team for funding' (Bowen 2009).

The Commission of the European Communities has announced similar programmes for 'stimulatory' investment in European broadband. The Commission argues that, 'Investment in broadband has a positive impact on economic development, innovation and territorial cohesion.' Accordingly, it is introducing measures which aim to achieve '100% high-speed Internet coverage for all citizens by 2010 as part of the European Economic Recovery Plan'. The programme includes a €1 billion investment 'to help rural areas get online, bring new jobs and help businesses grow'. The Commission claims that on average, 93 per cent of Europeans access a high-speed online connection but in some countries broadband covers less than half of the rural population. The focus of the EU strategy is unambiguously about economic recovery in depressed times: 'Broadband Internet connection is expected to create 1 million jobs and boost the EU's economy by €850 billion between 2006 and 2015' (European Commission, press release 2009).

All these national broadband investment strategies indicate the dilemma of providing broadband in rural, regional and remote areas in advanced economies by large communications corporations. Where the choice is between an investment strategy directed at corporate clients and affluent residential areas, or investment in underserved, less populous rural and regional areas, the outcome is fairly clear. The investment will occur in markets where these companies already have a presence, and strong profits guaranteed. Inevitably, for these purely economic reasons, investment by these corporations in **backhaul** infrastructure in less populous markets is limited, compared with more densely populated markets. In the context of economic doldrums, the argument was also about how 'local networks open the door to local innovation and economic growth in ways that are impossible with absentee-owned networks' (Bowen 2009).

Accounting for broadband

Documenting an accurate overview of the state of broadband services at a national level is a difficult task, let alone making comparisons internationally. In fact, John Horrigan of the Pew Internet and American Life Project has argued that currently there is no reliable national map of where broadband is available in the USA because telecommunications and cable corporations are loath to release such commercially sensitive information (Kaste 2009). One Pew survey interprets the 14 per cent of Americans still using dial-up Internet to mean that this group remains unable to access broadband in the area where they live. As with all comparative analyses, the need to use an evaluation approach that takes into account key differences and yet is still able to render national and international data into a useful analysis is the core challenge. The OECD has identified a range of indicators that can be used to evaluate comparative national take-up of broadband, including the actual number of available lines in an area; households which are in a position to access broadband; the actual geography and land mass; the prices of broadband services; and, the speeds, products and services (including data caps) on offer in a given location (OECD 2009). Not without critics for some of its inbuilt assumptions (for instance, regarding the assumed ability of people to acquire relevant knowledge, or lack of distinguishing between domestic and workplace access), the sum of the parts of these statistics produces the analytical value. The number of broadband subscribers per 100 inhabitants (Figure 5.1) becomes more significant when it is cross-checked with the chart of population density (Figure 5.2) or the size of the total landmass (Figure 5.3), the pricing structures of particular product and service offerings (Figure 5.4), and the price of these for specific access speeds (Figure 5.5).

Behind these statistics of highly politicized rollout processes is a need for the recognition of a new reality of broadband communications policy. One's access to a broadband network at speeds capable of using content-rich audiovisual media is an important precondition for social participation at the close of the first decade of the twenty-first century. Public infrastructure provision, then, is simultaneously concerned with social, cultural and economic policies. Broadband provision can now be regarded as an important component of 'universal' infrastructure; a policy position that is consistent with nations who proselytize their place as information societies/knowledge economies.

Rethinking USOs for broadband networks

In many western democracies there have been mechanisms in place for decades that ensured citizens would have a basic level of communications services at affordable prices. This usually translated to at least a 'plain old telephone' (or POTS) service no matter where you lived in the nation. Many people are now realizing that access to affordable broadband services should be the core universal service obligation for the twenty-first century. From children's access to education resources, to everyone shopping online and e-commerce in general, to access to health services and all kinds of consumer information and audiovisual entertainments; a fast and affordable Internet connection has become an essential requirement for contemporary living. Unfortunately, in a time of neoliberal politics and the removal of safety nets addressing inequities of provision, in favour of market provision, such a move has been met with resistance. Many analysts agree that the funding of minimum levels

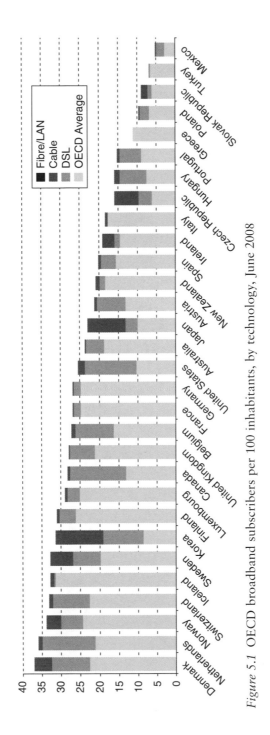

Figure 5.1 OECD broadband subscribers per 100 inhabitants, by technology, June 2008

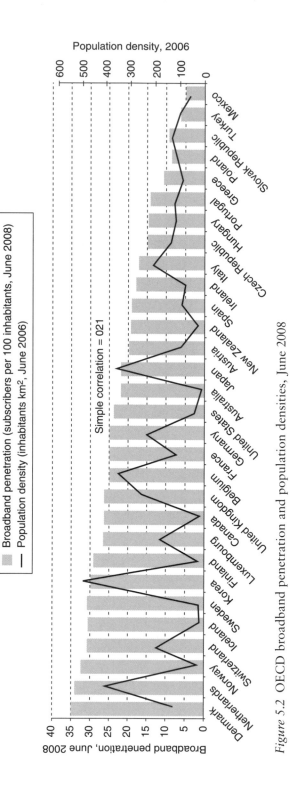

Figure 5.2 OECD broadband penetration and population densities, June 2008

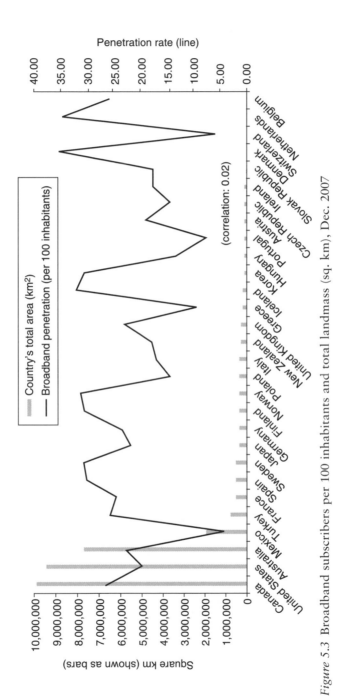

Figure 5.3 Broadband subscribers per 100 inhabitants and total landmass (sq. km), Dec. 2007

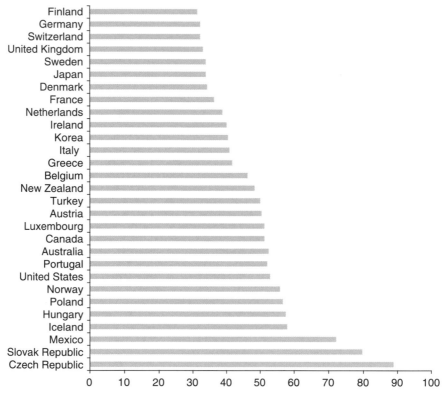

Figure 5.4 Broadband average monthly subscription price, October 2007, US$ ppp (Purchasing Power Parities/currency conversion rates)

of broadband should be a priority matter for renovating existing universal service obligations by governments.

An early study of **universal service obligation (USO)** conducted for the European Commission claimed that 'for a service to be considered for inclusion in the universal service obligation it ought to have already grown to a 75 per cent market penetration under normal market conditions' (Analysys, cited in ACA 1998: 121). In a submission to an Australian government telecommunications review in 2007 into universal service obligations I have argued that on the basis of this criterion, if total wireline broadband penetration is added to wireless, and mobile Internet access as well, then a USO for broadband access is now overdue for implementation (Dwyer and Ramsay 2007).

In my view, there is also considerable merit in the suggestion by Patrick Xavier in an OECD-commissioned study that mobile services should be included in an expanded USO. Given the ubiquity of mobile services and devices compared with fixed line services, his recommendation is hardly surprising. Xavier argued

Japan	3.09
France	3.70
Italy	4.61
United Kingdom	5.29
Korea	5.96
Luxembourg	7.31
Switzerland	8.17
Germany	8.44
Norway	9.81
Portugal	11.52
United States	12.60
Finland	13.45
Hungary	14.31
Ireland	14.92
Netherlands	15.26
New Zealand	16.75
Czech Republic	17.54
Austria	17.66
Denmark	17.70
Sweden	18.40
Belgium	18.55
Slovak Republic	19.59
Australia	21.34
Iceland	22.22
Spain	22.85
Poland	25.03
Canada	28.14
Greece	29.13
Mexico	63.89
Turkey	97.43

Figure 5.5 Average broadband monthly price per advertised Mbit/s Oct. 2007, US$ ppp (Purchasing Power Parities/currency conversion rates)

that this should be not in the sense of mandating universal availability 'but a USO defined in terms of basic voice and data service without specifying the means would allow technology-neutrality and flexibility for USO to be cost effectively delivered by fixed wireless, mobile or other means' (OECD 2005: 36).

Against mandating universal service, the argument is made that it could discourage investment in the network and impede the development of broadband services. But the question about the inclusion of data in a USO has been included in policy debates for over a decade. For instance, in 1998, Australia's then Minister for Communications Richard Alston directed the telecommunications regulator to conduct an inquiry into 'whether a carriage service that provides digital data capability broadly equivalent to 64 kilobits per second (Kbit/s) . . . should be incorporated into the Universal Service Obligation' (ACA 1998: 11). Importantly, in the Digital Data Inquiry report, the ACA articulated a rationale for government intervention in the provision of a digital data capability to ensure accessibility, including:

- to correct for market failures in an attempt to make market outcomes more efficient;
- to produce public goods and promote strategic national benefit;
- to improve equity or fairness of market outcomes;
- where the service or good is considered essential; or;
- where the provision of a service affects the rights of citizens.

However, a succession of government policy reports from the mid-1990s have framed the provision of broadband communications in varying ways. The general rhetorical trend that emerged was a trajectory away from presenting broadband as a service for citizens and as being a policy priority for social inclusiveness, to being a policy priority for the economy. Broadband was increasingly talked about as a 'market' that needed to be developed because it would be a driver of Gross Domestic Product, jobs and wages growth.

The rhetoric now is that ubiquitous, multi-megabit broadband will primarily underpin Australia's future economic, and social capital that accrues is an added bonus. This is broadly the approach in the other nations discussed earlier in the book, but the point of difference is the configuration of existing players and regulatory frameworks, and the cultural expectations about private and public sector roles. In an aspirational way the policy objective is for Australians to have always-on, multi-megabit-per-second (Mbps) access no matter where they live. The benefits of broadband are mostly cast mainly in economic terms; how broadband access will benefit a recessed economy.

Policy statements have expanded the reach and levels of access to the various broadband platforms available, and argue that Australians are able now to access broadband services of comparable speed to those being offered internationally (see Figure 5.5). The rollout of ADSL2+ services is recognized to be dependent on hundreds more exchanges being switched on, without necessarily mentioning the power of the former monopoly provider and market failure. The majority of the underutilized equipment is Telstra Corporation's, and to date in a 'head-to-head' strategy it has only offered ADSL2+ services from exchanges where its competitors are also selling ADSL2+. In exchanges where no competition exists, Telstra has left its DSL equipment dormant, refusing to turn it on until the competition regulator gives it 'greater regulatory certainty'; code critics refer to meaning an 'access holiday', where competitors are banned from seeking access to Telstra equipment and services for resale. The suggestion is that this was *de facto* allowing Telstra to re-monopolize the wireline telecoms market.

In 2007, the previous conservative government awarded the Optus-Elders consortium (OPEL) more than $900m in funding to build a regional broadband network constituted by both ADSL2+ and WiMAX wireless technologies.

The plan was for most of regional Australia to be serviced by ADSL2+, with the most remote parts of the country getting WiMAX coverage (which it claimed would deliver download speeds of up to 12Mpbs). The announcement was highly controversial, with Telstra crying foul over the tender process, and instituting court proceedings against the government. There were also concerns about the feasibility of the WiMAX component of the network, as services were to be delivered via unlicensed spectrum (with Unwired and the pay TV operator Austar then owning the licences for the preferred operating spectrum of WiMAX in Australia). There were added concerns that interference could cause OPEL's WiMAX service to drop out.

The announcement was made within the context of an election year, where the creation of a broadband fibre-to-the-node (FTTN) network was a core election promise. While the policy as expressed through the OPEL deal was a pledge to deliver at least 12Mbps to all Australians as soon as OPEL can build its network, Federal Labor (now in government) had proposed rolling out a more expensive fibre-to-the-node network to provide 98 per cent of the population with speeds of up to 50Mbps. Both plans have been subject to robust criticism, with critics claiming neither policy was capable of delivering uniform speed to all Australians.

The Rudd Government had previous publicly committed to honouring the contract between the Commonwealth and OPEL consortium as long as it could provide coverage equivalent to 90 per cent of under-served premises within its coverage area. In the event, when analysis performed by Department of Broadband, Communications and the Digital Economy (DBCDE) found that the OPEL network would cover only 72 per cent of identified under-served premises, and that the OPEL network would create an overbuild with its own planned FTTN broadband plan, it cancelled the contract (Bingemann 2008).

In evidence before the Senate Select Committee's NBN inquiry, the Queensland, South Australian and Western Australian governments all expressed concerns that the government's 98 per cent coverage claims may not be accurate; generally they doubted the meaningfulness of any claimed future NBN coverage when applied to various population densities in different states. The South Australian government argued that the actual NBN coverage may be significantly less than 98 per cent 'due to the economics and practicalities of an FTTN architecture solution' (Senate Select Committee 2008: 19). 'The remaining two per cent' remained problematic for the NBN inquiry Committee, and it concluded:

> neither the department nor the Australian Government had provided any guidance or further clarification of the composition of the 98 per cent NBN coverage footprint. The committee believes that the government needs to provide this clarification to proponents and stakeholders alike to

ensure a level of confidence that the significant A\$4.7 bn funding will benefit in particular those Australians that are already underserved or unserved. Particular attention is required to address the needs of those remote areas that are currently generating a large percentage of Australia's wealth yet are in the most underserviced areas.

(Senate Select Committee 2008: 20)

The most recent Australian debates focus on the future direction of broadband rollout in terms of optic fibre networks, or more specifically a fibre-to-the-home (FTTH) network that could be capable of delivering download rates of up to 100 megabits per second (Mbps). But the controversial element of the latest post-election proposal by the Rudd Government, is not the speed or technologies on the wish list, but rather the fact that the government has announced that it will *own* 51 per cent of the new network via a broadband company in which it intends to invest up to AUS\$43 billion. This is a sign of the economically recessed times we now live in. The proposal as it now stands, before any of the parliamentary horse-trading that will undoubtedly ensue, is that the Rudd Government will be the owner of what is, effectively, a re-nationalized monopoly-style network for a period of 13 years (until 2022), when the network would be privatized, and sold to the highest bidder. The network, the government claims, would be structured as an open access one, wholesale-only infrastructure (Hudson 2009).

Some content providers have suggested that for IPTV, movie or TV on-demand services over the Internet to thrive, consumers will need widespread access to download speeds of at least 25Mbps – a far cry from the typical 1.5Mbps ADSL services currently used by most Australians, despite the fact that the advertised speed is often much higher. By contrast, a study by Ofcom of typical broadband speeds in the UK found consumers 'receive an average broadband speed of 3.6 Mbs' which Ofcom claims is less 'than the average maximum possible speed of 4.3 Mbs across the UK and significantly below advertised headline speeds'. The research found that 60 per cent of UK consumers currently subscribe to packages promising speeds of up to 8 Mbs, and yet one in five of these subscribers actually receive an average speed of less than 2 Mbs. The average the actual speed consumers receive is 45 per cent of the advertised headline speed (Ofcom 2009).

Although a fibre optic network is frequently invoked, clearly it is not the only solution to deliver next generation broadband, with high-speed wireless 3G and ADSL networks already making up the mix of available technologies. It seems inescapable that in using a mix of technologies the speed of service will continue to be determined by geographic location and population densities, which in turn affects affordability, as the unevenly distributed national access in the

OECD data corroborates. With regional, rural and remote Australians receiving slower services than those living in metropolitan Australia, questions remain as to whether those living outside of our cities will be able to access the levels of functionality they will need to, as the government asserts, to fully participate in an online economy and society.

The discursive framing of these debates will also affect the response by governments and regulatory authorities. Murdock and Golding have argued that media markets address people as consumers rather than citizens, presenting the freedom to choose between competing products as the central freedom of the modern world. Within such marketizing frameworks, citizen's rights are narrowed to a set of economic rights (Murdock and Golding 1989, 2004). Other media analysts have argued that neoliberal policy discourses of leaving the development of media and communications to market forces is problematic, unable to provide equitable access to new communications spaces (see Burgelman 1997; Lax 2001).

Broadband convergence

If the Internet is the archetypical example of media convergence, then broadband infrastructures and applications are its preeminent forms. Yet the diversification of convergence processes means a variety of formerly disparate services can now be delivered over any one of several technology platforms. An example of this technological convergence can be witnessed in mobile networks. Previously used to deliver only voice services, many mobile networks are now designed to support text, broadband and video applications. A recent tally has calculated that there are 4 billion mobile devices worldwide, in effect, the most ubiquitous portable computer (Markoff 2009).

Recognition of this diversification is urgently required for any USO model developed by future governments. Unless this diversification of convergence processes is taken into account in future constructions of the USO, an unintended consequence may be to limit the universal provision of alternative voice telephony services that may otherwise develop through service and application competition. Since voice services are only one possible range of services delivered over increasingly bundled applications, there may be wider limitations on the growth of these markets.

At the same time that access to information and entertainment by broadband Internet in the home is occurring at varying national levels, Internet over PSTN infrastructure is rapidly declining in high broadband usage nations, according to telecommunications indicators (ACMA 2005). While broadband Internet is a key distribution technology, other access technologies (often with wireless

Internet connectivity), such as digital TV and 3G telephony, are also being used extensively for entertainment and information products; including for news and information delivery.

It is this context of the broader patterning of communications and media consumption that needs to be factored into assessments of the USO. But the inclusion of broadband home access in future USO frameworks will depend on multiple factors ultimately beholden to the political will of individual governments. And increasingly these assessments are influenced by international organizations such as the International Telecommunications Union (ITU) and the UN's Working Group on Internet Governance (WGIG). Although the need for universal broadband home access is upon us, a systematic procedure for evaluating this question was provided by Xavier several years ago (see Figure 5.6 OECD 2005: 40).

In the USA, the Universal Service Fund (USF) is administered by the FCC, and as in Australia, primarily funds universal telephone service (and Internet connections for schools and libraries). It is reported that there is now a strong lobbying effort underway to extend USF funds to broadband. In late 2008, the FCC sought comments on a proposal for a pilot programme that would see a subsidy for broadband Internet to low-income households. The proposal would require broadband Internet providers to meet eligibility criteria for the USF's Lifeline and Link Up funds – the latter being programmes used to defray costs of telephone service and connection charges for households that fall under a certain income threshold (Fineberg 2009).

It is evident that like the USA and elsewhere, the USO remains a battleground within the Australian telecoms sector, with Telstra complaining that the levels of funding it receives are too low, and its competitors complaining that they are forced to provide USO funds to Telstra, a company which maintains market dominance and remains vastly more profitable than competitors. There remains a reluctance to widen the USO in Australia, but supranational trends may gradually change the terms of these debates. The universal ability to access and effectively use the Internet in our everyday lives has emerged in the first decade of the twenty-first century as an urgent matter of fundamental social equity for policy-makers (Burgelmann 1997; Castells 2001; Castells and Himanen 2002; OECD 2005).

In the Introduction, we saw that the process of media convergence can be used to describe the 'disruptive' technology VoIP (or Voice Over Internet Protocol). More specifically, VoIP is an example of a convergent broadband application that is, by some accounts, contributing to the restructuring of the economics of telecommunications networks. By using specific software such as 'Skype', VoIP converts the voice signal from the caller's telephone into a digital signal then converts it back at the other end to enable voice communication with anyone

---

A systematic procedure for considering USO status for broadband

A sytematic process for considering the need to re-define USO should include:

1. Consideration of whether broadband is an essential service of significant 'social importance'.

2. Estimation of the degree of expected market penetration of broadband service.

3. Assessment of the nature and extent to which broadband will not be made available by the market and why.

4. Identification and specification of objectives and desired outcomes clearly and specifically.

5. Assessment of the extent to which market demand and delivery can/will meet the specified objectives.

6. Consideration of the social and economic disadvantages incurred by those without access to broadband if there is no government intervention in this expected market situation.

7. Estimation of the costs of intervention to widen broadband deployment through the use of the USO mechanism.

8. Estimation of the costs of intervention through the use of the USO mechanism compared against the use of other approaches to establish that the USO mechanism is superior.

9. Establishment that the benefits of intervention through the USO exceed the costs of doing so, taking into account the incidence of such benefits and costs (especially those on unsubsidised telecommunications/Internet/broadband Internet customers); and of effects on other communications and broader policy objectives. (Intervention should only occur where overall benefits persuasively outweigh overall costs and where a substantial increase in the level of USO expenditure would not result.)

Figure 5.6 A systematic procedure for considering USO status for broadband
Source: OECD (2005)

with a phone number. P2P video conferencing is a very popular application (see Figure 5.7). One commentator recently noted that, conservatively, there were 276 million accounts using Skype, 17 million people simultaneously logged in, and 264 billion international call minutes made through Skype, constituting around 4.4 per cent (and growing rapidly) of all international traffic (Marks 2009). VoIP is becoming more prevalent on mobile devices, meaning that people will no longer need to be sitting at a laptop or desktop computer in order to use it.

Using VoIP dramatically reduces costs for suppliers and users of the service, bypassing traditionally voice network infrastructures in domestic and business

Figure 5.7 Accessing Voice Over Internet Protocol (VoIP) telephony using the Skype application on a larger screen. This screen shows how to download the software for making voice or video calls.

contexts. With broadband IP networks, the costs to users are a fraction of those associated with traditional wired and wireless networks, and often the quality and reach are an improvement on the transmission it substitutes, although this can have more variation than with PSTN fixed line calls. VoIP services often include additional features without the costs that would usually be associated with them in fixed line services. These include voicemail, electronic notification of voicemails, call blocking, conference calls, routing to a selected number, instant messaging, video calls, the ability to send text, visual information or files during a conversation, and the ability to use your VoIP phone number regardless of one's geographic location. However, some of these features may not be available unless both call participants are using a computer-based VoIP service or the same VoIP provider (ACMA 2008a). According to Ofcom (2008a), VoIP revenue as a proportion of fixed telephony share was highest in Canada (5.6 per cent), followed by Japan (4.9 per cent) and the USA (4.7 per cent), so it is steadily beginning to eat into the revenue streams of telecommunications providers. Clearly, VoIP is a rapidly increasing convergent application where, for instance, in France and Japan, the number of subscribers is over 10 per cent of the population. A survey of the availability of Internet Protocol (IP) networks where voice, text and audiovisual content is transported as data packets, shows over 10 subscribers per 100 inhabitants in these two countries have VoIP services bundled with their broadband services.

Case study
VOIP and Skype

VoIP is a 'disruptive' technology that is reconfiguring media, telecommunications infrastructures, devices and entrenched cultural activities. It is a viable, cost-economic option for people to substitute mobile telephony for fixed line services and to run VoIP software such as Skype on smartphones/PDAs that may also have a capacity to switch between 3G and IP networks. There is a growing trend for people to replace fixed-line services with mobile ones in many countries. It is anticipated that, eventually, these trends will have significant impact on current regulatory arrangements and concepts, as they have with the growth in VoIP services in general (ACMA 2008a).

Skype users now number in the tens of millions. Small wonder then that in 2005 the company sold to EBay, the online auction site, for $2.6 billion (Goldsmith and Wu 2008: 125).

VoIP is also indicative of a trend for several networks to be used together. The term *network convergence* is used to describe the reconfiguration of distribution networks allowing them to carry more than one type of content. There is also evidence of the trend to proliferating 'device convergence' involving combinations of fixed and mobile networks, where voice and data originating from the same device travel over different networks depending on the location of the user and whether the available networks allow dual mode handsets, or handsets that can switch between fixed, WiFi or VoIP (Ofcom 2007, 2008a).

Net neutrality

As an increasingly important social and economic infrastructure, the issue of how, and in whose interests, governments regulate the Internet is an ongoing power struggle. As we have seen, not only is the Internet at the core of the economic success of national and international commerce and trade, but it has also become a key social and cultural infrastructure, as broadcasting did throughout the twentieth century.

In 2004–05, major US telecommunications and cable companies, who together control the telecommunications networks over which Internet data flows, put forward the idea of creating the electronic equivalent of a paid 'fast lane'. In other words, the suggestion was that some content or services would be given priority over others. The **net neutrality** debate was a response to these proposals by companies like AT&T and Verizon, who spend millions lobbying Congress to have their way. Proponents of net neutrality argued that whether a user searches for recipes using Google, reads an article online, visits a not-for-profit or community site, or looks at a friend's Facebook or MySpace profile, all of that data ought to be treated equally and delivered from the originating website to the user's Web browser with the same priority, and at the same speed. The alternative, it was argued, was a tiered Internet where access became a matter of affiliation to particular corporate groups who control preferential content delivery. A movement championing net neutrality, and warning of the inherent risks of the proposals, called 'Save the Internet' has had some limited success, even if only at a public awareness raising level (SavetheInternet.com 2009).

In this worst-case scenario, a few major corporations and their commercial affiliates alone would benefit. On the other hand, large telecommunications corporations argue that the ability to charge for services such as high-quality video from websites ranging from Google to eBay is crucial to being able to afford the multibillion-dollar price tag of upgrading its network-to-fibre links. Their argument is that in order to roll out bandwidth-hungry audiovisual services, they need to charge heavy users to make it more economically viable, and for them to compete. It is worth noting, however, that the European Union has warned telecommunications corporations that they will not tolerate discriminatory access regimes (Foroohar 2006). Other policy actors argue that network neutrality rules be dropped for wireless networks. In a submission to the National Telecommunications and Information Administration (NTIA) regarding how the Congressional economic stimulus funds for broadband should be allocated, the CTIA (the main lobby group for the wireless industry) argued that net neutrality rules 'should be applied to broadband stimulus grantees within the context of its existing parameters, and not more broadly'. Their submission argued that

> Wireless networks are inherently different than the networks for which the [net neutrality] policy statement was developed. The underlying network infrastructure, including spectrum, as well as the integration of the customer equipment, make wireless significantly different than other broadband networks.
>
> (Fierce Wireless 2009)

In the context of the US Congress legislating for an economic stimulus package including broadband, public interest groups continued to call for the government to take steps to enforce net neutrality. It is highly likely that the degree of 'open access' or 'non-discrimination' for competitor's content flow and network interconnection will be subject to ongoing legislative contestation. Nonetheless, open access provisions were 'attached as contractual requirements for any firms taking grant money', which some are reading as a purposeful intervention by legislators (Corbin 2009).

Digital delays

Media convergence, broadly conceived, has critical implications for the provision of universal communication services. We need to recognize that traditional media have evolved to the point where online platforms are now integrated and necessary components of their businesses. Therefore, the line between digital broadcasting and the Internet is no longer so clearly demarcated. Digital television has given 'further impetus to the technology convergence between the broadcasting, telecommunications and computer industries' (Starks 2007: 2). And in the process of conversion of analogue television services to digital services, the full potential of digital spectrum remains to be examined. The interplay between digital broadcasting and the Internet is indisputably an evolving and multifaceted project. In this sense, the ubiquitous penetration of digital television when switchover is completed offers enormous scope for universal connectivity to a full range of services. These include higher bandwidth applications in e-commerce, e-learning, e-health and general entertainment. However, the transition to digital has been smoother in some countries than others, with authorities underestimating the full range of mitigating factors.

In the USA, the passing of the Digital Television Delay Act 2009 sent an unequivocal signal that the policy and planning measures to switch from analogue to free-to-air television had not worked out as intended. But the original plans have not been that far off, considering the scale of the exercise. The change in the original US switchover date from 17 February 2009 to 12 June 2009, only approximately three months, has been attributed to a combination of planning and political factors:

- an underfunded coupon programme to help pay for analog converter boxes;
- public outreach in some markets that raised concerns about whether the switch could be accomplished without a big disruption;
- too little effort, too late by government agencies to deal with consumer confusion;
- President Barack Obama and Congressional Democrats having little to gain by rushing forward with the February switchover date.

It was reported that one month before the scheduled switchover, 5.7 per cent of households were 'completely unprepared for digital TV and would lose their TV signal'. Moreover, those surveys indicated that minority groups were more deeply affected than the bulk of the American population. The Nielsen survey data showed '9.9% of African American and 9.7% of Hispanic households were completely unready, with particular problems in big markets including Dallas, Houston, Phoenix and Los Angeles' (Tienowitz 2009).

Characteristic of most decision-making in the cultural industries where audience consumption, governance and business decision-making intersect, there is a great deal of financial and commercial risk involved in digital broadcasting transition processes (Hesmondhalgh 2007: 19). In the USA, network owners were confronted with the question, should they delay their move, or go ahead and switch, possibly putting a large number of very unhappy viewers into darkness? The FCC, responsible for implementing and monitoring the switch, released figures which told the transition story. By 17 February 2009, approximately 421 stations had switched off their analogue signals. Adding these to the 220 that had already switched off their analogue services, some 641 were switched over. This represented only 36 per cent of the total number of 1,800 full-power television stations in the US (FCC Media Release 2009). With a new President in the Oval Office and the FCC under the acting Chairmanship of Democrat appointee Michael Copps, the FCC announced that it reserved the right to deny requests from stations to switch early to digital-only 'if they do not serve the public interest' (FCC Public Notice 2009). Interventions invoking 'the public interest' have been extremely rare in the last few years at the FCC while under Republican control, and so this statement was a telling sign of the times.

It is clear that the contingencies of geography are playing a considerable role in DTV rollouts. In the US market, Hawaii is a case in point. Before even the specific digital transition issues arise, the 50th state has experienced less than parity in its television services – having only one or two poorly received stations. It was reported that following the switchover date for the Hawaiian market of 15 January, over 1,000 residents were put in the dark. It appears that a new set of poor reception issues arose because of decisions made about the location of transmission towers. Environmental impact now figures in ways that it would not have when free-to-air television was first introduced (Kaufman 2009).

In Australia, the government acknowledged in 2008 that the already amended timetable for digital switchover would be pushed out yet again, an extra year, to the end of 2013 (Conroy 2008). Adoption of DTTB reception technologies has been much slower than the predictions. The schedule therefore extends the simulcast (transmission of analogue and digital signals) period in metropolitan areas to around 13 years (it had initially been eight years and then nine years). This included the news that the switchover scheduling would be reversed: the decision was made to end the switchover in metropolitan rather than rural areas; a politically-attuned measure given that viewers are also voters, and the bulk of them live in cities, not in less densely populated rural, regional and remote areas. The conversion process commences in smaller regional markets in 2010, and it is hoped that these areas will be useful case studies to assist the planners. Data on the take-up of digital television indicate a national average DTTB take-up rate of 41.8 per cent of households in 2008 (ACMA 2008b). This compares to a figure approaching 90 per cent in the UK (Ofcom 2008b).

Digital conversion policy in Australia has required multiple ongoing adjustments, and exhibited characteristic signs of a process that is overly responsive to private, incumbent corporate interests (Given 2003). Major criticisms of the conversion include doubts over the merits of policy restricting the genres of multichannel services of the national (PSB) broadcasters and the creation of entirely new categories of services ('datacasting'), when there was no tangible interest from providers in these potential offerings. The planned auctioning of datacasting licences was abandoned because of a lack of commercial interest. Both of these policies were significantly modified following departmental reviews, and a new body 'Digital Australia' was established to boost interest among Australians. The agency became subsumed within the government when the Rudd Government came to power in late 2007. Since then the Minister, Stephen Conroy, has announced additional initiatives to facilitate digital conversion; this included research to track uptake of DTTB, public awareness of the digital switchover programme; and the development of a logo and labelling scheme to help consumers identify digitally-ready products (Conroy 2008).

But the slow rate of adoption is far from surprising when it is considered that commercial broadcasters have little incentive to promote rapid take-up of DTTB. After all, broadcasting their signals in both analogue and digital formats, and the commissioning and development of hit programmes on their multichannel services are a very expensive and risky business. Audience taste preferences are probably more complex than ever at a time of fragmenting mediaspheres. In this context of proliferating sources of media entertainment and information, and the shift of advertising expenditures to the Internet, the switchover process is a difficult one for any nation.

From a network edge perspective, there are geographical variations in the rollout between most countries, including in the UK. A protracted implementation in the UK was prefigured by a policy that sought to duplicate the coverage of the analogue network (98.5 per cent). This has meant the installation of over 1,000 small transmitters for the last few per cent of coverage. Elsewhere, nations such as Germany avoided this by recourse to satellite technology. But, overall, the UK implementation has been the exemplar for other nations to emulate; starting earlier (the first country beginning in 1998), and having a gradualist and relatively long rollout has guaranteed a high rate of take-up. It has not been without some flaws: for example, as Michael Starks has described, a hasty start by ITV Digital, using unproven technologies, was one of the reasons for its collapse in 2002, and analogue switchover only became possible when Freeview was so successful (Starks 2007).

Conclusion

In this chapter, in considering the transition to widespread take-up of Internet broadband and digital terrestrial television, my intention was to unpack the very politicized way that decision-making takes place, invariably involving the preferences of powerful media and communications corporations and governments. The chapter considered the argument that a mix of technologies will be required in attempts to suit the circumstances of universal broadband services in specific nations and regions. The potential role of new broadband technologies (including wireless infrastructures such as 'WiFi' and 'WiMAX') should not be underestimated, nor should the capacity of promised **next generation networks** to provide information and entertainment to communities 'at the network edge'. Against the neoliberal tide, there is renewed support for an economic model based on subsidies and grants as the only sustainable way that fast, reliable broadband reaches, markets that corporations deem 'uneconomic'.

A similar story can be seen in the much awaited, and yet insufficiently publicized, transition to digital terrestrial television. The digital TV conversion process tells us about the management of risk in a high profile cultural industry sector, and the need for an open dialogue between governments, market actors and the wider publics in whose benefit the whole process is said to be undertaken in the first place.

Further reading

Castells, M. (2001) *The Internet Galaxy: Reflections on the Internet, Business and Society*. Oxford: Oxford University Press.

Chester, J. (2007) *Digital Destiny: New Media and the Future of Democracy*. New York: The New Press.

European Commission (2008) *Broadband Access in the EU*. Brussels, 28 November DG INFSO/B3, COCOM08-41 FINAL. See http://www.broadband-europe.eu/Lists/DocumentsData/Attachments/70/Broadband_data_july_08_EN.pdf.

Lax, S. (2001) 'Information, education and inequality: Is new technology the solution?' in S. Lax (ed.) *Access Denied in the Information Age*. Basingstoke: Palgrave.

Murdock, G. and Golding, P. (2004) 'Dismantling the digital divide: Rethinking the dynamics of participation and exclusion,' in A. Calabrese and C. Sparks (eds) *Toward a Political Economy of Culture: Capitalism and Communication in the 21st Century*. Maryland, MD: Rowman and Littlefield.

OECD (2009) *Broadband Portal*. http://www.oecd.org/sti/ict/broadband.

Starks, M. (2007) *Switching to Digital Television: UK Public Policy and the Market*. Bristol: Intellect.

6 | CONCLUSION

Media convergence has provided an analysis of the key components of media industry change in the first decade of the twenty-first century. A core argument has been that changing industry and audience practices, including the increasing uptake of online and mobile media, and the continuing liberalization of media ownership rules are closely interconnected. My argument has been that a priority policy concern for governments and their regulatory agencies needs to be the way these components are threatening to diminish voice diversity in digital media systems. As one of the clearer instances of the long-term meaning for society of these changes, trends in convergent news production and distribution in particular have the potential for more immediate and serious ramifications for the construction of all social and cultural diversities. It is an area crying out for systematic empirical research in various comparative national settings.

Throughout the book we have seen that there is an ongoing trend for traditional media corporations that had a dominant role in the previous century, including for use by advertisers, to now colonize the online space. This is being achieved through the usual corporate techniques of mergers and acquisition as deals are continuously sought and negotiated through asymmetrical power relations. The way these deals restructure the media industries, both institutionally and in terms of work practices, and how media products are made, distributed and consumed will vary, depending on the sectors involved. Typically, however, there will be some recognizable patterning and consequences. For example, in the context of an analysis of 'convergent' newsrooms, it has been argued that 'technological convergence and corporate concentration must be understood as part of the strategy of media owners to acquire new sources for profit, extending their control over the relations of production and distribution of news' (see Deuze 2008, 2009). In this connection, as Napoli notes, there is a growing body of evidence that questions the often heard suggestion in policy-making circles, 'that regulation of traditional media's ownership and market structure is no longer necessary because the Internet provides a robust and viable alternative to them'. The implications of this are that 'the more the Web exhibits the characteristics of traditional media, the less relevant this argument becomes' (Napoli 2008: 66).

The account of media change and concentration of ownership presented in the book is a familiar process that we can describe as 'capitalist accumulation'. The updated description in the context of intensifying Internet protocol networks and e-commerce is 'digital capitalism' (Schiller 1999) or 'informational capitalism' (Castells 2000). A point that I want to emphasize in this concluding chapter is that citizens and consumers need to have a critical alertness to the bigger picture, where convergence and digitalization are being used by media corporations to redesign the terms of people's engagements with the media. In this process, place-based audience formations like publics and communities are being supplemented with, and in some cases replaced by, web-based global consumerist alternatives, virtual communities and social networks, often linked to particular services, brands and product flows. There are consequences for the relative availability of 'serious' and 'light' content, and a Giddensian structuration model would hold that both 'agents' and 'structures' co-determine how individuals actually access media content in a 'marketplace of attention' (Webster 2008: 31). An equally important question though, and which I have hopefully highlighted in previous chapters is, 'in what proportion, how are they aggregated, and which content prevails in particular genre, site or medium contexts?' A regular diet of Google News may give audiences a very different set of information resources than more active media-seeking habits based on specifically selected sources. There is no doubt that, in tandem with people's level of education and general media literacies, people do occupy a habitus of media consumption; and that it is possible to 'account' for these patterns on the basis of **audience taste publics** and hierarchies (Bennett et al. 1999).

The phenomenal growth of the Internet has approximately a quarter of the world's population 'using the Internet'; mobile phone penetration has reached twice that number, and Internet connectivity to an expanding array of devices is on an ever-upward spike (www.internetworldstats.com). Inevitably, media convergence as a rhetorical terminology has evolved in parallel to developments in media industries themselves. A Rubik's cube metaphor offers a heuristic calculus for media convergence: interacting industry/user elements and seemingly endless permutations can be used to explain market, audience and policy developments arising from different combinations of industry, technological, network and regulatory and media genres, as we saw in the Introduction. In this context, I agree with Fagerjord and Storsul's assessment that

> *Convergence* is used as a *rhetorical tool* in order to facilitate reform. The concept communicates a media landscape undergoing significant change. This has been instrumental in convincing politicians, regulators, investors and other market players that their strategies need to adapt.
>
> (2007: 28)

And so, in spite of the popularization of the term, it continues on its trajectory from the early 1980s and then the 1990s, and now through the noughties, to have cultural and politico-economic discursive affectivity for the particular constituencies who mobilize it.

Similarly, the idea of the Internet as a media convergence exemplar is both a simplification of complex and unfolding industry developments that aids understanding, and a set of unfolding developments that can be empirically verified. Napoli makes a compelling argument in this regard, citing an observation by Wellman that 'earlier Internet research focused primarily on prognostications. The second stage involved the basic mapping of user behaviour, and only now have we entered the stage where the dynamics of Internet usage are being subject to robust empirical analysis' (Napoli 2008: 66). Though he adds a further important qualification

> However, not all aspects of Internet research are at the same evolutionary stage. While we are developing a sophisticated understanding of the dynamics of Internet usage, our understanding of the production side is not so far along. Today we are still very much embedded in Wellman's second stage of analysis as it relates to the production and presentation of Web content. This 'mapping' of the online space is well developed. We are developing a strong sense of the distribution of links – of who links to whom and how often. However, we do not yet understand very well the dynamics of the linking decision-making process. What factors determine whether a site is linked to another site? Why do certain sites become important nodes in Web space while others languish in relative obscurity? Inquiries in this vein have been infrequent up to this point.
>
> (2008: 66)

The suggested agenda is one that would be familiar to many media researchers: investigating 'the dynamics of the linking decision-making process' in the online media space has become a subset of the researching wider conditions of media concentration and its consequences for the provision of media content. Obviously this field is a fast moving target. For example, Halavais argues that the 'long-predicted Semantic Web, a Web that provides both content and information about how that content is related has been slow in coming', but there are early signs of its arrival. Metadata in forms of tagging, usage data arising from certain content management systems, blogging tools, and other forms of 'reflexing hyperlinking' are rendering new meanings onto the practice of hyperlinking (Halavais 2008: 52; 2009: 29, 188). Hyperlinked networks are a social morphology that is necessarily scaffolded by human agency: its successor innovations will undoubtedly become the new media objects of our research agenda.

Information infrastructures, diversity, scale

We can reasonably ask the question, 'Is it possible to overstate the transformative powers of new media infrastructures?' Media theorist and cultural geographer, David Morley, has provided an historical analysis of the social and cultural construction of technologies within modernity, arguing that market fundamentalisms that rely on economic policies underpinned by science, technology and the 'rational' can be likened to a deity. He suggests that

> If Comte and Saint-Simon worshipped the beneficially transformative powers of the new communications systems of their day, in the form of canals and railways, and both early twentieth-century American capitalists and Soviet communists worshipped the benefits of electricity, today it is the Internet which is enshrined as the ultimate source of goodness and progress.
>
> (Morley 2007: 314)

Neoliberal ideologies (manifestly the most widely dispersed form of market fundamentalism) are coupled with a technologically determinist vision that anticipates 'a convergence in forms of social life (and values) around one, rational solution, which . . . is the nub of Fukuyama's hymn to the inevitable worldwide triumph of free-market capitalism' (2007: 314).

Predictably, with all new media technologies, as we discussed in the Introduction, their arrival is shaped by competing corporate interests, with governments being involved to varying extents, and they are always underwritten by prevailing ideologies, or ways of envisioning their utility. The current period of economic 'stimulus' measures by governments and investment in public works programmes, including for broadband 'nation-building' infrastructures, is surprisingly *contre-courant* of the prevailing 'let the market provide' ideologies of neoliberalism. In a timely policy research report for the US Congressional Research Service entitled *Infrastructure Programs: What's Different About Broadband*, the authors note that broadband in the United States may be distinguished in several ways from 'conventional infrastructure' programmes, and this warrants different treatment by government. These distinctive features include:

- Virtually all broadband networks in the United States are privately owned and financed through private capital markets.
- In most geographic markets, there are two or more broadband networks offering competing services over their own facilities, rather than a single provider.
- The competing broadband networks generally employ different technologies and each of these technologies has somewhat different capabilities.
- Each is also experiencing rapid technological progress, making it difficult to predict which technology will prove most successful from a technical or commercial perspective.
- Because the capabilities of these technologies are at various stages of development, some broadband network technologies may be better able than others to meet a stimulus package requirement to be quickly deployable, though perhaps at the expense of long-term productivity and innovation.
- Most broadband network providers are vertically integrated into the production of downstream services/applications that they provide to customers over their own networks.
- These applications compete with the offerings of independent applications providers that also must ride over the broadband networks to reach customers and therefore are dependent on access to those networks.

(Goldfarb and Kruger 2009)

Moreover, the report notes that, in rural areas, limited demand and the high costs of rolling out broadband networks preclude private investment in the absence of government subsidy programmes. There is a twin-edged problem of scale economies neither allowing affordable services, nor the subsidy of multiple providers because of the small markets. In comparison to urban dwellers, rural dwellers will always be disadvantaged in this sense.

As the authors of the report argue, one of the principal complexities of designing a programme to support privately-owned infrastructure is that the private profit-maximizing objectives of different providers will rarely match the public policy objectives. There are many supply-side and demand-side factors, then, which make government policies to accelerate broadband take-up a very problematic policy object. Even on the demand-side there are fundamental computer access issues that several 'digital divide' studies have documented, showing constraints on Internet access, such as this US one:

But many observers believe that the cost of a home computer – the customer premise equipment needed to gain access to broadband services – is a greater deterrent to households purchasing broadband access service. According to an October 2008 study by Connected Nation 74%t of all U.S. households own home computers, but computer ownership levels are significantly lower for specific demographic groups: 44% for households with annual income less than $25,000, 44% for older households (65 or older), 51% for people with disabilities, 60% for households headed by adults with no college education, and 64% for African-American households. Some observers therefore have proposed that any broadband infrastructure package include a subsidy program for targeted populations to purchase household computers.

(2009: 18)

These kinds of subsidy programmes are being increasingly discussed. And as media industries evolve, including importantly the rollout of faster and higher bandwidth broadband and growing online news consumption, these issues will remain a high priority for national governments. The UK's regulator Ofcom has promised a 'flexible' 'private sector-led' interventionist policy role that offers the promise of meeting both competitive industry and 'customer' needs for 'super-fast broadband' by:

- allowing wholesale pricing flexibility to enable returns appropriate to the considerable risks of building new networks, but constrained by the market in the interests of customers;
- ensuring that any regulatory pricing allows investors the opportunity to earn a rate of return that genuinely reflects the cost of deployment and the associated level of risk;
- minimizing unnecessary inefficiencies in network design and build as a result of regulatory policies, while continuing to protect the consumer interest;
- supporting the use of new, more flexible wholesale services by BT to offer super-fast services to other service providers and consumers at competitive prices;
- safeguarding the opportunity for further competition based on physical infrastructure, by facilitating fair opportunities for companies to synchronize their investments with BT's deployments, should reasonable demand arise, and encouraging network design that takes future potential competition into account.

(Ofcom 2009)

Inevitably, some of the main features of both infrastructure and content provision will be shaped by these and other basic economic forces. In this regard,

Napoli's 'forces of massification thesis' observes that some fundamental processes of audience media consumption, media economics and institutional arrangements all tend to compel new media technologies, and most notably the Internet, to function in evolutionary ways similar to traditional media systems (Napoli 2008: 56). Therefore, audiences in Internet contexts still seek out higher production budgeted content 'typically geared to mass appeal'. This tendency in itself works against the availability of a more diverse repertoire of content. As Napoli argues: 'It is somewhat telling that the typical television viewer, in an environment of channel abundance, regularly consumes only about 13 of the available channels – and that is roughly the same as the number of Web sites that the typical person visits on a regular basis.'

Powerful economies of scale together with the key characteristics of 'public goods' (high fixed costs, low variable costs, nondepletability) are another force operating to make online media like traditional media, and to *distribute* media products made by traditional media outlets. The high risks that could be borne by traditional media corporations in originating new content, by virtue of their scale and market capitalization are also working in the online world to the appeal of very large audiences. This is not to say there are not also exceptions working on the one-to-one and one-to-many model, as has been discussed previously in this book. However, it is now an empirically well-documented backdrop to new media industries growth that concentration and conglomeration of large media corporations have been defensive mechanisms under capitalist organization from the latter half of the twentieth century (Murdock and Golding 1977: 28).

Furthermore, there is an evident pattern of web searchers who tend to not go beyond the first page of links, thus constraining the potential interaction. Similarly, the prominence of the hugely popular content aggregators such as YouTube, MySpace, Hulu, Joost and their ilk have been achieved on the back of their ability to 'confine the vastness and complexity of the Web into a simpler and more manageable framework' (Napoli 2008: 61). Clustering around a relatively small number of content options is a mirror to the traditional media **'power law' of distribution of audience** attention (and/or the amount spent), with '20% of available content attracting 80% of the audience'. This pattern is being replicated in online spaces, and the presence of traditional media (as discussed in Chapter 2) underlines the similarity of traditional media institutional arrangements. And very importantly for the shape and organization of online media, 'this clustering of audiences also continues to be associated with patterns in advertiser behaviour that are consistent with the massification effects of audience measurement' (Napoli 2008). This means that 'established audience measurement systems naturally favour sites that attract large audiences (in the perception of advertisers)' and consequentially, explains why the 'most popular websites attract a share of online advertising dollars that exceeds their share of the online audience . . . and creates important economic disincentives for serving narrower, more specialized audiences online' (2008: 62). The recurring patterning in legacy and new media organization points to systemic failures in the economics of content provision.

New welfarist models of media communications policy

In my view, there is renewed merit and substantive appeal in revisiting 'welfarist' media communications policy models: events in financial markets make this return even more salient than ever. In economies around the globe, economic policy is now being rewritten, and earlier models reconsidered and updated. And so too should we take an integrated, contextualized approach to media and communications policies. Welfarist theories of governance provide frameworks for citizen-centred arguments based on a view that future media and communications infrastructure models can include ideas of diversity of content, platforms and ownership.

Burgelman has made a persuasive case for revisiting welfarist policy frameworks for communications media (Burgelman 1997). He writes, 'The rise of new conservatism, the pressures of financial capitalism, the economic recession since the seventies' oil crisis and all kinds of technological innovations put an increasing strain on this social contract and/or render it illegitimate in many people's eyes.' By 'social contract,' he is referencing the typical set of policies in advanced Western democracies for the construction of the welfare state post-World War II, being based on the existence of an implicit or explicit understanding between the individual and the state that there should be a safety net of provision, in employment, health, education and other services, not exposed to a ruthless market society. These set of policies provided a universal guarantee for the protection of citizens. For Burgelman, welfarist policies in general, and for communications in particular, offer an alternative to neoliberal orthodoxy. If they are not taken up,

> It remains to be seen for how long this model can be maintained, taking into account the fundamental social transformations that accompany the change towards the information society (marginalisation of the working classes, degradation of the middle classes, polarisation of the social field and ageing of the population in general).
>
> (Burgelman 1997)

More specifically in the context of the growth of an informational or network society, Burgelman reflects on whether everyone will be able to access the new services on the information infrastructure, on 'whether there will be a real choice between the 400 available channels, and whether or not the average citizen will fall victim to the feared social polarisation brought about by the information infrastructure'. His concern, then, is with the potential for communication systems to deliver a broadly conceived, and socially representative, 'social diversity'. He is critical of conceptualizations which construct a binary of state/pure market actors, preferring more dynamic understandings of ideas such as 'universal service' or 'public service' that include a renewed social contract between labour, capital and government.

A question that has moved to the foreground in discussions of changing media industries is whether maintaining democracy and economic prosperity are simultaneously achievable goals. The answer, as is often the case, may partially lie in existing studies. For instance, Castells and Himanen, in their classic case study of Finnish society, conclude that

> Finland has been able to combine technological innovation and economic dynamism with the welfare state and legitimizing identity. In a time of increasing stress in the model of global development, it is worthwhile for all of us to reflect on the conditions and processes underlying the emergence of a socially sustainable network society, as represented by the recent experience of Finland.
>
> (2002: 14)

They do not put Finland forward as the example *par excellence* and 'do not wish to imply that Finland is an ideal model that other should try to imitate'. Instead, they argue that the information society can exist in a 'plurality of models, the same way that the industrial society developed in very different, and even antagonistic, models of modernity, for instance, in the United States and the Soviet Union, as well as in Scandinavia or Japan' (2002: 2). Their suggestion is that information societies share common structural features:

> It is based on knowledge generation and information processing, with the help of micro-electronics based information technologies; it is organized in networks; and its core activities are networked on a global scale, working as a unit in real time thanks to the infrastructure of telecommunications and transportation. This socio-technical structure develops and expands on the basis of its superior performing capacity, by phasing out through competition the organizational forms from the industrial era that are based on vertical, less flexible forms of management and implementation, less able to globalize their operating models.
>
> (2002: 3)

So the argument is that societies at various stages of informationalization are on a trajectory towards these characteristics. Coming off disparate base levels of development, as a by-product of unique cultural histories, there will be divergent interpretations and implementations. As they argue, 'there is no one model of the information society, ultimately represented by the United States and California, that serves as the standard of modernity', precisely because the significance of the Information Age is that 'it is a global, diverse, multicultural reality' (2002: 3).

Interestingly, the authors set out to ask the question 'Is the welfare state a contributing force to the full development of informationalisation?' Their answer is that in addition to the nation's top position in technological, economic development, social justice and exclusion, access to education, public health care indices, Finland's sense of national identity underpins a legitimacy that authorizes state intervention in their information society (2002: 4–14).

Clearly, Finland does very effectively combine, as their data shows, the information society with the welfare state. Their analysis is focused on the Finnish model of 'informational welfare state', whose core is 'the virtuous cycle of the informational economy and the welfare state' (2002: 89). There are many interacting, and in certain respects, unique elements in the Finnish informational welfare state. Notwithstanding this, Castells and Himanen offer several concluding 'lessons' as proof of the existing alternatives to Silicon Valley. They argue that a dynamic new economy is not incompatible with a 'fully fledged welfare state'; indeed, they see it is a decisive factor in its growth and stability. Contrary to neoliberal orthodoxy, 'this welfare state is not sustainable without a high level of taxation' but this is not problematic with growing productivity and competitiveness and the valuing of a higher quality of life for all. There are, of course many other contributory factors in their story, such as industrial relations, targeted state policies, and cultures of technological innovation and identity politics behind their success. As always, there are caveats. Significantly, it is quite *atypical* in their cultural diversities: Finnish society is in many ways a very homogeneous society that has been sheltered from foreign investment and participation, and this is their greatest challenge.

Informationalism and democracy

At a fundamental level, the information society is underpinned by the traditions of representative liberal democracy and capitalism. While information and communications have increased in significance within these economic systems, capitalist priorities and pressures remain, and market criteria and pressures decisively influence innovation and informational developments.

Capitalism is colonizing the online media space and there is commodification of information at a time when transnational corporate capitalism is a dominant form. It is not that surprising, then, that the information society will embed capitalist imperatives and information will be developed for predominantly private, not public ends. The term 'Information Society' is not without its critics. Frau-Meigs, for instance, notes that it is increasingly 'criticized for its unified and hegemonic version of globalisation . . . Unesco and civil society actors tend to prefer "Knowledge Societies" ' (Frau-Meigs 2007: 34).

Yet the problem is that the commodification of information and cultural experiences more generally creates tension with concepts of democracy and citizenship as we considered previously. Lévy (1997) argues that the information society is characterized by the creation of a new anthropological space, the knowledge space, and our prosperity depends on how nations, regions, businesses and individuals navigate this space. Lévy's view of the future is one where society is organized around two trajectories: the recreation of the social bond through our relation to knowledge, and the development of a collective intelligence. However, the development of Lévy's concept of collective intelligence and renewal of the social bond assumes public use and access to knowledge.

But the dominant capitalist (or consumerist) model rewards and favours the commodification of information and the corporatization of information production. Information will be produced mostly for private, rather than public use. The marketizing nature of consumer capitalism frames how rights are defined, and social goals are achieved. Murdock and Golding have argued that markets address people as consumers rather than citizens, presenting the freedom to choose between competing products as the central freedom of the modern world. So the problem is that within a market society, citizen's rights are narrowed to a set of economic rights (Murdock and Golding 1989). Burgelman (1997, 2000) considers the dominant policy discourse of leaving the development of communications to market forces is as problematic as it is unsustainable, and Mansell (1999) considers it as being unable to provide unfettered access to new communications spaces.

In my view, what this points to is a significant narrowing of citizen's rights, at the precise time when the communications media sector is becoming the ground on which debates on labour, education and democracy are potentially given oxygen. And it is also at a time when communication policy must be considered as part of the framework from within which social policy itself arises (Burgelman 2000). Since communications policy increasingly underpins social policy, the tendency is for the dominant rhetoric to focus on economic (or more accurately consumer) rights, and civil, social and political rights tend to fall outside its scope. In other words, the dominant policy rhetorics, including those connected with media convergence, falls short of considering all aspects of what citizenship means within the information society.

Neoliberalism, at the very least, has very visibly failed at a populist ideological level in the so-called 'global financial crisis', giving renewed legitimacy to calls for interventionist policies by governments in the interests of all citizens. Such intervention can be in very practical ways, with long-term consequences, as the role of public service broadcasting has provided ample evidence of in 80-plus years.

Utopian visions of converging media and communications technologies have often carried a democratic inflection of a participatory polity: convergence will bring 'the good life' along with democracy, citizenship and participation (Storsul and Stuedahl 2007: 12). This was seen in the 1970s 'cable fable' fantasy of an informational, interactive world brought about by new cable technologies (Streeter 1987). In the past 50 years we've seen the inexorable 'rise of the verticals' (vast media empires or just 'big media') and now we are witnessing their continuing rise at the same time as a flattening out, and accelerating growth of horizontal social networks. However, ultimately, these enormously popular horizontal networks have arisen under the imprimatur of the same vertically organized media conglomerates. This is not to argue that such horizontal (and other more independent networking structures) have not allowed emancipatory countertrends in participatory communications, including mobilizing large-scale social movements, at times with 'smart mobs' using their mobile media devices (Rheingold 2002; Goggin 2006).

The view from here

As should be apparent from the discussion in this book, there are strong pressures to further liberalize ownership policies in all the nations considered, where core components of their regimes have been retained. Recent developments in the UK indicate that further radical liberalization may only be just around the corner. One report suggests that legislation (an outcome of the *Digital Britain* review) is being prepared 'that would tear up merger regimes for television, regional newspapers and local radio as part of the biggest shake-up in media regulation since the beginning of the decade' (Sabbagh 2009). The final report of the *Digital Britain* review does in fact recommend sweeping changes to cross-media laws at the local level:

> The government believes that an arguable case could now be made for greater flexibility in the local radio and cross-media ownership rules to support consolidation of local media groups which taken together would

allow for greater economies of scale and a sustainable local voice alongside that of the BBC. For example, a local radio station and local newspaper could consolidate and share news gathering resources, reduce overheads and help build local brands through cross-promotion.

(DCMS/BIS 2009: 155)

If we look at this issue historically, though, the UK has periodically 'relaxed' cross-media and foreign ownership, as has the USA. And now Australia, in passing radically deregulatory media ownership rules, has allowed the merging of traditional media. Financial engineering in media corporations is, quite rightly, under the microscope in the wake of the financial tsunami in 2008, and specific high-profile debacles such as Sam Zell's failed takeover of Tribune Newspaper Company in the USA, which filed for bankruptcy due to its inability to meet vast debt repayments. The financial health of parts of Australia's commercial free-to-air television sector is in doubt, also labouring under a mountain of debt arising from private equity refinancing. In the event that the sector collapsed, it could trigger a wave of cross-media rationalizations with significant implications industry and audiences.

These circumstances of continuing media consolidation will therefore require innovative public policy, laws and regulation for promoting and maintaining democratic values of diversity and pluralism for the media and communications industries. Media businesses are closely implicated in the performance of neoliberal ideologies and determining the direction, scope and pace of new media audience engagement. The ongoing contest between proprietary media content and more participatory structures of social networking and user created content provision is clearly an ongoing battleground. Access to 'super-fast' broadband is high on the policy agenda of those nation-states that express a desire to participate in the twenty-first-century information society and economies. As the archetypical example of media convergence, broadband infrastructures and applications are now seeing formerly disparate categories of content delivered to a variety of fixed domestic and mobile screen devices. Such diversification of convergence processes will need to be taken into account in future constructions of the universal service provision, for nations which regard themselves as participants in inclusive, globally connected, information societies.

At stake in the debates canvassed throughout this book are the capacities for digital media cultures for shaping a well-informed citizenry. It is to be hoped that the analysis and discussion of these issues will help inform students and other readers' understanding and expectations of the role played by media and communication in society, as well as contributing to ongoing policy development and law reform processes.

Further reading

Castells, M. (2000) *The Information Age: Economy, Society and Culture* (2nd edn). Oxford: Oxford University Press.

Castells, M. and Himanen, P. (2004) *The Information Society and the Welfare State: The Finnish Model*. New York: Oxford University Press.

Deuze, M. (2009) 'Convergence culture and media work,' in J. Holt and A. Perren (eds) *Media Industries: History, Theory, and Method*. Malden, MA: Wiley-Blackwell.

Morley, D. (2007) *Media, Modernity and Technology: The Geography of the New*. London: Routledge.

Napoli, P. (2008) 'Hyperlinking and the forces of massification', in J. Turow and T. Lokman (eds) *The Hyperlinked Society: Questioning Connections in the Digital Age*. Ann Arbor, MI: University of Michigan Press.

GLOSSARY OF KEY TERMS

Audience taste publics: A term that derives from Bourdieu's classic work *Distinction: A Social Critique of the Judgement of Taste*. Media researchers have variously applied the term to correlate 'taste' choices of cultural products and social and cultural capital, or hierarchies, which audiences bring to their media consumption.

Backhaul: The backhaul portion of the network comprises the intermediate links between the core, or backbone, of the network and the small sub-networks at the 'edge' of the entire hierarchical network. For instance, while mobile (cell) phones communicating with a single tower constitute a local sub-network, the connection between the cell tower and the rest of the global telecommunications network begins with a backhaul link to the core of the telecoms company's network (via a point of presence).

Collective intelligence: Pierre Lévy defines collective intelligence as 'A form of universally distributed intelligence, constantly enhanced, coordinated in real time, and resulting in the effective mobilization of skills' (1997: 13). He clarifies this definition by adding that, 'No one knows everything, everyone knows something, all knowledge resides in humanity. There is no transcendent store of knowledge and knowledge is simply the sum of what we know' (1997: 13–14).

Diversity: As well as the notion of a heterogeneity of views and opinion, particularly in relation to news and current affairs content, diversity has also been defined as:

- an inclusive representation of cultural diversity;
- the development of a strong national, regional or local identity in an increasingly internationalized media;
- representation of regional and local issues to regional and local communities;
- a range of viewpoints within media formats and genres; and
- a range of media platforms and output that delivers content relevant for a divergent range of societal groups and interests.

Debates over changes to media ownership laws often reflect different political understandings of what we mean by 'diversity' in media policy discourses. Use of the term has tended to conflate often competing definitions, and has, on occasion, rendered the concept of diversity to mean little more than a multitude of content on proliferating media platforms. As Karpinnen argues: 'It needs to be recognised that any act of constructing the differences against which diversity is analysed or measured is itself an act of power' (Karpinnen 2007: 14).

Gutenburg Galaxy: The term derives from *The Gutenberg Galaxy: The Making of Typographic Man*, a book by Marshall McLuhan, in which he analyses the effects of mass media, especially the printing press, on European culture and human consciousness. McLuhan popularized the term 'Gutenberg Galaxy' which we may now regard today as referring to the accumulated body of recorded works of human art and knowledge, especially books. In particular, the invention of movable type in the development of the printing press was a decisive moment in the change from a culture based on visual logics.

Internet Protocol (IP): The packet data protocol used for routing and carriage of messages across the Internet and similar networks.

Internet Protocol TV (IPTV): IPTV combines new methods of television and/or video programme signal distribution over Internet Protocol platforms and access devices. IPTV, quite literally, combines a managed (or closed Intranet) Internet broadband network with elements of traditional TV, in terms of content, scheduling and generally its overall packaging for audiences to view. These IPTV services hosted on servers in an exchange, means they can be delivered with assured Quality of Service (QoS), as the ISP has more control over the network. IP-VoD or Internet Protocol-Video-on-Demand over the public Internet, which offers services using streaming TV, is sometimes seen as similar to IPTV.

Mediasphere: The sum total of interconnecting texts that may be accessed by people in specific contexts. The mediasphere is shaped by prevailing discourses of power and control in any given society. The term was popularized by John Hartley (1996) who used it to account for the output of media in all its forms. The terms mediasphere and public sphere are linked: ultimately mediaspheres are subsumed within wider public spheres, although the former contributes a great deal to the latter's operations. Public spheres extend beyond mediaspheres because they embrace all unmediatized social interactions, for example, conversations in the pub or café, or discussing a movie. Eschewing singular or unity notions of a 'mediasphere' or 'public sphere', many theorists prefer to talk about the plurality of mediaspheres, public spheres, and the more complex ways in which media can contribute to democracies.

Mediatization: We can understand the term as referencing experiences of how the media are implicated in the production and transmission of messages (Thompson 1995; De Zengotita 2005; Fortunati 2005). In the context of media convergence and changing media industries, we can observe that circuits of mediated meaning are thus embedded in the discourses of media convergence. This kind of self-referentiality between disparate contexts and media texts is a consequence of living in a mediated world.

Nasdaq tech crash: Sometimes also referred to as the bursting of the 'dot-com bubble'; the 'Nasdaq tech crash' was a speculative bubble covering roughly 1995–2001 (which climaxed on 10 March 2000 with the NASDAQ peaking at 5132.52) during which stock markets in Western nations saw their value increase rapidly from growth in the new Internet sector and related fields, but then plunge spectacularly. ('NASDAQ', which stands for National Association of Securities Dealers Automated Quotations, is an American stock exchange that is oriented towards technology stocks. It is the largest electronic screen-based equity securities trading market in the United States. With approximately 3,200 companies, it has more trading volume per day than any other stock exchange in the world.)

Neoliberalism: In *A Brief History of Neoliberalism*, David Harvey defines Neoliberalism as the idea that 'the social good will be maximized' by 'bring[ing] all human action into the domain of the market' (2005: 3). Harvey explains that neoliberalism 'requires technologies of information creation and capacities to accumulate, store, transfer, analyse, and use massive databases to guide decisions in the global marketplace' (2005: 3).

The rival of doctrines of the 'free market' in the United States in the late 1970s, and a social and economic theory that argues that completely free and open markets are the best way of ordering society. Thus it is a return to a once discredited liberalism in political economics, the nineteenth-century espousal of *laissez-faire* economics for free trade in an international division of labour, and minimal state intervention within the nation. For governments in the West, from the 1940s through to the 1970s, neoliberalism was the conventional wisdom that capitalism had to be managed by the state, and that rewards needed to be equalized through welfare entitlements in order to maintain social cohesion (see McGuigan 2005: 230).

Net neutrality: The proposal by a coalition of private sector and public interest groups that no website's traffic should be privileged over any other site.

Next Generation Networks (NGNs): NGN is partly a marketing term but it is also a concept used to describe the replacement of 'legacy' fixed copper wire distribution networks with a more diverse range of higher speed and capacity, mobile and 'nomadic', fibre, wireless and satellite networks. At the heart of the concept is the integration of existing separate voice and data networks into a simpler more flexible network using packet switch and Internet protocols. This will enable voice, text and visual messages to be carried on the same network and for each type of message to be responded to in any of these formats on that network.

Paid and organic listings: Paid Listing is an advertising platform enabling marketers to list their advertisements when specific terms are searched for by Internet users. In doing so, they nominate the price they are willing to pay 'per click' when someone clicks on their advertisement.

An Organic Listing is a look-up service provided by search engines where web pages are categorized and ranked based on their relevancy to a search term query entered by a searcher. Organic results are not paid advertising, and websites cannot appear in organic search results by paying a search engine directly. Rather, these are the search engine's recommendations of content which is deemed most appropriate and relevant to the searcher (Hitwise 2007).

Peer-to-peer architecture (P2P): A Peer-to-peer (or P2P) computer network uses diverse connectivity between participants in a network and the cumulative bandwidth of network participants rather than conventional centralized resources where a relatively low number of servers provide the core value to a service or application (known as a client-server model where communication is usually to and from a central server). P2P networks are typically used for connecting nodes via largely ad hoc connections. Such networks are useful for many purposes. Sharing content files containing audio, video, data or anything in digital format is very common, and real time data, such as telephony traffic, is also passed using P2P technology.

Pluralism: According to Mouffe (2000: 18), the acceptance of pluralism, understood as 'the end of a substantive idea of the good life' is the most important single defining feature of modern liberal democracy that differentiates it from ancient models of democracy. In this sense, pluralism is understood not merely as a fact, something that must be dealt with, but rather as an axiological principle that is 'constitutive at the conceptual level of the very nature of modern democracy and considered as something that we should celebrate and enhance' (Mouffe 2000: 19, cited in Karpinnen 2007: 11).

Power law of distribution of audience: Audience research has noted the phenomenon of audiences clustering around relatively few content options. This so-called 'power law' of the distribution of audience attention (and/or the amount spent), with '20% of available content attracting 80% of the audience' (Napoli, 2008). The popular term is also associated with Anderson's idea of the 'long-tail' (or the 80/20 rule) of fragmented audience use of content, whereby media consumers can mine programme archives for niche programming, or a 'long-tail' of programming (Anderson 2006).

Private equity: Private equity financing refers to a debt-funded buyout of a publicly listed company. The *modus operandi* of private equity investors is to take out an enormous loan, buy a controlling interest in a publicly listed corporation and then 'take the company private' for several years. In this process, it moves the company away from public scrutiny required by stock exchanges. At the same time the principals behind this form of financial engineering reorganize the assets in an attempt to remove lower performing components. The end game is then to refloat the company with a view to selling it back to public ownership at a higher price than when they privatized it. The revenue streams of the company are used to finance the interest payments on their debt (Keen 2008).

Propaganda model: The propaganda model describes a decentralized and nonconspiratorial market system of control and processing, although at times the government or one or more private actors may take initiatives and mobilize coordinated elite handling of an issue. It is not claimed that the propaganda model explains everything or that it shows media omnipotence and complete effectiveness in manufacturing consent. It is a model of media behaviour and performance, not of media effects (Herman 2003).

Public sphere: According to Habermas:

> By the 'public sphere', we mean first of all a realm of our social life in which something approaching public opinion can be formed. Access is guaranteed to all citizens. A portion of the public sphere comes into being in every conversation in which private individuals assemble to form a public body.
>
> (Habermas 1984: 49)

In this idealized conception we include the public spaces of work, leisure, politics, religion, academia and mediaspheres, where issues and ideas are encountered, articulated, negotiated and discussed as part of the ongoing process of forming opinions in democratic societies.

Really simple syndication (RSS): Really simple syndication feeds are an easy way to be alerted when content that interests you appears on your favourite Web sites. Instead of visiting a particular Web site to browse for new articles and features, RSS automatically tells you when something new is posted online.

Semantic web: A web that provides both content and information about how that content is related has been slow in coming, but there are early signs of its arrival. Metadata in forms of tagging, usage data arising from certain content management systems, blogging tools, and other forms of 'reflexing hyperlinking' are rendering new meanings onto the practice of hyperlinking.

Silo structures: This term refers to the separate broadcasting, telecommunications, publishing, and information technology industries that can be described as 'preconvergence' and bound up with the previous industrial mass production organizations of the 'Fordist' period.

Structural/functional separation: Structural separation refers to the creation of separate companies with ownership controls, which prevent retail service providers, including the incumbent's downstream businesses, from having effective control in the network infrastructure. Functional separation, which is a similar term, refers to the practice of imposing and obligation of 'equivalence' on a vertically integrated network provider to ensure all retail service providers, including its own downstream business, are treated equally.

Technological determinism: A belief that technology develops independently of society and in so doing is the central cause of consequent social 'impacts'. Widely challenged, nevertheless the idea is found in many historical accounts of social change and lies behind countless predictions of future social trends. An alternative perspective on the use of new media technologies is to see them as part of social development and part of social and cultural practices.

Universal service obligation (USO): USO arrangements refer to the fundamental access and service provision regimes offered by networks that have traditionally been regulated by governments in developed countries. USO arrangements vary from country to country, but, in general, the current understanding of the term is that all users regardless of location can access quality voice service at an affordable price. Increasingly, governments are under pressure to include new media, including broadband, in these arrangements.

Value chain: The value chain is a conceptual tool used to disaggregate the activities of a firm or industry sector into a series of sequential processes moving from supply to demand or, inputs to outputs. These processes are the set of tasks performed to create goods and services. Each task, for example, 'production' or 'packaging' or 'distribution', is reviewed from the perspective of the 'value' it adds to the final product or service. With the introduction of the Internet changes to value chains brought by, for example, 'disintermediation', meant that 'unbundled' or new value elements were introduced.

Voice over Internet Protocol or VoIP: This works by converting voice into a digital signal (using Internet Protocol packets) that travels over the Internet via a broadband connection. Using specific software, VOIP converts the voice signal from the caller's telephone into a digital signal then converts it back at the other end to enable voice communication with anyone with a phone number. Typically, callers use the software on their computer, a handset connected to their broadband modem, or certain kinds of mobile (cell) handsets, to send and receive calls. VoIP offers several benefits including cost savings and nomadicity – or the ability to use the service in different locations.

Web 2.0: A term used to describe a perceived second generation of web-based communities and services (such as social networking sites and wikis) which facilitate collaboration and sharing between users. It refers to the idea of 'Network as platform' – delivering (and allowing users to use) applications entirely through a Web browser; users own the data on the site and can exert some control over the data; an architecture of participation and democracy that encourages users to add value to the application as they use it, often with a rich, interactive, user-friendly interface. The growing prevalence (and popularity) of Web 2.0 sites, which for many users have made using the Internet a more creative, engaging experience are another factor that may be driving increasing average times online. Social networking websites such as Facebook, Wikipedia and YouTube allow users to create their own profiles and/or upload content (such as text, pictures and video) for others to view and comment on.

REFERENCES

AAP (2005) 'News Corp continues online push', *Sydney Morning Herald Online*, 9 September 2005. Available at: http://www.smh.com.au/news/breaking/news-corp-con-tinues-online-push/2005/09/09/1125772669368.html.

AAP (2009) 'AAP offshoot aims for the stars', *Business Day*, 20 January.

ACCC (2008) Media Release, 26 August.

ACMA (2005) *Digital Media in Australian Homes, Monograph 1. Telecommunications Performance Report, 2004–2005*. Available at: www.acma.gov.au.

ACMA (2008a) *Fixed-mobile Convergence and Fixed-mobile Substitution in Australia, ACMAsphere*, Issue 34, September.

ACMA (2008b) *The Australian VoIP Market*. Canberra: Australian Communications and Media Authority.

ACMA (2008c) Media Release, 23/2008, 14 March 2008.

Agar, J. (2003) *Constant Touch – A Global History of the Mobile Phone*. Cambridge: Icon.

Agence France Press (2007) 'NBC, Viacom join in YouTube copyright battle', 8 May.

Agence France Press (2008) 'Canada restricts media ownership', AFP, 15 January.

Allan, S. (2006) *Online News: Journalism and the Internet*. Maidenhead: Open University Press.

Allan, S. (2007) 'Citizen journalism and the rise of "mass self-communication": reporting the London bombings', *Global Media Journal*, Australian edition, volume 1, issue 1.

Allan, S. and Matheson, D. (2004) 'Online journalism in the information age', *Knowledge, Work & Society*, 2(3): 73–94.

Anderson, B. (1983) *Imagined Communities: Reflections on the Origin and Spread of Nationalism*. London: Verso.

Anderson, C. (2006) *The Long Tail: Why the Future of Business is Selling Less of More*. New York: Random House.

Anderson, N. (2007a) 'Viacom sues YouTube for "brazen" copyright infringement', *Ars Technica*, 13 March.

Anderson, N. (2007b) 'Filter this: new YouTube filter greeted by concerns over fair use', *Ars Technica*, 16 October.

Appadurai, A. (1996) *Modernity at Large: Cultural Dimensions of Globalization*. Minneapolis: University of Minnesota Press.

Australian Communications Authority (1998) *Digital Data Inquiry*. Melbourne: ACA.

Australian Communication and Media Authority (2008) *Digital Television in Australian Homes – 2007*. Available at: http://www.acma.gov.au/WEB/STANDARD/pc=PC_311307.

Australian Competition and Consumer Commission (2008) Media Release, 26 August.

Bagdikian, B. (2004) *The New Media Monopoly*. Boston: Beacon Press.

Baker, C. E. (2007) *Media Concentration and Democracy: Why Ownership Matters*. New York: Cambridge University Press.

Balogh, S. (2007) 'Press baron, Conrad Black, 63, sent to prison', 12 December. Available at: heraldsun.com.au.

Barr, T. (2000) *Newmedia.com.au: The Changing Face of Australia's Media and Communications*. Sydney: Allen and Unwin.

BBC (2007) 'Terra Nova private equity group to buy EMI', 21 May.

Beck, U. and Beck-Gernsheim, E. ([2001] (2002)) *Individualization – Institutionalized Individualism and its Social and Political Consequences*. London: Sage.

Benkler, Y. (2006) *The Wealth of Networks: How Social Production Transforms Markets and Freedom*. New Haven, CT: Yale University Press.

Bennett, T., Emmison, M. and Frow, J. (1999) *Accounting for Tastes: Australian Everyday Cultures*. Cambridge: Cambridge University Press.

Benton Foundation (2008) 'House subcommittee votes to stop FCC media ownership rule', 17 June. Available at: Benton.org.

Bettig, R. and Hall, J. (2003) *Big Media, Big Money: Cultural Texts and Political Economics*. Lanham, MD: Rowman and Littlefield.

Bingemann, M. (2008) 'Conroy pulls the plug on $1billion Opel Broadband Project', ITNews, 2 April. Available at: http://www.itnews.com.au/News/73118.

Boltanski, L. and Chiapello, E. ([1999] (2006)) *The New Spirit of Capitalism*. London: Verso.

Bolter, J.D. and Grusin, R. (1999) *Remediation: Understanding New Media*. Cambridge, MA: The MIT Press.

Bolton, T. (2006) 'News on the Net: a critical analysis of the potential of online alternative journalism to challenge the dominance of mainstream news media', *Scan: News and the Net: Convergences and Divergences*, 3(1), June. Available at: http://scan.net.au/scan/journal/display.php?journal_id=71.

Boltz, N. (1993) *Am Ende der Gutenberg-Galaxis: Die neuen Kommunikationsverhältnisse*. München: Fink Verlag.

Bourdieu, P. and Wacquant, L. (2001) 'New liberalspeak: Notes on the new planetary vulgate', *Radical Philosophy*, 105: 2–5.

Bowen, W. (2009) 'Speak your piece: let local networks deliver broadband', *Daily Yonder*, 27 January.

Briggs, A. and Bourke, P. (2002) *A Social History of the Media: From Gutenberg to the Internet*. Cambridge: Polity.

Broadcasting Services Amendment (Media Ownership) Bill (2006) *Explanatory Memorandum*. Canberra: AusInfo.

Bull, M. (2008) *Sound Moves: iPod Culture and Urban Experience*. London: Routledge.

Burgelman, J.C. (1997) 'Communication, citizenship and social policy: rethinking the limits of the welfare state', paper presented at 12th EURICOM (European Institute for Communication and Culture) symposium, University of Colorado, Boulder, US.

Burgelman, J.C. (2000) 'Regulating access in the information society: the need for rethinking public and universal space', *New Media & Society*, 2(1): 51–66.

Butler, D. and Rodrick, S. (2007) *Australian Media Law* (3rd edn). Sydney: Lawbook Company.

Calabrese, A. and Sparks, C. (eds) (2004) *Toward a Political Economy of Culture: Capitalism and Communication in the Twenty-First Century*. Lanham, MD: Rowman and Littlefield.

Cammaerts, B. and Carpentier, N. (2007) *Reclaiming the Media: Communication Rights and Democratic Media Roles*. Bristol: Intellect.

Canadian Parliament (1997) *Direction to the CRTC (Ineligibility of Non-Canadians)*, 8 April, Canadian Parliament.

Carey, J. W. (1989) *Communication as Culture*. Winchester, MA: Unwin Hyman.

Carnegie Corporation (2005) 'Abandoning the news', *Carnegie Reporter*, 3(2).

Castells, M. ([1996] 2000) *The Rise of the Network Society*. Oxford: Basil Blackwell.

Castells, M. (2000) *The Information Age: Economy, Society and Culture* (2nd edn). Oxford: Blackwell.

Castells, M. (2001) *The Internet Galaxy: Reflections on the Internet, Business and Society*. Oxford: Oxford University Press.

Castells, M. (2007) 'Communication, power and counter-power in the Network Society', *International Journal of Communication*, 1: 238–66. Available at: http://ijoc.org.

Castells, M. and Himanen, P. (2002) *The Information Society and the Welfare State: The Finnish Model*. Oxford: Oxford University Press.

Cauley, L. (2009) 'Feel like someone's watching you?', USAtoday.com, 9 February.

Chaffin, J. (2007) 'Media groups challenge Google on copyright', FT.com, 18 October.

Cheer, U. (2003) 'Media and communication', *1 Laws NZ*, para 78.

Chester, J. (2007) *Digital Destiny: New Media and the Future of Democracy*. New York: The New Press.

Collins, R. (2008) cited in House of Lords (2008) *The Ownership of the News*, Vol. 1: Report HL paper 122–1, House of Lords, Select Committee on Communications, 2008, UK Parliament. London: TSO.

Collins, R. (2009) 'Trust and trustworthiness in fourth and fifth estates,' *International Journal of Communication*, 2: 61–86.

Collins, R. and Murroni, C. (1996) *New Media, New Policies: Media and Communications Strategies for the Future*. Cambridge: Polity Press.

ComScore MediaMetrix (2008) www.comscore.com, accessed 11 November 2008.

Conroy, S. (2008) Media Release, 'Conroy sets digital TV switchover timetable', 19 October.

Copps, M. J. (2005) 'Where is the public interest in media consolidation?', in R. McChesney, R. Newman and B. Scott (eds) *The Future of Media: Resistance and Reform in the 21st Century*. New York: Seven Stories Press, pp. 117–25.

Corbin, K. (2009) 'IT, network neutrality groups praise stimulus plan', 12 February, Internetnews.com.

Crikey.com (2007) 'Dow Jones is not for sale, at any price, to Rupert Murdoch', 7 May.

Croteau, D. and Hoynes, W. (2006) *The Business of Media: Corporate Media and the Public Interest* (2nd edn). London: Sage.

Crovitz, L. G. (2009) 'Time to reinvent the Web (and save Wall Street)', *Wall Street Journal*. Available at: http://online.wsj.com/article/SB123413741814261521.html?mod=todays_us_opinion.

CRTC (1997) *Public Notice 1997–99: Building on Success – A Policy Framework for Canadian Television*. Ottawa: CRTC.

CRTC (2001) 'Licence renewals for the television stations controlled by Global (Canwest): Decision: 2001–458'. Ottawa: CRTC.

Dallow, P. (2007) 'Mediatizing the Web: the new modular extensible media', *Journal of Media Practice, Intellect*, 8(3): 341–58.

DCMS (Department of Culture, Media and Sport) (2008) *Government Response to the House of Lords Select Committee on Communications Report on the Ownership of the News*, (HL 122-1). Session 2007–2008. Available at: www.dcms.gov.uk.

Deibert, R. (1997) *Parchment, Printing, & Hypermedia: Communication in World Order Transformation*. New York: Columbia Univ. Press.

Dennis, E. and Merrill, J. (eds) (2006) *Media Debates: Great Issues for the Digital Age* (4th edn). Toronto: Thomson Wadsworth.

Dessauer, C. (2004) 'New media, Internet news, and the news habit', in P. Howard and S. Jones (eds) *Society Online: The Internet in Context*. London: Sage, pp. 121–36.

Deuze, M. (2008) 'Understanding journalism as newswork: how it changes, and how it remains the same', *Westminster Papers in Communication and Culture*, 5(2): 4–23.

Deuze, M. (2009) 'Convergence culture and media work', in J. Holt and A. Perren (eds) *Media Industries: History, Theory, and Method*. Malden, MA: Wiley-Blackwell.

De Zengotita, T. (2005) *Mediated: How the Media Shape Your World*. London: Bloomsbury.

Downie, C. and Macintosh, A. (2006) 'New media or more of the same? The cross-media ownership debate', *The Australia Institute*, May pp. 1–15. Available at: http://www.tai.org.au/documents/downloads/WP86.pdf.

Doyle, G. (2002) *Media Ownership: The Economics and Politics of Convergence and Concentration in the UK and European Media*. London: Sage.

Dunbar, J. (2005) 'Who is watching the watchdog?', in R. McChesney, R. Newman and B. Scott (eds) *The Future of Media: Resistance and Reform in the 21st Century*. New York: Seven Stories Press.

Dwyer, T. and Ramsay, G. (2007) *Submission to the Australian government's 'Telecommunications Universal Service Obligation Review'* (Department of Broadband, Communications and the Digital Economy, November 2007). Canberra.

Dwyer, T., Wilding, D., Wilson, H. and Curtis, S. (2006) *Content, Consolidation and Clout: How Will Regional Australia be Affected by Media Ownership Changes?* Melbourne: UNSW/Victoria University, Communications Law Centre.

The Economist (2006) 'More media, less news', 24 August.

Erdal, I. J. (2007) 'Negotiating convergence in news production', in T. Storsul and D. Stuedahl (eds) *Ambivalence Towards Convergence: Digitalization and Media Change*. Göteborg University: Nordicom.

European Commission (2009) Press Release, 'Commission earmarks €1bn for investment in broadband', 28 January, MEMO/09/35, Brussels. Available at: http://europa.eu/rapid/pressReleasesAction.do?reference=MEMO/09/35&format=HTML&aged=0&language=EN&guiLanguage=en.

Evans, P. and Wurster, T. E. (2000) *Blown to Bits: How the New Economics of Information Transforms Strategy*. Boston: Harvard Business School Press.

Fagerjord, A. and Storsul, T. (2007) 'Questioning convergence,' in T. Storsul and D. Stuedahl (eds) *Ambivalence Towards Convergence: Digitalization and Media Change*. Göteborg University: Nordicom.

Farbstein, A. (2001) 'A look at merger review in the light of corporate consolidations in communications', *Appeal*. 7.

FCC (2009a) Media Release, 'Preparations in high gear for stations going all-digital this week. FCC seeks to protect access to analog news and emergency information'. Available at: http://hraunfoss.fcc.gov/edocs_public/attachmatch/DOC-288530 A1.pdf.

FCC (2009b) Public Notice 'FCC requires public interest conditions for certain analog TV terminations on February 17, 2009', 11 February, FCC 09-7.

Feintuck, M. (2004) *The Public Interest in Regulation*. Oxford: Oxford University Press.

Feintuck, M. and Varney, M. (2006) *Media Regulation, Public Interest and the Law* (2nd edn). Edinburgh: Edinburgh University Press.

Fell, J. (2009) 'Centre of gravity has shifted in media M&A', Foliomag.com, 8 January.

Financial Services Authority (FSA) (2006) *Private Equity: A Discussion of Risk and Regulatory Engagement*, Discussion Paper 06/6, London: FSA.

Fine, J. (2009) 'Who will be the last media giant left standing?', *Businessweek*, 8 January.

Fineberg, A. (2009) 'With stimulus fight complete, advocates shift focus to universal service', 16 February. Available at: BroadbandConcensus.com

Finnemann, N. (2006) cited in U. Carlsson (ed.) (2006) 'The Internet and the public space', in *Nordic Media Trends*. Gothenburg: Nordicom.

Fitzpatrick, M. (2007) 'Why mobile Japan leads the world', *The Guardian*, 27 September.

Flew, T. (2008) *New Media: An Introduction* (3rd edn). Melbourne: Oxford University Press.

Flew, T., Cunningham, S., Bruns, A. and Wilson, J. (2008) 'Social innovation, user-created content and the future of the ABC and SBS as public service media', Submission to ABC and SBS Review, Department of Broadband, Communications and the Digital Economy. Available at: http://www.dbcde.gov.au/media_broadcasting/consultation_and_submissions/abc_sbs_review/_submissions/t/2580.

Foroohar, R. (2006) 'The Internet splits up', *Newsweek*, 16 May.

Fortunati, L. (2005) 'Mediatization of the net and internetization of the mass media' *Gazette: The International Journal for Communication Studies*, 67(1): 27–44.

Frank, T. (1997) *The Conquest of Cool: Business Culture, Counterculture, and the Rise of Hip Consumerism*. Chicago: University of Chicago Press.

Frank, T. (2001) *One Market Under God: Extreme Capitalism, Market Populism, and the End of Economic Democracy*. New York: First Anchor Books.

Frau-Meigs, D. (2007) 'Convergence, internet governance and cultural diversity', in T. Storsul and D. Stuedahl (eds) *Ambivalence Towards Convergence: Digitalization and Media Change*. Göteborg University: Nordicom.

Freedman, D. (2008) *The Politics of Media Policy*. Cambridge: Polity.

Friends of Canadian Broadcasting (2001) *Brief to the House of Commons Standing Committee on Cultural Heritage*, 10 September, 2. Submission. House of Commons. Canadian Parliament.

Froud, J. and Williams, K. (2007) 'Private equity and the culture of value extraction', CRESC Working Paper Series, Working Paper No. 31. Manchester: University of Manchester.

Fuchs, C. (2009) 'Social networking sites and the surveillance society', paper presented at Forschungsgruppe 'Unified Theory of Information' – Verein zur Förderung der Integration der Informationswissenschaften, Salzburg/Vienna, Austria.

Given, J. (2003a) *America's Pie: Trade and Culture after 9/11*. Sydney: UNSW Press.

Given, J. (2003b) *Turning off Television*. Sydney: UNSW Press.

Goggin, G. (2006) *Cell Phone Culture: Mobile Technology in Everyday Life*. New York: Routledge.

Goggin, G. (2007) 'Dancing with the stars, or dancing in the dark', in A. Kenyon (ed.) *TV Futures: Digital Television Policy in Australia*. Melbourne: Melbourne University Press.

Goldfarb, C. and Kruger, L. (2009) *Infrastructure Programs: What's Different about Broadband?* Washington, DC: Congressional Research Service.

Goldgar, A. (2007) *Tulipmania, Money, Honour, and Knowledge in the Dutch Golden Age*. Princeton, NJ: Princeton University Press.

Goldsmith, J. and Wu, T. (2008) *Who Controls the Internet? Illusions of a Borderless World* (2nd edn). New York: Oxford University Press.

Goldstein, K. J. (2002) 'The myth of media concentration,' *The National Post*, 2 December.

Goldstein, P. (2009) 'CTIA urges net neutrality rules be dropped for wireless networks', CTIA live, forum. 16 April. Fiercewireless.com.

Graham, P. (2006) *Hypercapitalism: New Media, Language, and Social Perceptions of Value*. New York: Lang.

Greenslade, R. (2008) *ABC Radio National, The Media Report, 'Survival of Media Platforms for Journalism'*, 8 May.

Habermas, J. (1984) *The Theory of Communicative Action*, vol. 1, *Reason and the Rationalization of Society*. Boston: Beacon Press.

Habermas, J. (1989) *The Structural Transformation of the Public Sphere*. Cambridge: Polity Press.

Halavais, A. (2008) 'The hyperlink as organising principle', in J. Turow and T. Lokman (eds) *The Hyperlinked Society: Questioning Connections in the Digital Age*. Ann Arbor, MI: University of Michigan Press.

Hallin, D. (2008) 'Neoliberalism, social movements and change', in D. Hesmondhalgh and J. Toynbee (eds) *The Media and Social Theory*. London: Routledge.

Hallin, D. C. and Mancini, P. (2004) *Comparing Media Systems: Three Models of Media and Politics*. Cambridge: Cambridge University Press.

Hart, C. (2008) 'Split network and broadband: Google'. Business. *The Australian*, 3 July.

Hart, K. and Goldfarb, Z. (2007) 'You can hear Google now: Internet giant looking to expand into cellphones', November. Available at: Washington Post.com.

Hartley, J. (1996) *Popular Reality: Journalism, Modernity, Popular Culture*. London: Arnold.

Harvey, D. (1990) *The Condition of Postmodernity: An Enquiry into the Origins of Cultural Change*. Oxford: Blackwell.

Harvey, D. (2001) *Spaces of Capital: Towards a Critical Geography*. Edinburgh: Edinburgh University Press.

Harvey, D. (2005) *A Brief History of Neoliberalism*. Oxford: Oxford University Press.

Harvey, M. (2009) 'YouTube to launch music video site with Universal', 10 April. Times Online.

Hassan, R. (2004) *Media, Politics and the Network Society*. Maidenhead: Open University Press.

Hayes, D. (2007) 'Viacom, Microsoft online Deal', *Variety*, Variety Technology, 19 December. Available at: www.variety.com/techology.

Held, D. (2004) *Global Covenant: The Social Democratic Alternative to the Washington Consensus*. Cambridge: Polity.

Henton, A. and Tadayoni, R. (2008) 'The impact of the Internet on media technology, platforms and innovation', in L. Kung, R. Picard and R. Towse (eds) *The Internet and the Mass Media*. London: Sage.

Hesmondhalgh, D. (2007) *The Cultural Industries* (2nd edn). London: Sage.

Herman, E. (2003) 'The propaganda model: a retrospective', *Journalism Studies*, 1(1): 101–12.

Herman, E. and Chomsky, N. (1994) *Manufacturing Consent*. London: Vintage.

Hitchens, L. (2006) *Broadcasting Pluralism and Diversity: A Comparative Study of Policy and Regulation*. Oxford: Hart Publishing.

Hitwise (2007) *Best Practice Search Engine Optimisation*. October, Hitwise. Available at: www.hitwise.com.au

Hoffman-Reim, W. (1996) *Regulating Media*. New York: Guilford Press.

Holton, K. and Cowan, M. (2007) 'Bebo and "Lonelygirl15" creators launch UK version', Reuters, 25 May.

House of Lords (2008a) *The Ownership of the News*, Vol. 1: report HL paper 122-1, House of Lords, Select Committee on Communications, 2008, UK Parliament. London: The Stationery Office.

House of Lords (2008b) Presentation of Ownership of the News report, Lord Fowler, 5 November, Hansard.

Hudson, P. (2009) 'Internet company to be sold by 2022', *The Sydney Morning Herald*, 10–12 April.

Internetworld Statistics (2009) *World Internet Users and Population Statistics*. Available at: http://www.internetworldstats.com/stats.htm.

Jenkins, H. (2001) 'Convergence? I diverge', *Technology Review*. Digital Renaissance, June.

Jenkins, H. (2006) *Convergence Culture: Where Old and New Media Collide*. New York: New York University Press.

Johnson, B. (2009a) 'Microsoft and Yahoo revive talks as Google leaps ahead', *The Guardian, Business*. 10 April. http://www.guardian.co.uk/business/2009/apr/10/microsoft-yahoo-merger-talks

Johnson, B. (2009b) 'Does YouTube actually make any money?' *The Guardian*, 9 April. Available at: http://www.guardian.co.uk/technology/2009/apr/09/youtube-google-money

Jones, D. (2005) *iPod, Therefore I Am – A Personal Journey Through Music*. London: Weidenfeld & Nicolson.

Kang, C. (2009) 'Broadband program oversight Questioned', 12 February. Available at: WashingtonPost.com.

Karpinnen, K. (2007) 'Making a difference to media pluralism: a critique of the pluralistic consensus in European media policy', in B. Cammaerts and N. Carpentier, *Reclaiming the Media: Communication Rights and Democratic Media Roles*. Bristol: Intellect.

Karpinnen, K. (2008) 'Media and the paradoxes of pluralism', in D. Hesmondhalgh and J. Toynbee (eds) *The Media and Social Theory*. London: Routledge.

Kaste, M. (2009) 'National public radio, "effort to increase broadband access spurs debate" ', 11 February. Available at: http://www.npr.org.

Kaufman, D. (2009) 'DTV leaves some Hawaiians in the dark', 5 February. Available at: http://www.tvnewsday.com.

Keen, S. (2008) Personal email communications.

Keown, J. (2008) 'TVNZ strikes major IPTV deals', *The Independent*, May, p. 3.

Kiehl, S. (2009) 'As journalism remakes itself, students follow', *The Baltimore Sun* (online edition), 31 March. Available at: http://www.baltimoresun.com.

Kohler, A. (2006) 'Journalists will be first casualties when radio-TV mergers begin', Business, *The Age*, 15 March.

Kung, L., Picard, R. and Towse, R. (eds) (2008) *The Internet and the Mass Media*. London: Sage.

Larsen, J., Urry, J. and Axhausen, K. (2006) *Mobilities, Networks, Geographies*. Aldershot: Ashgate.

Lash, S. (2002) *Critique of Information*. London: Sage.

Lax, S. (2001) 'Information, education and inequality: Is new technology the solution?' in S. Lax (ed.) *Access Denied in the Information Age*. Basingstoke: Palgrave.

Leadbeater, C. (2000) *Living on Thin Air: The New Economy*. London: Penguin.

Leadbeater, C. (2008) *We-Think: Mass Innovation, Not Mass Production*. London: Profile.

Lealand, G. (2000) 'Regulation – what regulation? Cultural diversity and local content in New Zealand television', 95 *Media International Australia, Incorporating Culture & Policy*.

Lessig, L. (2004) *Free Culture: How Big Media Uses Technology and the Law to Lock Down Culture and Control Creativity*. New York: Penguin Press.

Lévy, P. (1997) *Collective Intelligence: Mankind's Emerging World in Cyberspace*, trans. R. Bononno. Cambridge, MA: Perseus Books.

Los Angeles Times (2008) 'Fox unit to miss revenue target', Business section, 5 April.

Ludes, P. (2008) *Convergence and Fragmentation: Media Technology and the Information Society*. Bristol: Intellect.

Lund, A. B. (2007) 'Media markets in Scandinavia: political economy aspects of convergence and divergence', *Nordicom Review*, Jubilee Issue, *Media Structures and Practices: As Time Goes By*, pp. 121–134.

Lunt, P. and Livingstone, S. (2007) 'Regulation in the public interest', *Consumer Policy Review*, 17(2).

Lury, C. (2004) *Brands: The Logos of the Global Economy*. New York: Routledge.

Mackenzie, A. (2008) 'Wirelessness as an experience of transition', in Fibreculture, Issue 13, *After Convergence: What Connects?* http://journal.fibreculture.org/.

Mansell, R. (1999) 'New media competition and access: The scarcity-abundance dialectic', *New Media & Society*, 1(2): 155–82.

Markoff, J. (2009) 'The cellphone, navigating our lives', 16 February. Available at: http://NyTimes.com.

Marks, P. (2009) 'Tech report: Skype', ABC, Radio National, 2 April.

Martell, D. (2008) 'Yahoos fear loss of fun culture', *Sydney Morning Herald* (Reuters), 4 February.

Martin, F. (2008) 'Convergence, online and new media news', *State of the News Print*, Sydney: Australian Press Council.

Maule, C. (2003) 'State of the Canada-US relationship: culture', *The American Review of Canadian Studies*, (Spring): 121.

McCarthy, C. (2007) 'Fox unit confirms photobucket, Flektor Buys', CNET news, 30 May.

McChesney, R. W. (1999) *Rich Media, Poor Democracy: Communications Politics in Dubious Times*. New York: New Press.

McChesney, R., Newman, R. and Scott, B. (eds) (2005) *The Future of Media: Resistance and Reform in the 21st Century*. New York: Seven Stories Press, pp. 117–25.

McGuigan, J. (2004) *Rethinking Cultural Policy*. Maidenhead: Open University Press.

McGuigan, J. (2005) 'NeoLiberalism, culture and policy', *International Journal of Cultural Policy*, 11(3): 229–41.

McGuigan, J. (2006) 'The politics of cultural studies and cool capitalism', *Cultural Politics*, 2(2): 137–58.

McGuigan, J. (2007) 'Technological determinism and mobile privatisation', in V. Nightingale and T. Dwyer (2007) (eds) *New Media Worlds: Challenges for Convergence*. Melbourne: Oxford University Press.

McLuhan, M. (1964) *Understanding Media: The Extensions of Man*. Cambridge, MA: MIT Press.

Media Access Project (2006) (Joint Public Interest Research Groups FCC Filing), *In the Matter of the 2002 and 2006 Review of the Commission's Broadcast Ownership Rules and Other Rules Adopted Pursuant to Section 202 of the Telecommunications Act of 1996*. Washington. Available at: http://www.mediaaccess.org.

Mika, N. (2009) 'Mobile connections surpass 4 billion mark worldwide', 11 February. Accessed at Reuters.com. http://www.reuters.com/article/technologyNews/idUSTRE51A2I820090211.

Mitchell, W.J. (1996) *City of Bits: Space, Place and the Infobahn*. Cambridge, MA: MIT Press.

Mitchell, W.J. (1999) *E-topia Urban Life, Jim – But Not as We Know It*. Cambridge, MA: MIT Press.

Moravec, H. (1998) *Simulation, Consciousness, Existence*. Available at: http://www.frc.ri.cmu.edu/~hpm/project.archive/general.articles/1998/SimConEx.98.html (accessed 13 Oct. 2003).

Moravec, H. (2000) *Robo9s, Re-Evolving Mind*. Available at: http://www.frc.ri.cmu.edu/~hpm/project.archive/robot.papers/2000/Cerebrum.html (accessed 13 Oct. 2003).

Morley, D. (2007) *Media, Modernity and Technology: The Geography of the New*. London: Routledge.

Mosco, V. (2004) *The Digital Sublime: Myth, Power and Cyberspace*. Cambridge, MA: MIT Press.

Mouffe, C. (2000) *The Democratic Paradox*. London: Verso.

Murdock, G. (2000) 'Digital futures: European television in the age of convergence', in J. Wieten, G. Murdock and P. Dahlgren (eds) *Television Across Europe*. London: Sage, pp.35–57.

Murdock, G. (2005) 'Building the digital commons: public broadcasting in the age of the internet', in G.F. Lowe and P. Jauert (eds) *Cultural Dilemmas in Public Service Broadcasting*. Göteborg University: Nordicom.

Murdock, G. (2007) 'Digital technologies and moral economies', in V. Nightingale and T. Dwyer (eds) *New Media Worlds: Challenges for Convergence*. Melbourne: Oxford University Press.

Murdock, G. and Golding, P. (1977) 'Capitalism, communication and class relations', in J. Curran et al. *Mass Communication and Society*. London: Edward Arnold/Open University Press.

Murdock, G. and Golding, P. (1989) 'Information poverty and political inequality:

citizenship in the age of privatised communications', *Journal of Communication*, 39(3): 180–95.

Murdock, G. and Golding, P. (2004) 'Dismantling the digital divide: rethinking the dynamics of participation and exclusion', in A. Calabrese and C. Sparks (eds) *Toward a Political Economy of Culture: Capitalism and Communication in the 21st Century*. Maryland, MD: Rowman and Littlefield.

Murdoch, R. (2009) 'Does Rupert Murdoch have kindle envy? News Corp. mulls an e-book reader investment', MediaMemo (Peter Kafka). 2 April. Available at: www.allthingsdigital.com.

Nakashima, E. (2007) 'Feeling betrayed, Facebook users force site to honor their privacy', 30 November. Available at: www.washingtonpost.com.

Napoli, P. (2008) 'Hyperlinking and the forces of massification', in J. Turow and T. Lokman (eds) *The Hyperlinked Society: Questioning Connections in the Digital Age*. Ann Arbor, MI: University of Michigan Press.

Napoli, P. (2003) *Audience Economics: Media Institutions and the Audience Marketplace*. New York: Columbia University Press.

Negroponte, N. (1995) *Being Digital*. New York: Alfred A. Knopf, Inc.

Nielsen, J. (1998) *The End of Legacy Media*. Alertbox. Available at: http://www.useit.com/alertbox/980823.html.

Nightingale, V. and Dwyer, T. (2006) 'The audience politics of "enhanced" television formats', *International Journal of Media and Cultural Politics*, 2(1): 25–42.

Nightingale, V. (2007a) 'New Media Worlds: Challenges for Convergence' Chapter 2, in Nightingale, V. and Dwyer, T. (2007) (eds) *New Media Worlds: Challenges for Convergence*. Melbourne: Oxford University Press.

Nightingale, V. (2007b) 'Emergence, Search and Social Networking', Chapter 17, in Nightingale, V. and Dwyer, T. (2007) (eds) *New Media Worlds: Challenges for Convergence*. Melbourne: Oxford University Press.

Nightingale, V. (2007c) 'Lost in space: television's missing publics', in R. Butsch (ed.) *Media and Public Spheres*. Basingstoke: Palgrave Macmillan.

Noam, E. (2007) 'Private equity is a problem for public media', *Financial Times*, 19 February.

Norris, P. (2002) 'Media ownership in NZ', in J. McGregor and M. Comrie (eds) *What's News? Reclaiming Journalism in New Zealand*. Wellington: Dunmore Press.

OECD (2005) 'Rethinking universal service for a next generation network environment'. Working Party on Telecommunication and Information Services Policies, Directorate for Science, Technology and Industry, Committee for Information, Computer and Communications Policy. (Xavier, P.), DSTI/ICCP/TISP (2005)5/FINAL. Brussels: OECD.

OECD (2007) *Participative Web: User-Created Content*. Paris: OECD.

OECD (2008) 'Convergence and next generation networks', Ministerial Background Report. DSTI/ICCP/CISP/(2007)2/FINAL, OECD Ministerial Meeting on the Future of the Internet Economy, Seoul, Korea, June.

OECD (2009) Broadband Portal. Available at: http://www.oecd.org/sti/ict/broadband.

Ofcom (2007a) *The Communications Market 2007*, 'Converging Communications Markets,' August. London: Ofcom.

Ofcom (2007b) *The International Communications Market 2007*, 'Convergence', December. London: Ofcom.

Ofcom (2007c) 'What is convergence?', Submission to the Convergence Think Tank by Ofcom, December.

Ofcom (2008a) *The International Communications Market 2008*, 'Convergence', December. London: Ofcom.

Ofcom (2008b) *The Communications Market 2008*. Available at: http://www.ofcom.org.uk/research/cm/cmr08/.

Ofcom (2008c) Response to the House of Lords Select Committee on Communications Report on the Ownership of the News (HL 122–1). Session 2007–2008. Available at: www.ofcom.gov.uk.

Ofcom (2009a) *UK Broadband Speeds 2008*. Available at: http://www.ofcom.org.uk/research/telecoms/reports/bbspeed_jan09/bbspeed_jan09.pdf.

Ofcom (2009b) *Delivering Super-Fast Broadband in the UK: Promoting Investment and Competition*. March. London: Ofcom.

Patterson, C. and Domingo, D. (2008) *Making Online News: The Ethnography of New Media Production*. New York: Peter Lang.

PC World (2007) 'The viral video hall of fame. From crooning politicians to a grocery store manager who can crush windpipes with his mind, these are the greatest hits of the YouTube age,' 12 November.

Perez-Pena, R. (2007) 'News Corp. completes take-over of Dow Jones', *New York Times*, 14 December.

Pew Center for the People and the Press (2008) *News Interest Index*. December 19–22.

Pew Center for the People and the Press (2009) Project for excellence in Journalism, *State of the News Media*. Available at: http://www.stateofthenewsmedia.org/2009/narrative_overview_intro.

Pool, I. de Sola. (1984) *Technologies of Freedom*. Cambridge, MA: Harvard University Press.

Poster, M. (1995) *The Second Media Age*. Cambridge: Polity Press.

Price, M.E. and Weinberg, J. (1996) 'United States (2)', in V. MacLeod (ed.) *Media Ownership and Control in the Age of Convergence*. London: International Institute of Communications.

Productivity Commission (2000) *Broadcasting*, Report no. 11. Canberra: AusInfo.

Quinn, S. (2004) 'Better journalism or better profits?: A key convergence issue in an age of concentrated ownership', *Pacific Journalism Review*, 10(2): 111–29.

Quinn, S. (2006) *Conversations on Convergence: Insiders' Views on News Production in the 21st Century*. New York: Peter Lang.

Rampell, C. and Ahrens, F. (2007) 'Google's ad reach may be unrivaled: FTC approves DoubleClick deal', December. Available at: WashingtonPost.com.

Reiss, S. (2006) 'His space', *Wired*, Issue 14.07, July. Available at: http://www.wired.com/wired/archive/14.07/murdoch.html.

Reuters (2008) 'Fox interactive media appoints Adam Bain President of FIM Audience Network', 4 April. Available at: http://www.reuters.com/news.

Rheingold, H. (1993) *The Virtual Community*. New York: Addison-Wesley.

Rheingold, H. (2002) *Smart Mobs: The Next Social Revolution*. Cambridge, MA: Perseus.

Rosen, J. (2008) 'A most useful definition of citizen journalism,' *PressThink: Ghosts of Democracy in the Media Machine*. July 14. Available at: http://journalism.nyu.edu/pubzone/weblogs/pressthink/2008/07/14/a_most_useful_d.html.

Rosenberg, B. (2008) *Media Ownership in New Zealand*. Updated at website of the Campaign Against Foreign Control of Autearoa. Available at: http://canterbury.cyberplace.co.nz/community/CAFCA/publications/Miscellaneous/index.html.

Rosenbush, S. (2005) 'News Corp.'s place in MySpace', BusinessWeek Online, 19 July. Available at: http://www.businessweek.com/technology/content/jul2005/tc20050719_5427_tc119.htm.

Saarinen, J. (2006) 'Telstra buys Chinese SouFun real estate website for A$342. Million', The Techsploder Blog, 31 August. Available at: http://www.geekzone.co.nz/juha.

Sabbagh, D. (2009) 'Digital economy bill to pave way for shake-up of rules governing media mergers', 16 April. Available at: Timesonline.com.

SavetheInternet.com (2009).

Schiller, D. (1999) *Digital Capitalism: Networking the Global Market System*. Cambridge, MA: MIT Press.

Schneider, H. and Whoriskey, P. (2008) 'Microsoft bids $44.6 billion for Yahoo', Washington Post.com, 1 February.

Schwartzman, A., Leanza, C. and Feld, H. (2005) 'The legal case for diversity in broadcast ownership', in R. McChesney, R. Newman and B. Scott (eds) *The Future of Media: Resistance and Reform in the 21st Century*. New York: Seven Stories Press, pp. 149–61.

Senate Select Committee (2008) *Select Committee on the National Broadband Network, Interim Report*. Canberra: Commonwealth of Australia, Senate Printing Unit.

Senate of Canada (2004) *Interim Report on the Canadian News Media, Standing Senate Committee on Transport and Communications*, April, Ottawa: Senate.

Shoebridge, N. (2008) 'CVC seeks bankers' backing for PBL', *Australian Financial Review*, 28 October.

Shultz, J. (2006) 'Google ads cash to news', *The Australian*, 9 August.

Skiba, K. (2008) 'Senate opposes media ownership rule', *US News and World Report*, 16 May.

Sky Network Television Limited (2005) 'Sky and INL merger complete', News Release, 1 July. Available at: http://www.skytv.co.nz/files/Miscellaneous/SKY_and_INL_Merger_Complete.pdf.

Sky Network Television Limited (2008) Available at: http://skytv.co.nz/investor-relations.aspx.

Smith, G. (2007) Times Online. Available at: www.timesonline.com.uk.

Sorauf, F. J. (1957) 'The Public Interest Reconsidered', *The Journal of Politics*, 19(4): 616–39.

Sørensen, K.H. and Williams, R. (eds) (2002) *Shaping Technology, Guiding Policy: Concepts, Spaces and Tools.* Cheltenham: Edward Elgar.

Sorkin, A. (2008) 'Workers pay for debacle at tribune'. Available at: nytimes.com, 8 December.

Sorkin, A. and Peters, J. (2006) 'Google to acquire YouTube for $1.65 billion', *New York Times*, 9 October. Available at: http://www.nytimes.com.

Sparks, C. (2004) 'The impact of the Internet on the existing media', in A. Calabrese and C. Sparks (eds) *Toward a Political Economy of Culture: Capitalism and Communications in the 21st Century.* Maryland, MD: Rowman & Littlefield.

Spurgeon, C. (2006) *Advertising and New Media.* New York: Palgrave Macmillan.

Standing Committee for Canadian Heritage (2003) *Our Cultural Sovereignty: The Second Century of Canadian Broadcasting*, House of Commons. Ottawa: Canada.

Starks, M. (2007) *Switching to Digital Television: UK Public Policy and the Market.* Bristol: Intellect.

Steffens, M. (2008) *Sydney Morning Herald*, Business Day, 24 March.

Steffens, M. (2009) 'AAP offshoot aims for the stars', *Sydney Morning Herald*, 20 January.

Storsul, T. and Stuedahl, D. (2007) *Ambivalence Towards Convergence: Digitalization and Media Change.* Göteborg University: Nordicom.

Streeter, T. (1987) 'The cable fable revisited: discourse, policy, and the making of cable television,' *Critical Studies in Mass Communication*, 4(2): 174–200.

Stursberg, R. (2002), cited in J. Barron (2002) 'Globalism and national media policies in the United States and Canada: a critique of C. Edwin Baker's *Media, Markets and Democracy*', *International Law*, 27.

Techtree News Staff (2008) 'Facebook: largest, fastest growing social network'. Techtree.com. ITNation. Accessed on 14 August 2008.

Teinowitz, I. (2009) 'Tracking the path to digital transition delay', 8 February. http://www.tvweek.com.

Thompson, J. (1995) *The Media and Modernity: A Social Theory of the Media.* Cambridge: Polity.

Thussu, D. (2009) *News as Entertainment: The Rise of Global Infotainment.* London: Sage.

Townsend, A. (1984) 'Regulation of newspaper/broadcasting, media cross-ownership in Canada', UNBLJ 261, Autumn.

Townsend, A. (1999) 'Cable television 1999: a history of the winding road to competition', *UNBLJ*, 48.

Turner, G. (2005) *Ending the Affair: The Decline of Television Current Affairs in Australia.* Sydney: UNSW Press.

Turow, J. (1997) *Breaking Up America: Advertisers and the New Media World.* Chicago: University of Chicago Press.

Turow, J. and Tsui, L. (2008) *The Hyperlinked Society: Questioning Connections in the Digital Age (The New Media World).* Ann Arbor, MI: University of Michigan Press.

Vise, D. (2005) *The Google Story.* New York: Random House.

Wallingford, T. (2005) 'What is VOIP?' OReillynet.com Accessed 6 June 2008.

Webster, J. (2008) 'Structuring a marketplace of attention', in J. Turow and T. Lokman (eds) *The Hyperlinked Society: Questioning Connections in the Digital Age*. Ann Arbor, MI: University of Michigan Press.

Williams, G. (2001) 'Selling off cyberspace', in S. Lax (ed.) *Access Denied in the Information Age*. Basingstoke: Palgrave Macmillan.

Williams, R. (1974) *Television: Technology and Cultural Form*. London: Fontana.

Williams, R. (1985) *Towards 2000*. London: Penguin.

Winseck, D. (2002) 'Netscapes of power: convergence, consolidation and power in the Canadian mediascape', *Media, Culture & Society*, 24: 795–819.

Winston, B. (1998) *Media, Technology and Society: A History from the Telegraph to the Internet*. London: Routledge.

Wurff, Richard van der and Lauf, Edmund (eds) (2005) *Print and Online Newspapers in Europe. A Comparativce Analysis in 16 Countries*. EU-COST a 20. Amsterdam: Het Spinhuis.

Zerbisias, A. (2001) 'Ready or not, CRTC takes on media convergence', *The Toronto Star*, 14 April.

Zittrain, J. (2008) *The future of the Internet, and How to Stop It*. New Haven, CT: Yale University Press.

INDEX